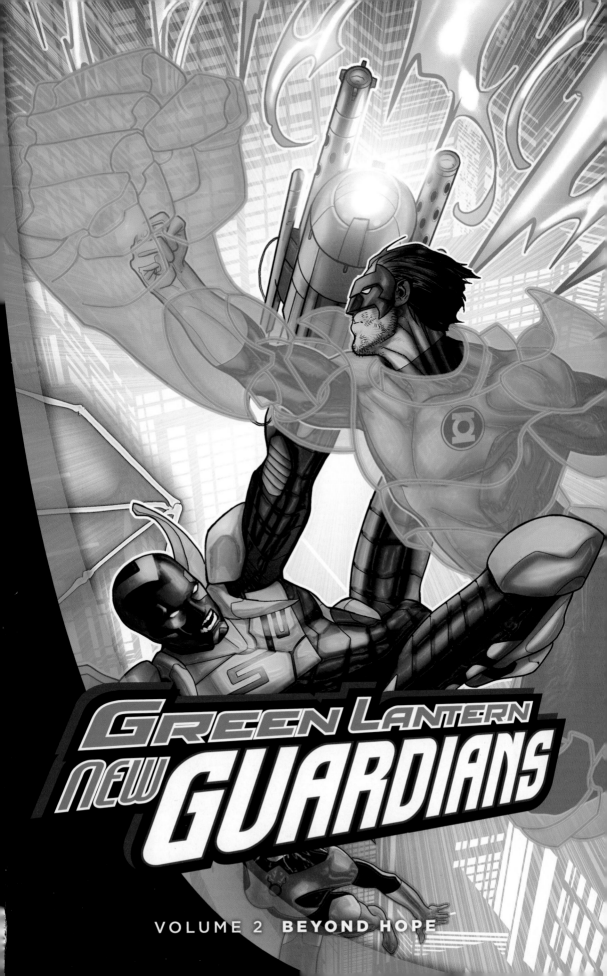

GREEN LANTERN
NEW GUARDIANS

VOLUME 2 BEYOND HOPE

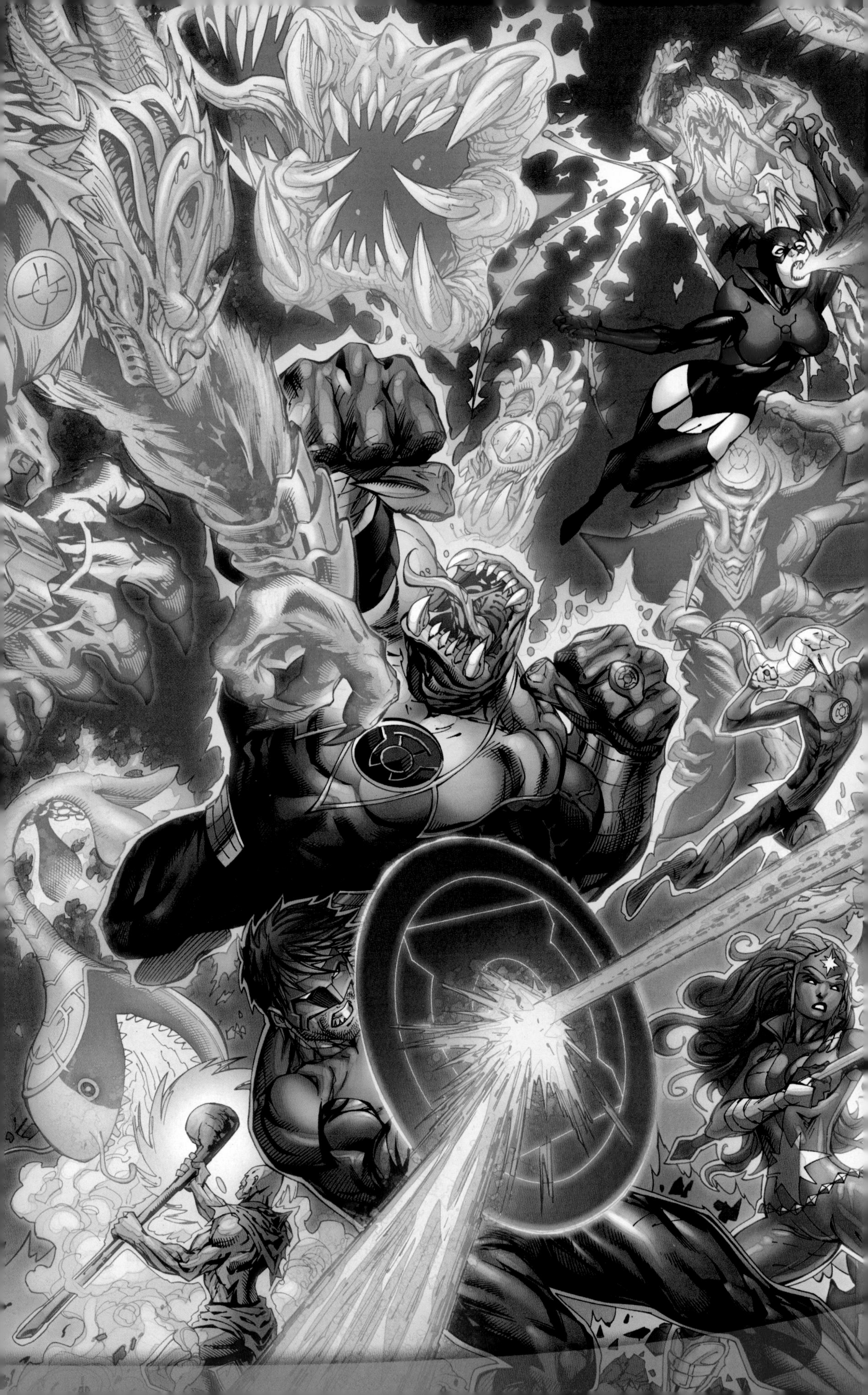

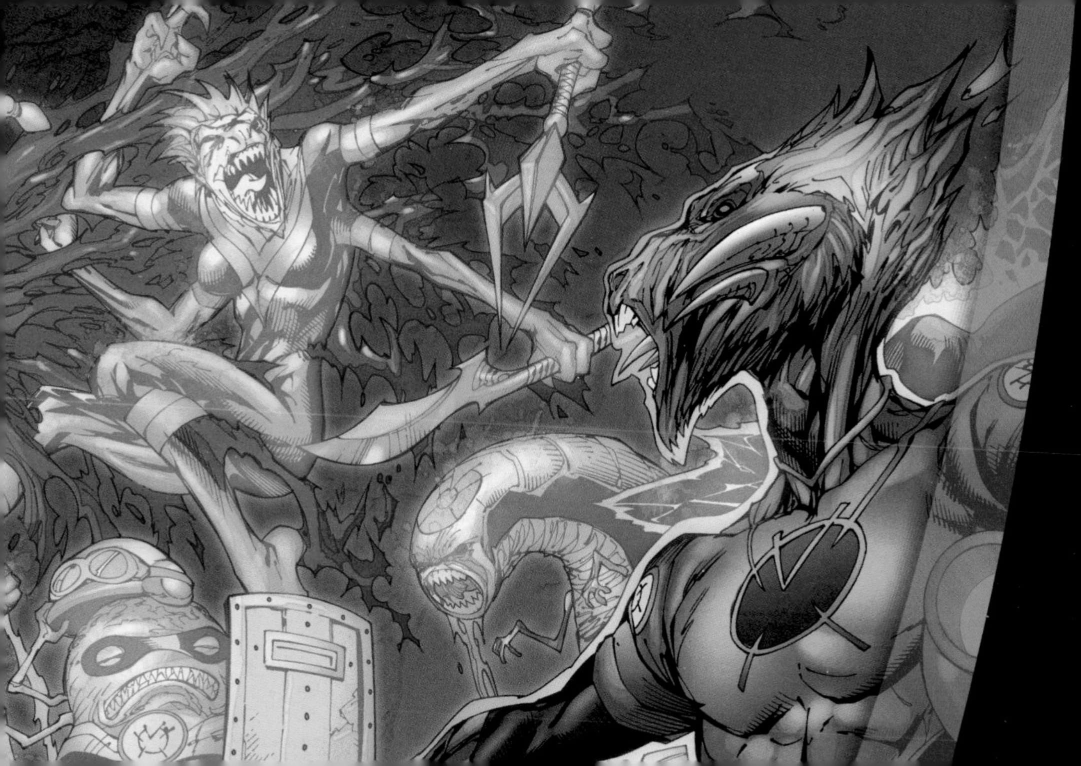

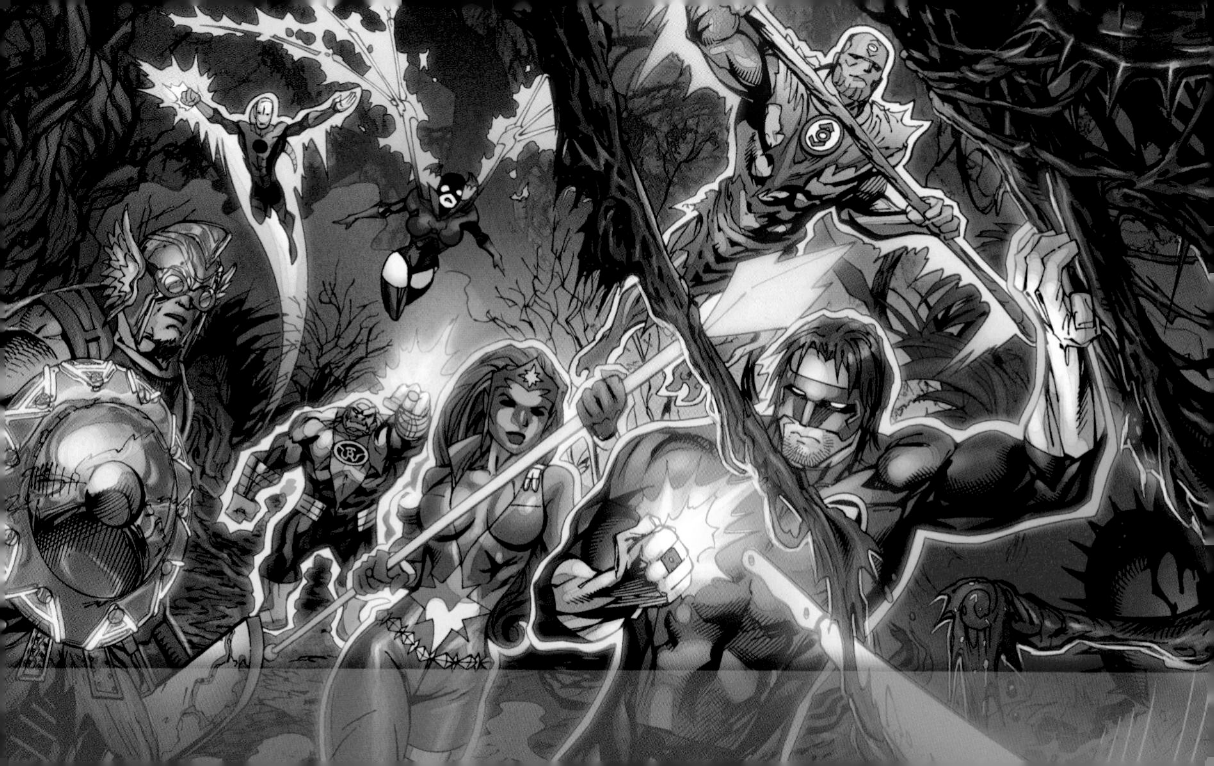

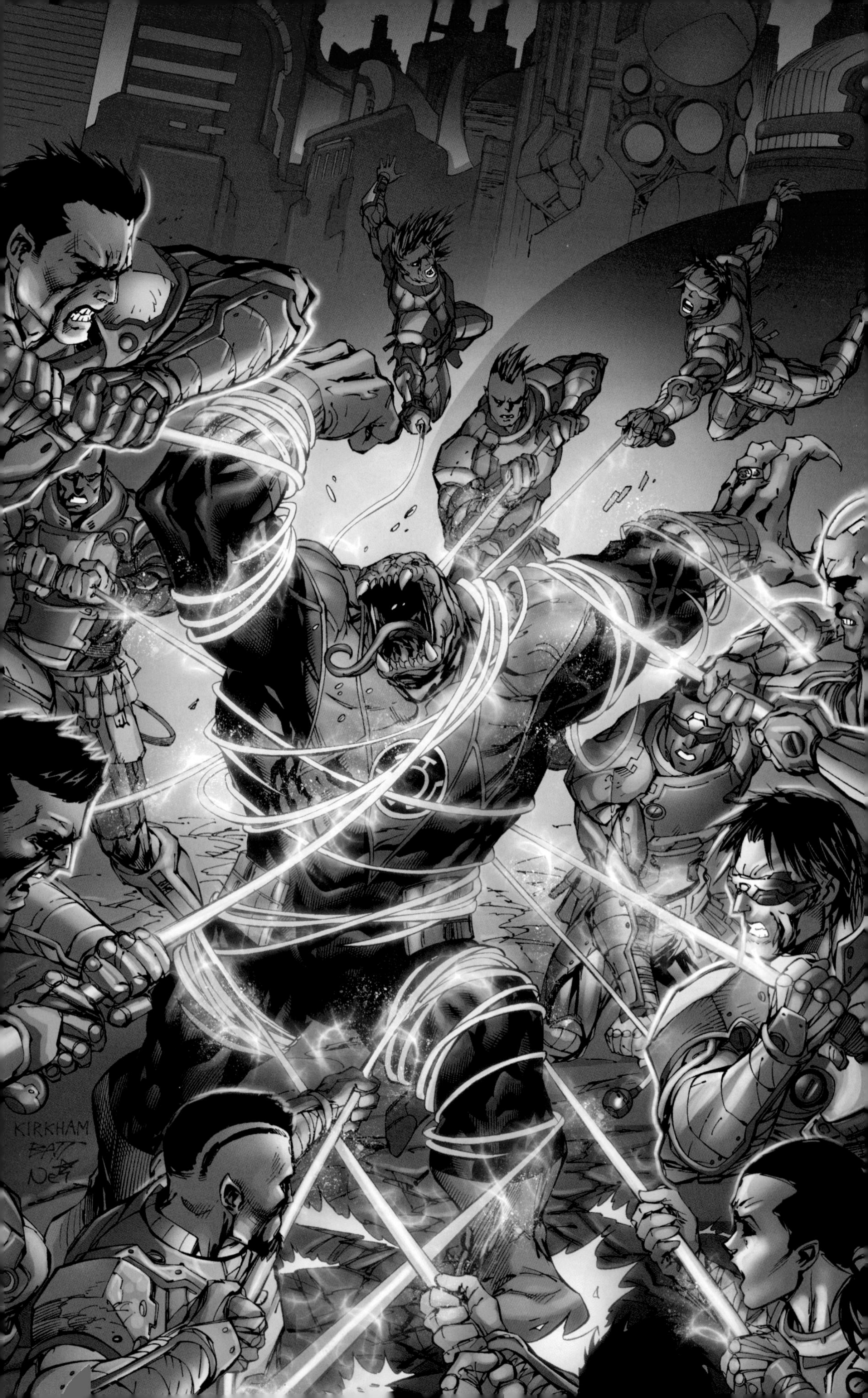
KIRKHAM

TONY BEDARD writer TYLER KIRKHAM penciller BATT inker cover by TYLER KIRKHAM, BATT & NEI RUFFINO

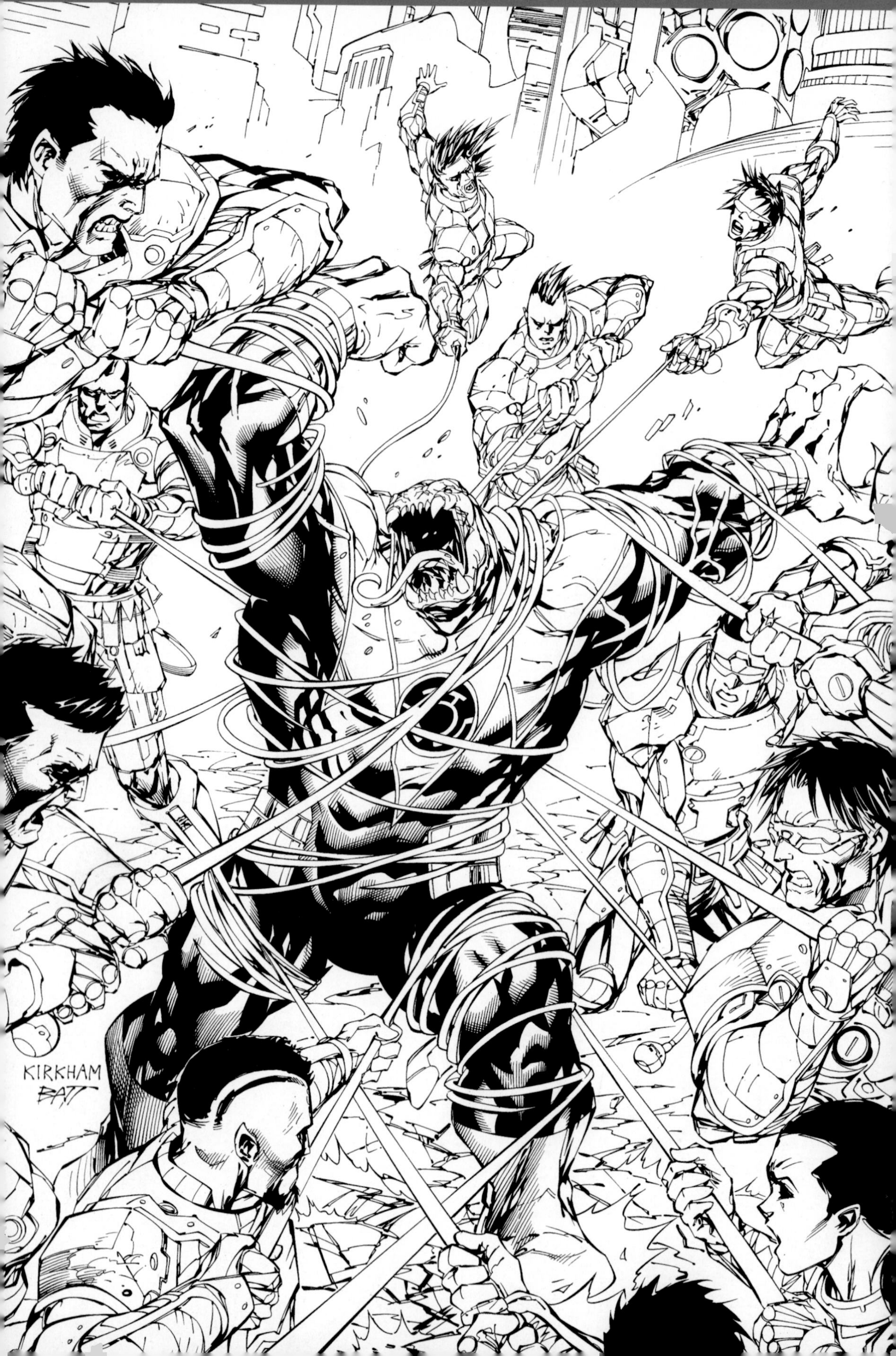
KIRKHAM
BATT

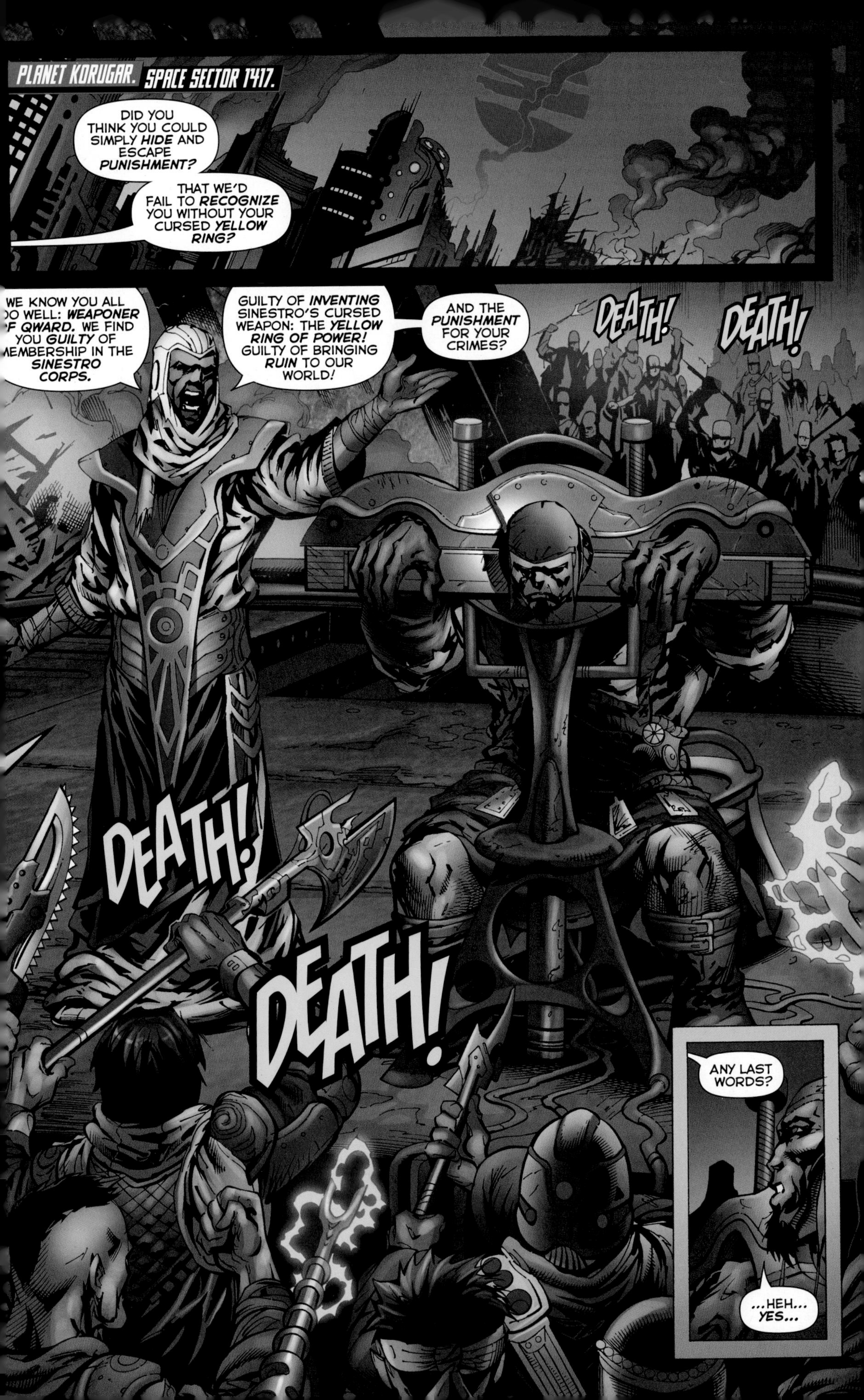

PLANET KORUGAR. SPACE SECTOR 1417.
DID YOU THINK YOU COULD SIMPLY HIDE AND ESCAPE PUNISHMENT?
THAT WE'D FAIL TO RECOGNIZE YOU WITHOUT YOUR CURSED YELLOW RING?
WE KNOW YOU ALL OO WELL: WEAPONER F QWARD. WE FIND YOU GUILTY OF MEMBERSHIP IN THE SINESTRO CORPS.
GUILTY OF INVENTING SINESTRO'S CURSED WEAPON: THE YELLOW RING OF POWER! GUILTY OF BRINGING RUIN TO OUR WORLD!
AND THE PUNISHMENT FOR YOUR CRIMES?
DEATH!
DEATH!
DEATH!
DEATH!
ANY LAST WORDS?
...HEH... YES...

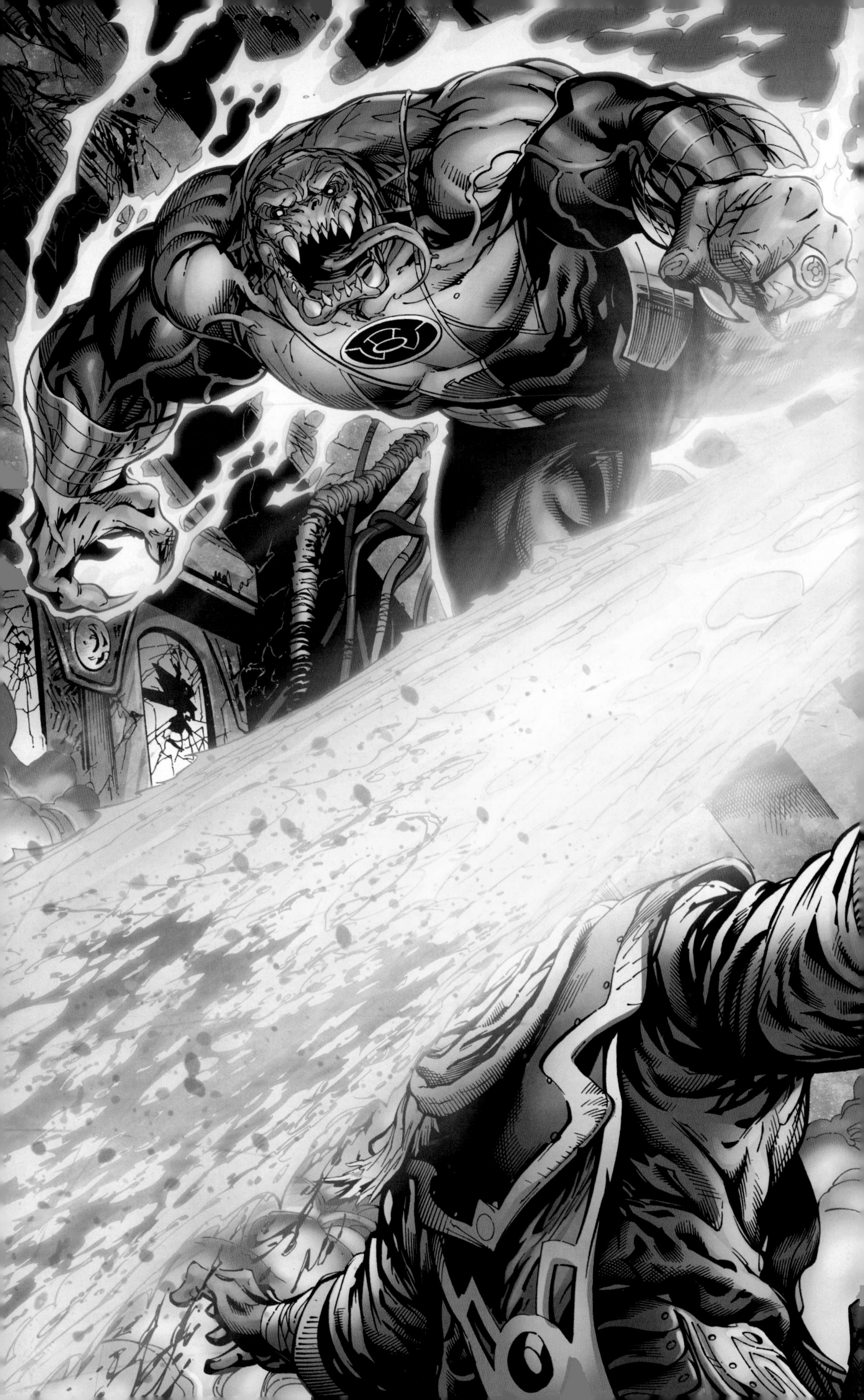

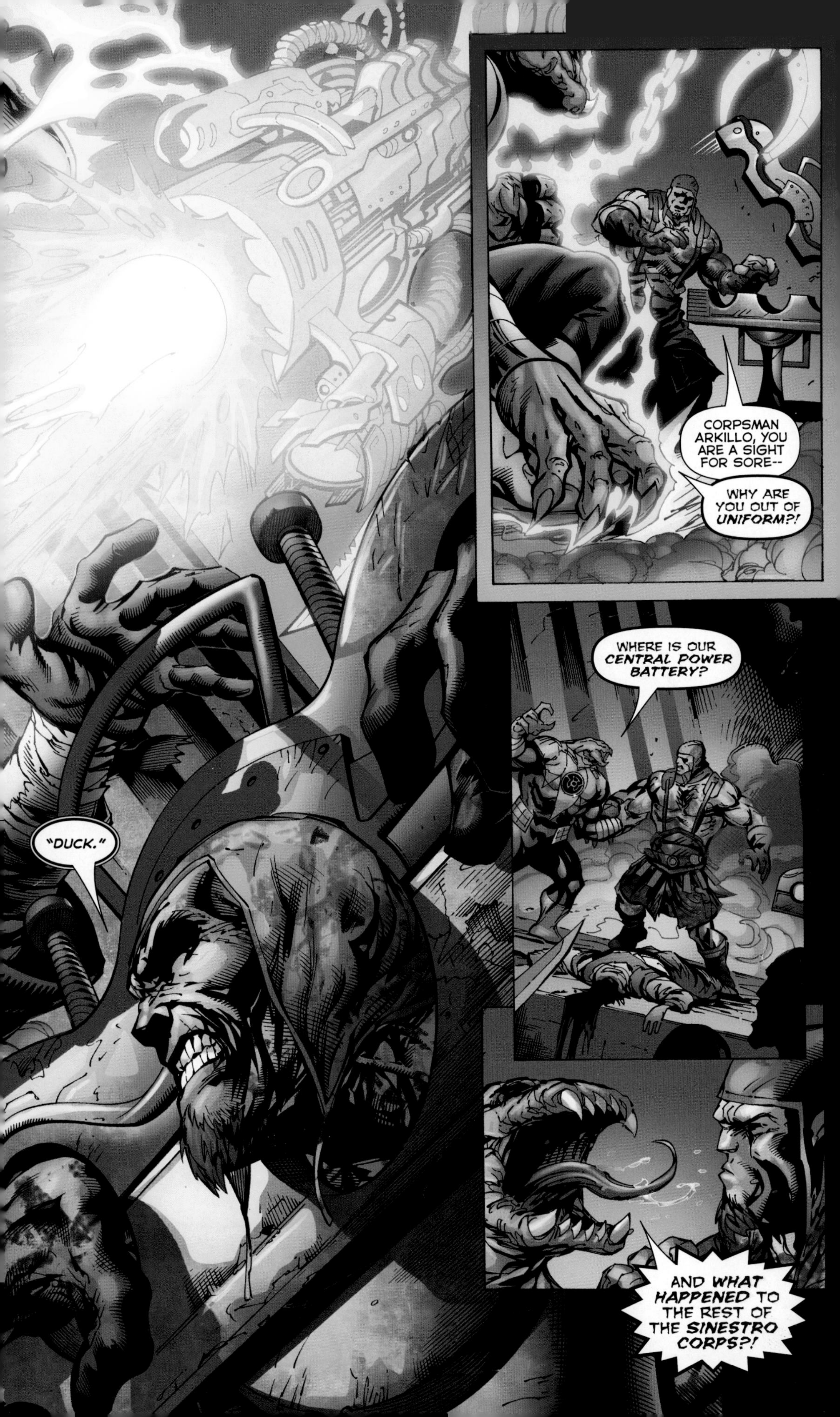
CORPSMAN ARKILLO, YOU ARE A SIGHT FOR SORE--
WHY ARE YOU OUT OF UNIFORM?!
WHERE IS OUR CENTRAL POWER BATTERY?
"DUCK."
AND WHAT HAPPENED TO THE REST OF THE SINESTRO CORPS?!

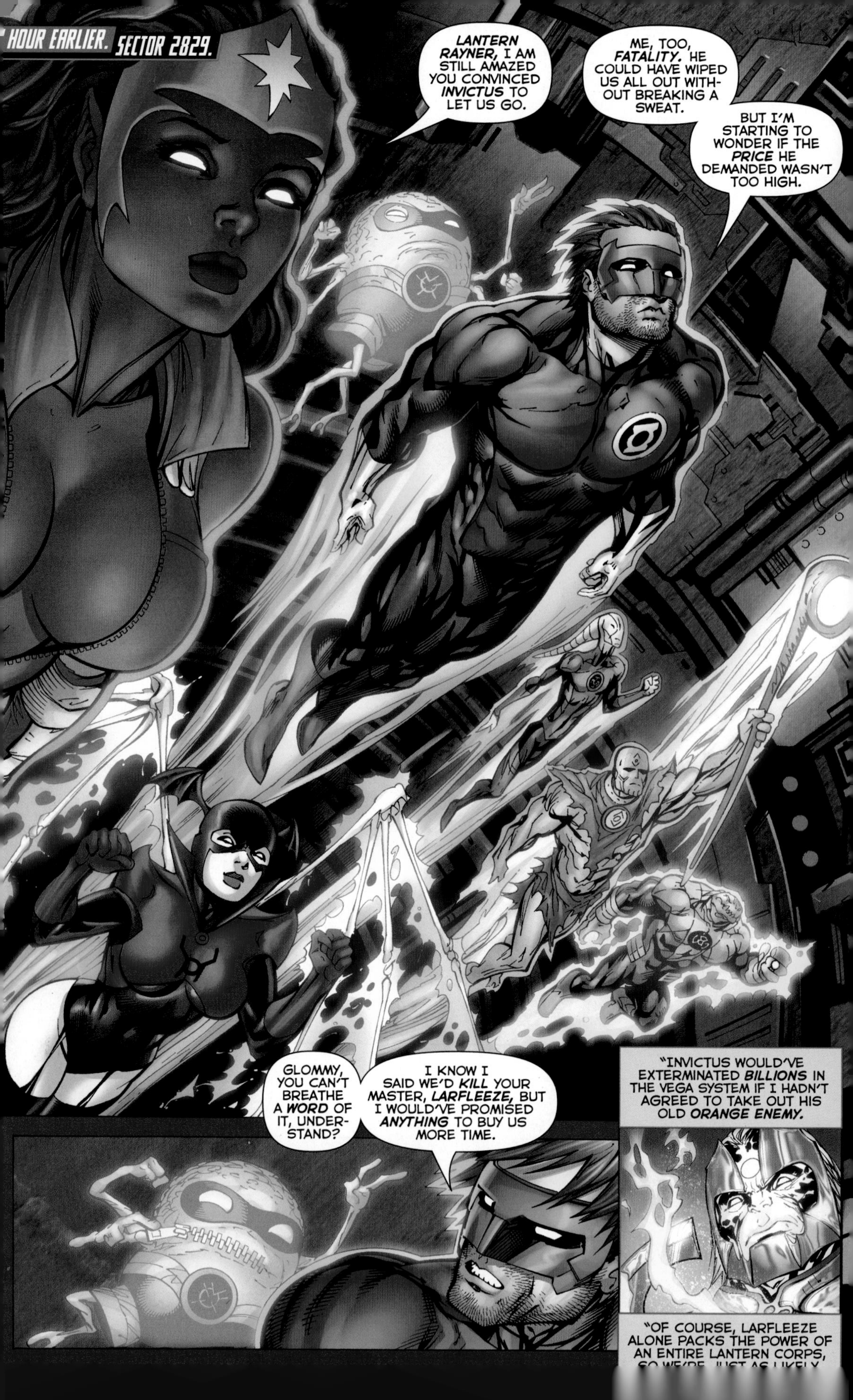
HOUR EARLIER. SECTOR 2829.
LANTERN RAYNER, I AM STILL AMAZED YOU CONVINCED INVICTUS TO LET US GO.
ME, TOO, FATALITY. HE COULD HAVE WIPED US ALL OUT WITH-OUT BREAKING A SWEAT.
BUT I'M STARTING TO WONDER IF THE PRICE HE DEMANDED WASN'T TOO HIGH.
GLOMMY, YOU CAN'T BREATHE A WORD OF IT, UNDER-STAND?
I KNOW I SAID WE'D KILL YOUR MASTER, LARFLEEZE, BUT I WOULD'VE PROMISED ANYTHING TO BUY US MORE TIME.
"INVICTUS WOULD'VE EXTERMINATED BILLIONS IN THE VEGA SYSTEM IF I HADN'T AGREED TO TAKE OUT HIS OLD ORANGE ENEMY.
"OF COURSE, LARFLEEZE ALONE PACKS THE POWER OF AN ENTIRE LANTERN CORPS,

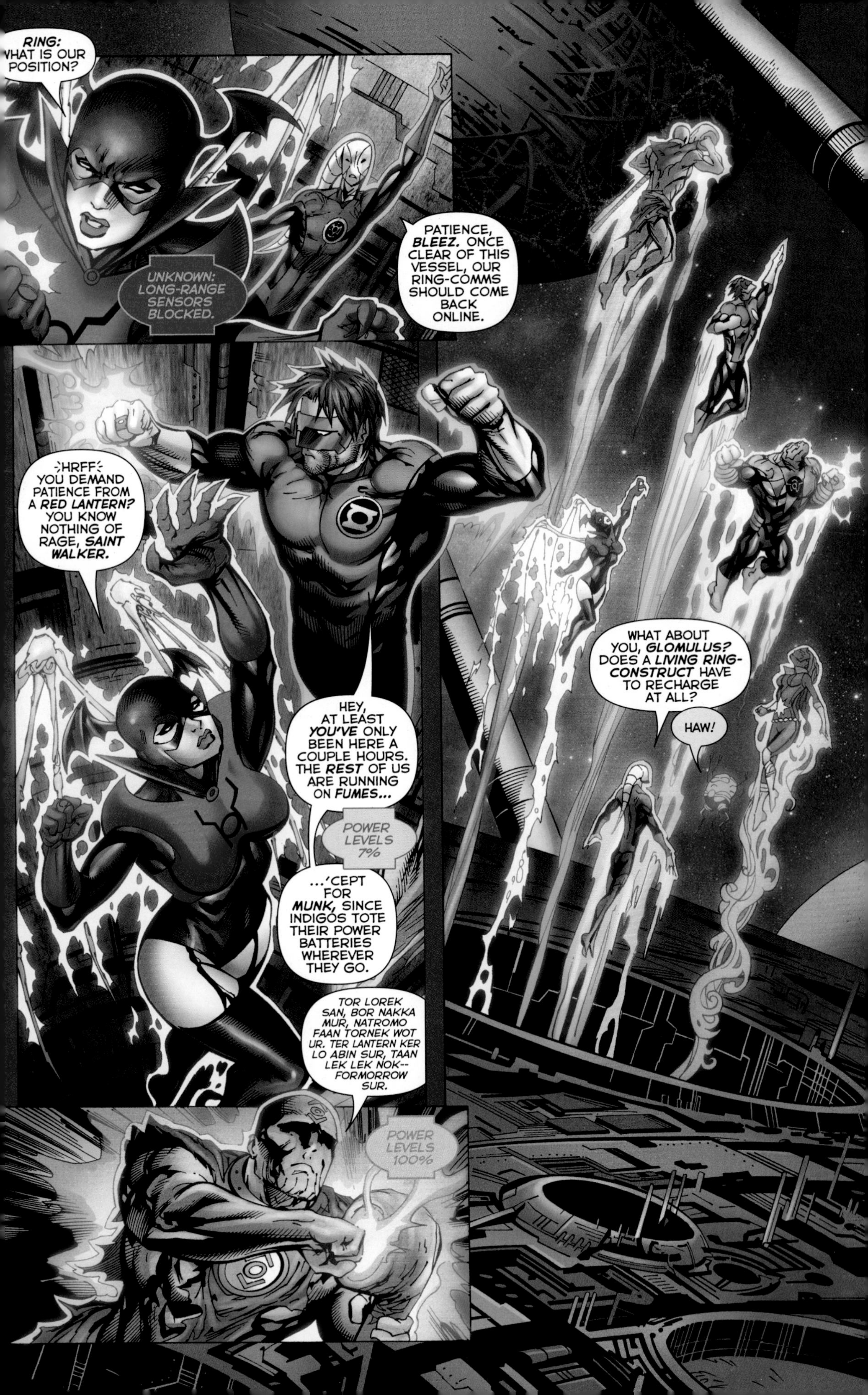
RING: WHAT IS OUR POSITION?
UNKNOWN: LONG-RANGE SENSORS BLOCKED.
PATIENCE, BLEEZ. ONCE CLEAR OF THIS VESSEL, OUR RING-COMMS SHOULD COME BACK ONLINE.
HRFF YOU DEMAND PATIENCE FROM A RED LANTERN? YOU KNOW NOTHING OF RAGE, SAINT WALKER.
HEY, AT LEAST YOU'VE ONLY BEEN HERE A COUPLE HOURS. THE REST OF US ARE RUNNING ON FUMES...
POWER LEVELS 7%
...'CEPT FOR MUNK, SINCE INDIGOS TOTE THEIR POWER BATTERIES WHEREVER THEY GO.
WHAT ABOUT YOU, GLOMULUS? DOES A LIVING RING-CONSTRUCT HAVE TO RECHARGE AT ALL?
HAW!
TOR LOREK SAN, BOR NAKKA MUR, NATROMO FAAN TORNEK WOT UR. TER LANTERN KER LO ABIN SUR, TAAN LEK LEK NOK--FORMORROW SUR.
POWER LEVELS 100%

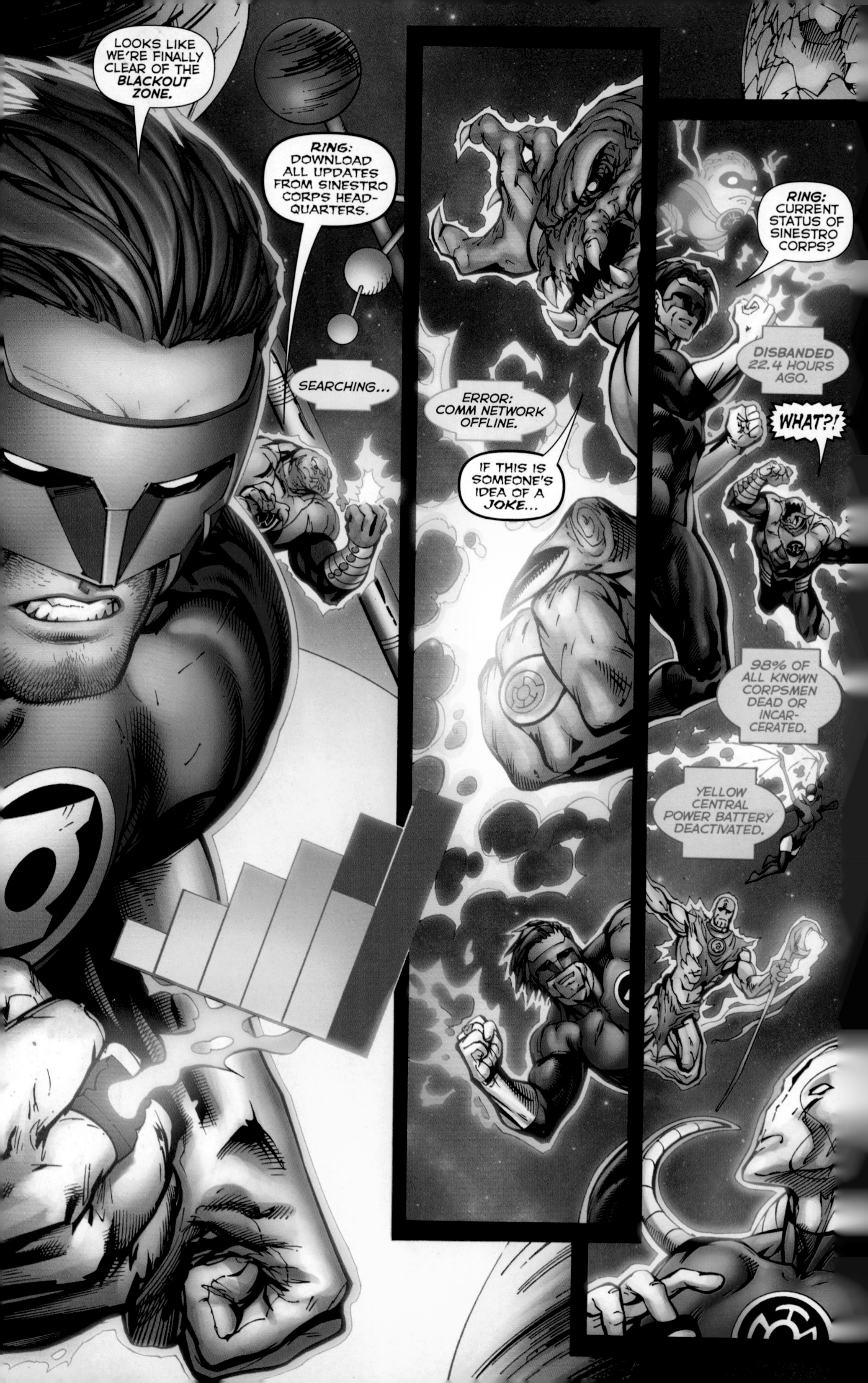
LOOKS LIKE WE'RE FINALLY CLEAR OF THE BLACKOUT ZONE.
RING: DOWNLOAD ALL UPDATES FROM SINESTRO CORPS HEAD-QUARTERS.
SEARCHING...
ERROR: COMM NETWORK OFFLINE.
IF THIS IS SOMEONE'S IDEA OF A JOKE...
RING: CURRENT STATUS OF SINESTRO CORPS?
DISBANDED 22.4 HOURS AGO.
WHAT?!
98% OF ALL KNOWN CORPSMEN DEAD OR INCAR-CERATED.
YELLOW CENTRAL POWER BATTERY DEACTIVATED.

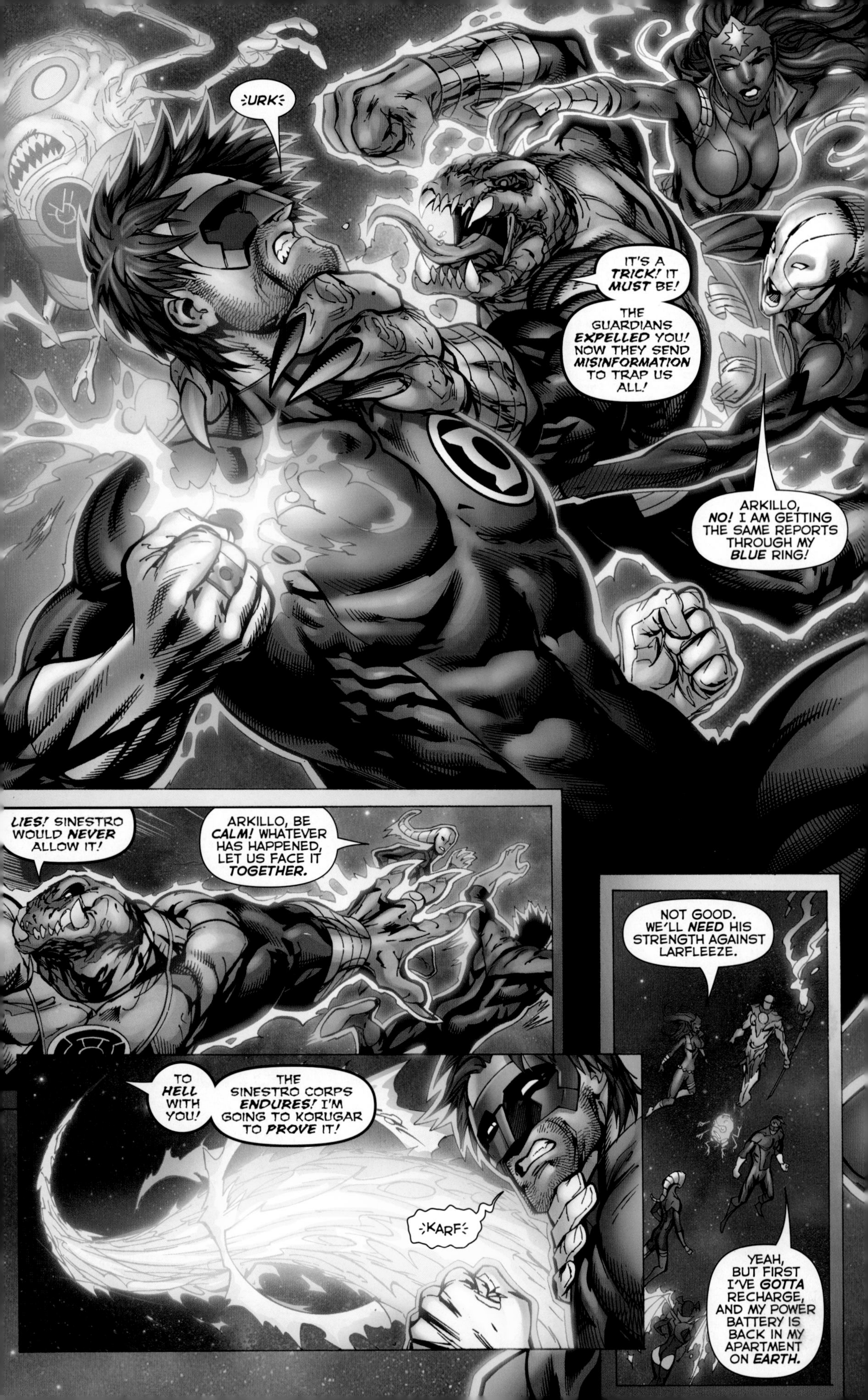
URK
IT'S A TRICK! IT MUST BE!
THE GUARDIANS EXPELLED YOU! NOW THEY SEND MISINFORMATION TO TRAP US ALL!
ARKILLO, NO! I AM GETTING THE SAME REPORTS THROUGH MY BLUE RING!
LIES! SINESTRO WOULD NEVER ALLOW IT!
ARKILLO, BE CALM! WHATEVER HAS HAPPENED, LET US FACE IT TOGETHER.
TO HELL WITH YOU!
THE SINESTRO CORPS ENDURES! I'M GOING TO KORUGAR TO PROVE IT!
KARF
NOT GOOD. WE'LL NEED HIS STRENGTH AGAINST LARFLEEZE.
YEAH, BUT FIRST I'VE GOTTA RECHARGE, AND MY POWER BATTERY IS BACK IN MY APARTMENT ON EARTH.

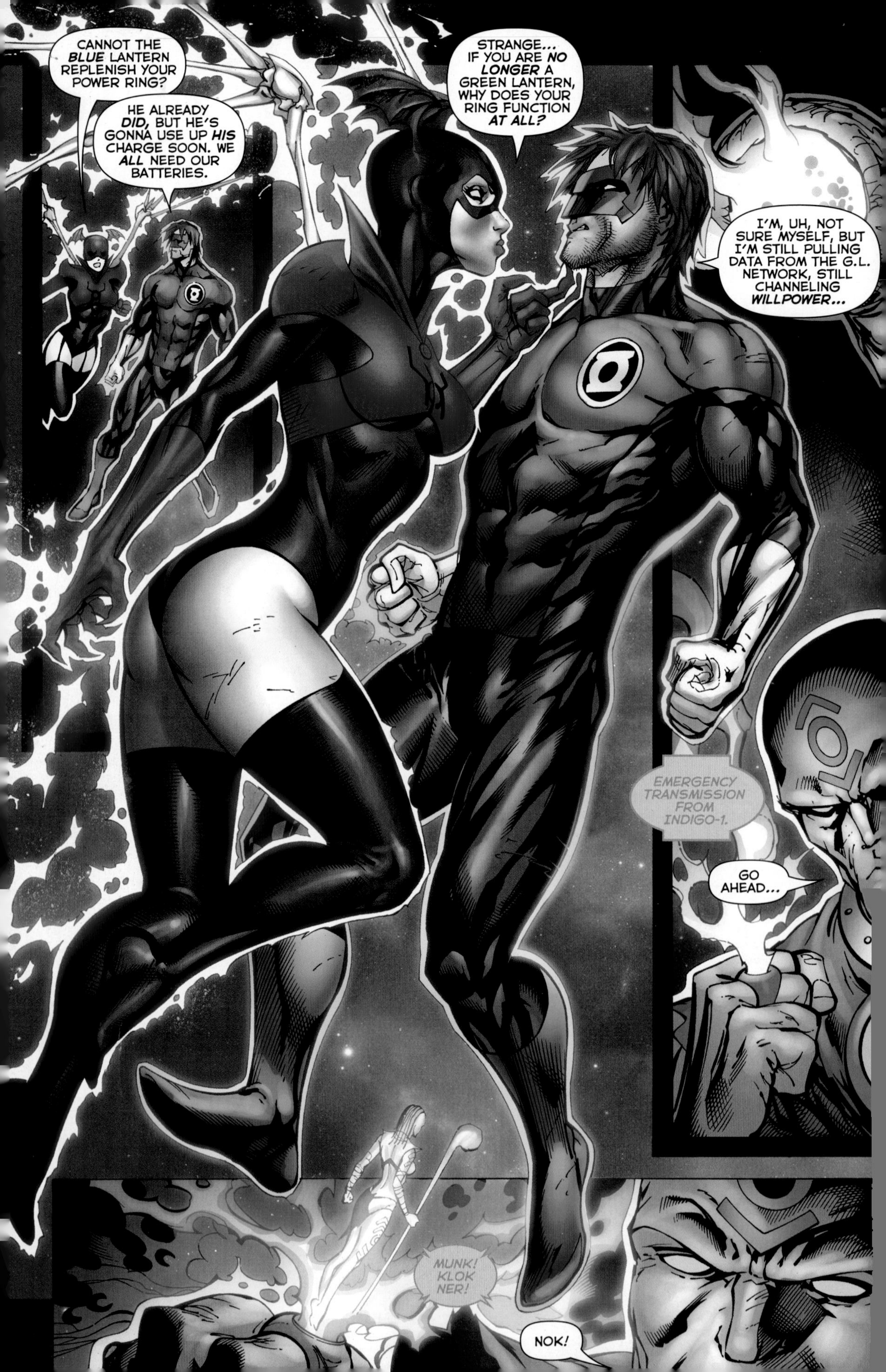
CANNOT THE *BLUE* LANTERN REPLENISH YOUR POWER RING?
HE ALREADY *DID,* BUT HE'S GONNA USE UP *HIS* CHARGE SOON. WE *ALL* NEED OUR BATTERIES.
STRANGE... IF YOU ARE *NO LONGER* A GREEN LANTERN, WHY DOES YOUR RING FUNCTION *AT ALL?*
I'M, UH, NOT SURE MYSELF, BUT I'M STILL PULLING DATA FROM THE G.L. NETWORK, STILL CHANNELING *WILLPOWER...*
EMERGENCY TRANSMISSION FROM INDIGO-1.
GO AHEAD...
MUNK! KLOK NER!
NOK!

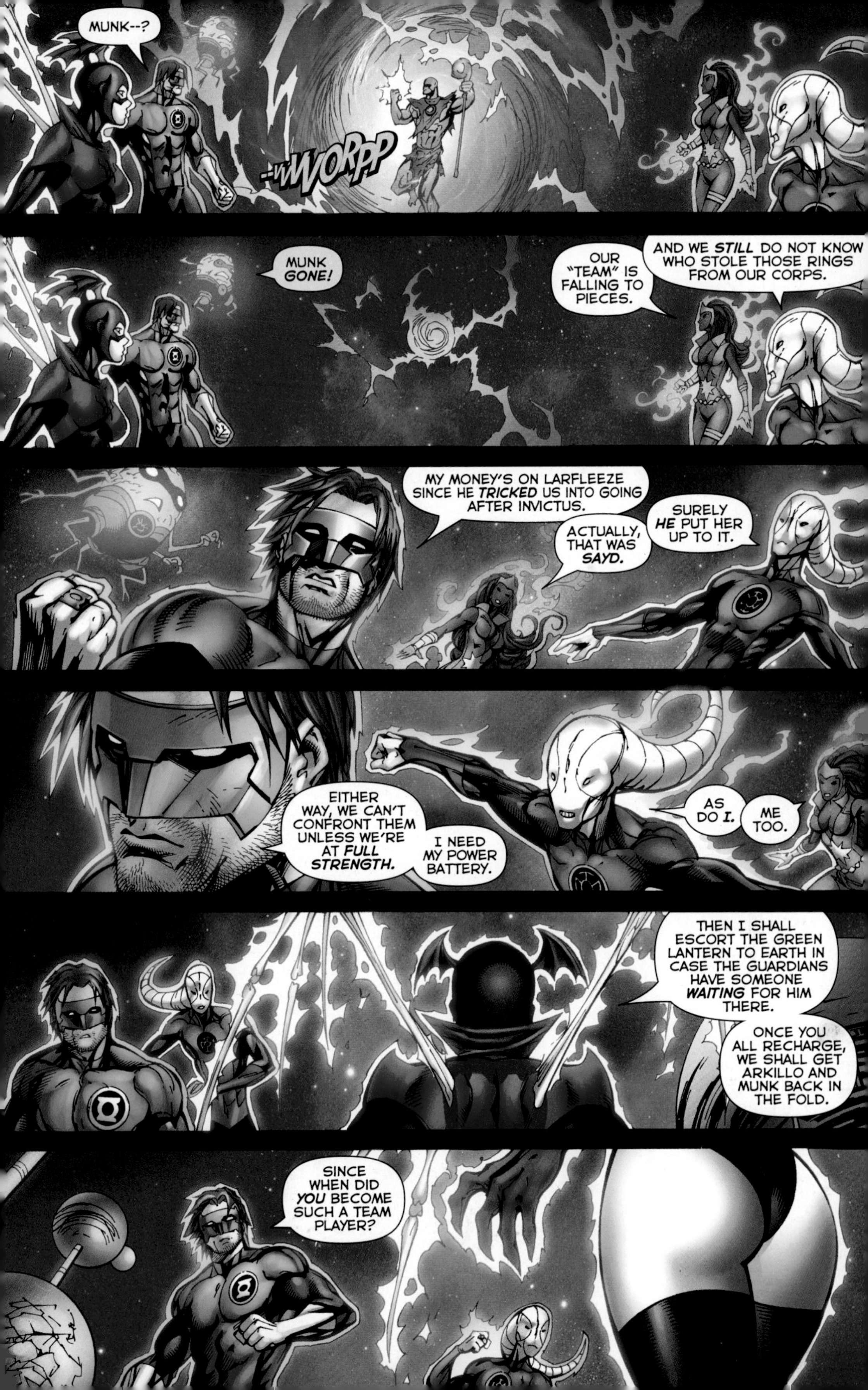
MUNK--?
-VVWORPP
MUNK GONE!
OUR "TEAM" IS FALLING TO PIECES.
AND WE STILL DO NOT KNOW WHO STOLE THOSE RINGS FROM OUR CORPS.
MY MONEY'S ON LARFLEEZE SINCE HE TRICKED US INTO GOING AFTER INVICTUS.
ACTUALLY, THAT WAS SAYD.
SURELY HE PUT HER UP TO IT.
EITHER WAY, WE CAN'T CONFRONT THEM UNLESS WE'RE AT FULL STRENGTH.
I NEED MY POWER BATTERY.
AS DO I.
ME TOO.
THEN I SHALL ESCORT THE GREEN LANTERN TO EARTH IN CASE THE GUARDIANS HAVE SOMEONE WAITING FOR HIM THERE.
ONCE YOU ALL RECHARGE, WE SHALL GET ARKILLO AND MUNK BACK IN THE FOLD.
SINCE WHEN DID YOU BECOME SUCH A TEAM PLAYER?

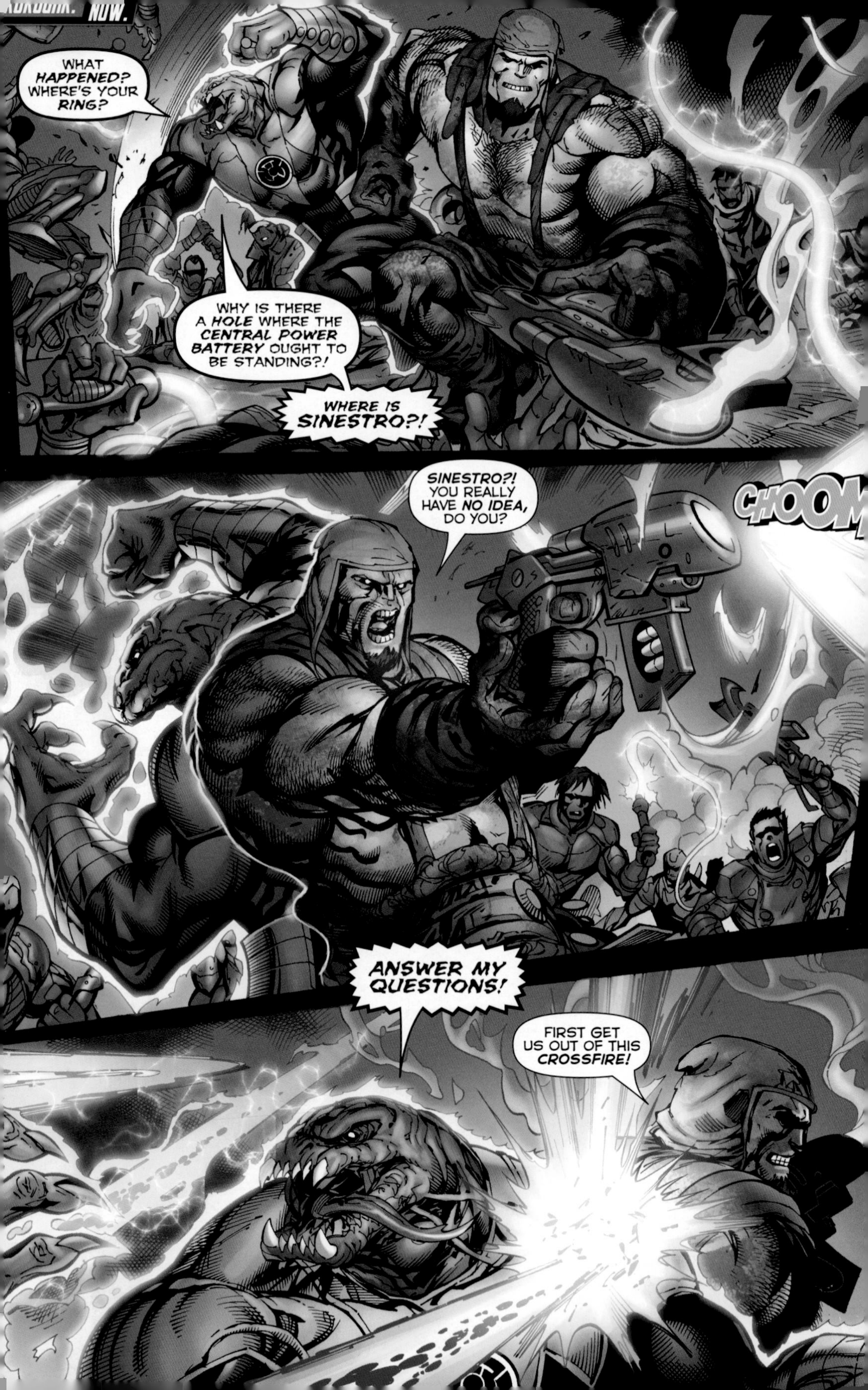
NOW.
WHAT HAPPENED? WHERE'S YOUR RING?
WHY IS THERE A HOLE WHERE THE CENTRAL POWER BATTERY OUGHT TO BE STANDING?!
WHERE IS SINESTRO?!
SINESTRO?! YOU REALLY HAVE NO IDEA, DO YOU?
CHOOM
ANSWER MY QUESTIONS!
FIRST GET US OUT OF THIS CROSSFIRE!

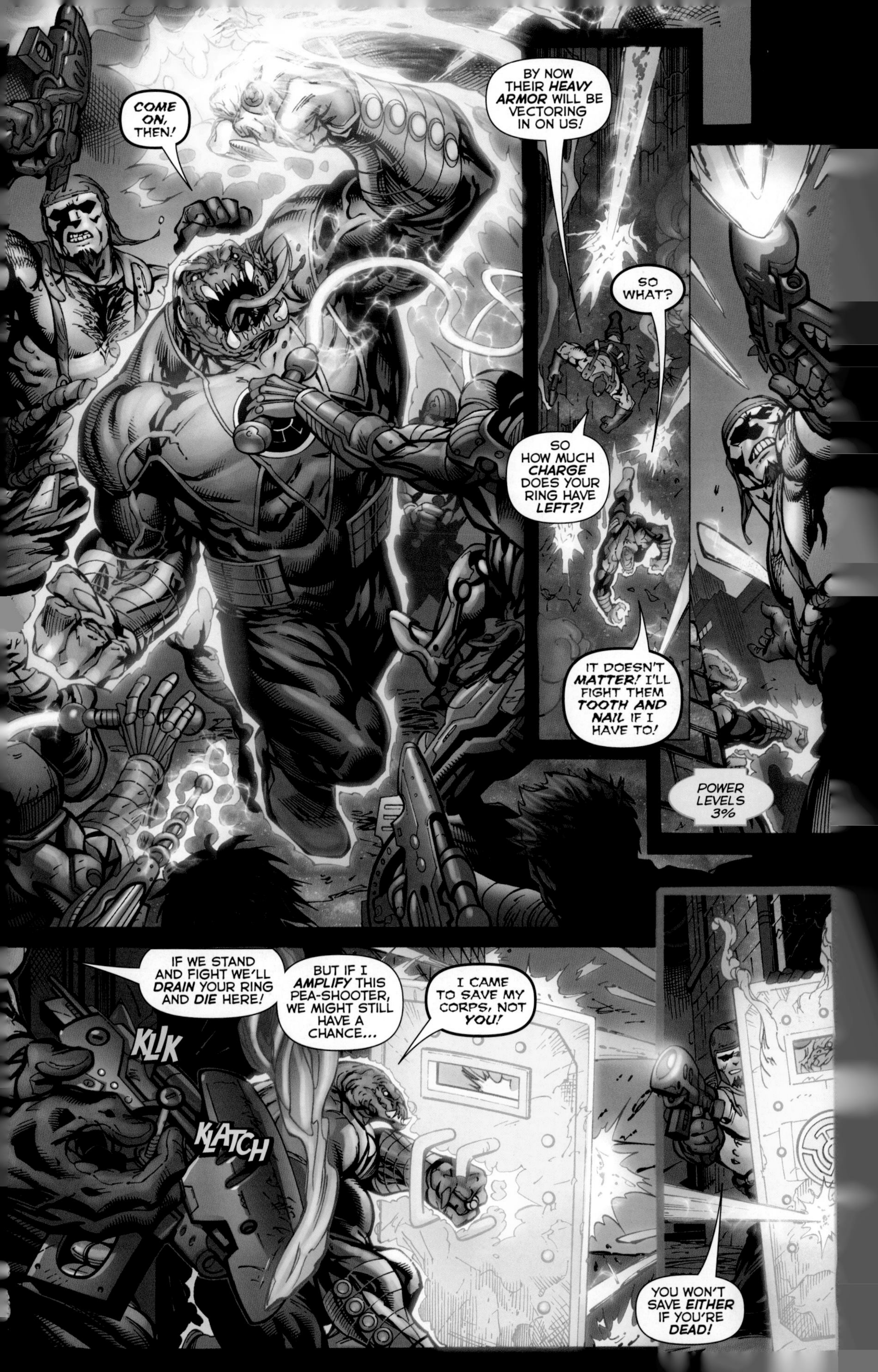
COME ON, THEN!
BY NOW THEIR HEAVY ARMOR WILL BE VECTORING IN ON US!
SO WHAT?
SO HOW MUCH CHARGE DOES YOUR RING HAVE LEFT?!
IT DOESN'T MATTER! I'LL FIGHT THEM TOOTH AND NAIL IF I HAVE TO!
POWER LEVELS 3%
IF WE STAND AND FIGHT WE'LL DRAIN YOUR RING AND DIE HERE!
BUT IF I AMPLIFY THIS PEA-SHOOTER, WE MIGHT STILL HAVE A CHANCE...
I CAME TO SAVE MY CORPS, NOT YOU!
KLIK
KLATCH
YOU WON'T SAVE EITHER IF YOU'RE DEAD!

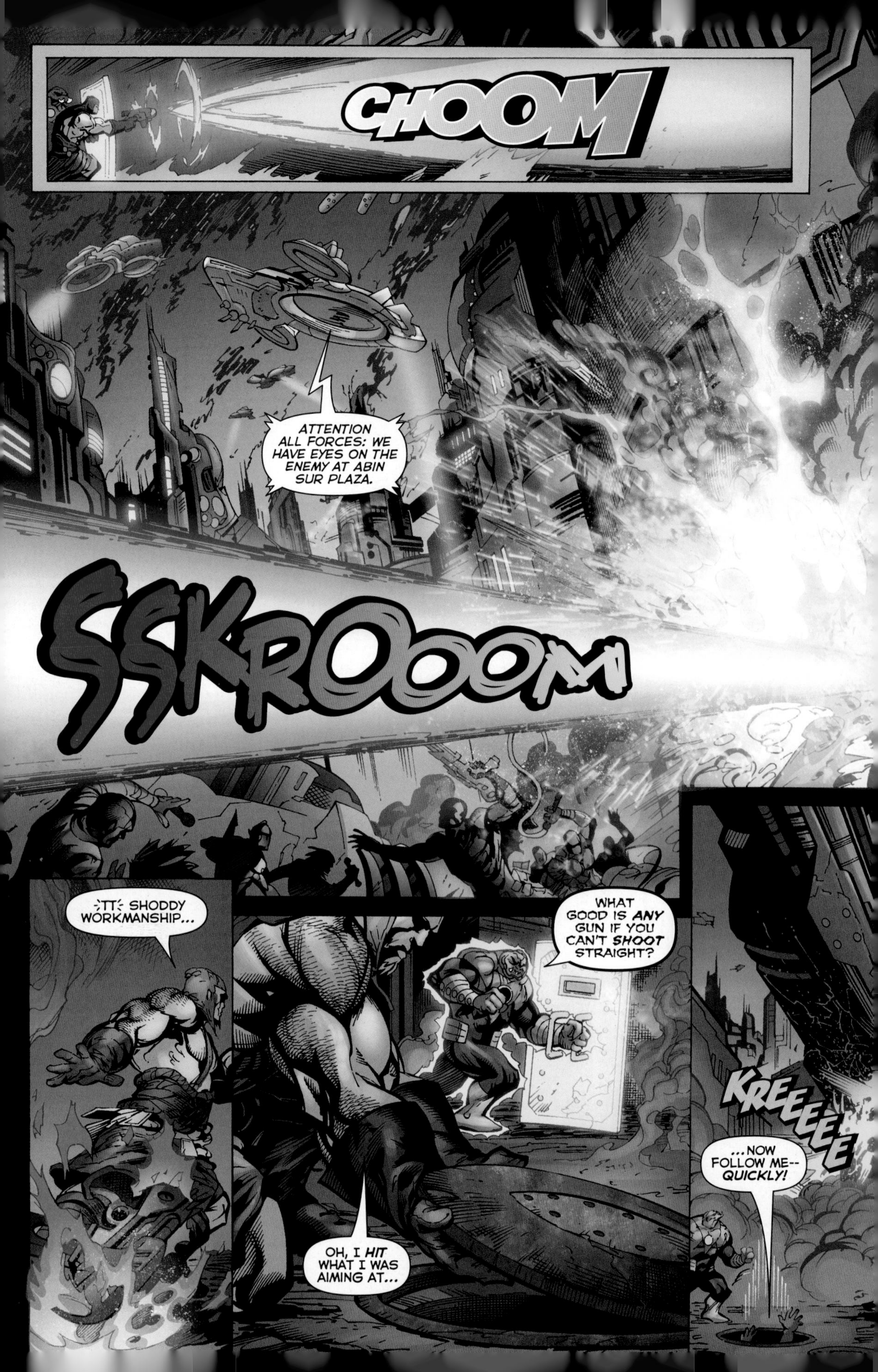
CHOOM
ATTENTION ALL FORCES: WE HAVE EYES ON THE ENEMY AT ABIN SUR PLAZA.
SSKROOOOM
-TT- SHODDY WORKMANSHIP...
WHAT GOOD IS ANY GUN IF YOU CAN'T SHOOT STRAIGHT?
OH, I HIT WHAT I WAS AIMING AT...
KREEEEEE
...NOW FOLLOW ME-- QUICKLY!

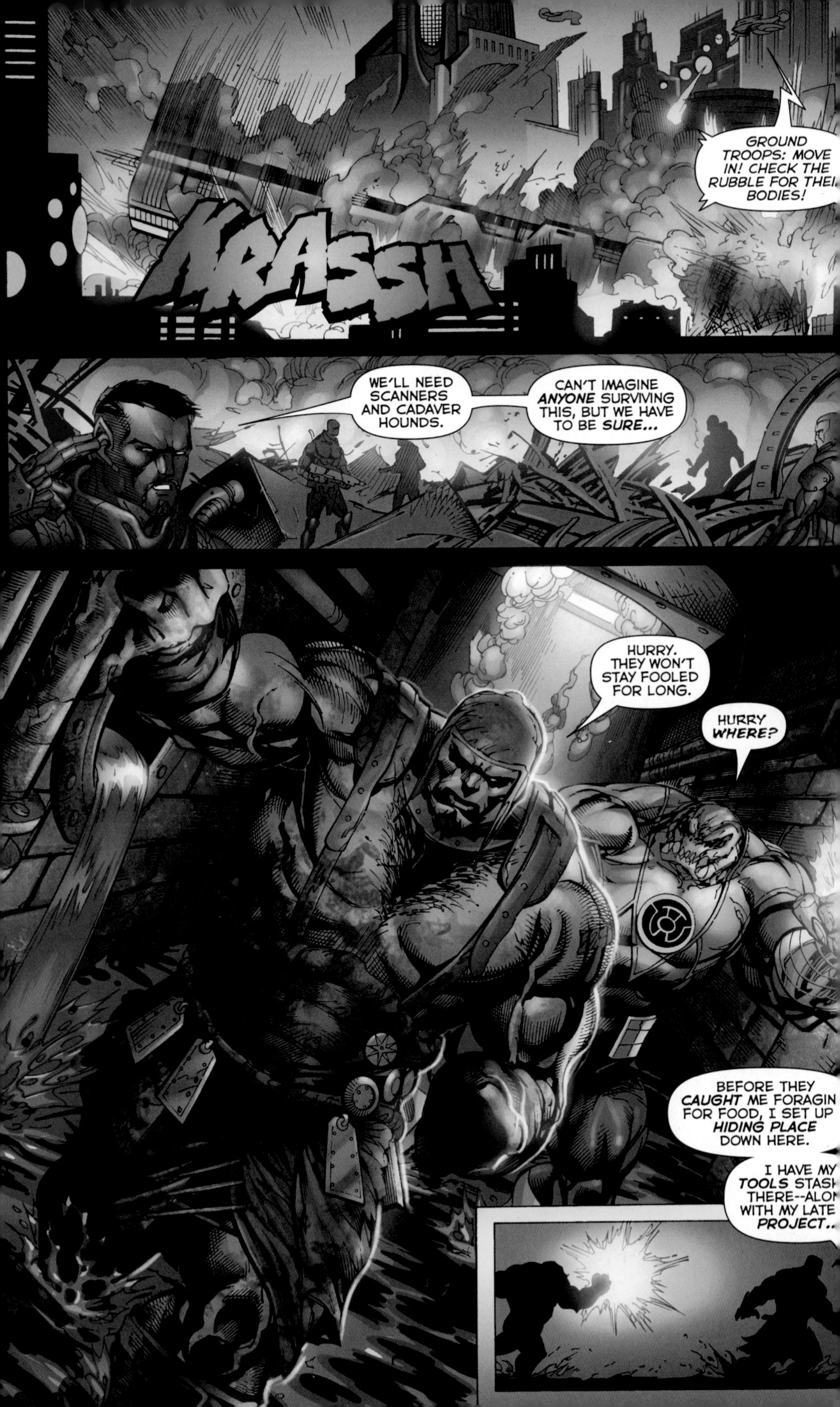
KRASSH
GROUND TROOPS: MOVE IN! CHECK THE RUBBLE FOR THEI BODIES!
WE'LL NEED SCANNERS AND CADAVER HOUNDS.
CAN'T IMAGINE ANYONE SURVIVING THIS, BUT WE HAVE TO BE SURE...
HURRY. THEY WON'T STAY FOOLED FOR LONG.
HURRY WHERE?
BEFORE THEY CAUGHT ME FORAGIN FOR FOOD, I SET UP HIDING PLACE DOWN HERE.
I HAVE MY TOOLS STAS THERE--ALO WITH MY LATE PROJECT..

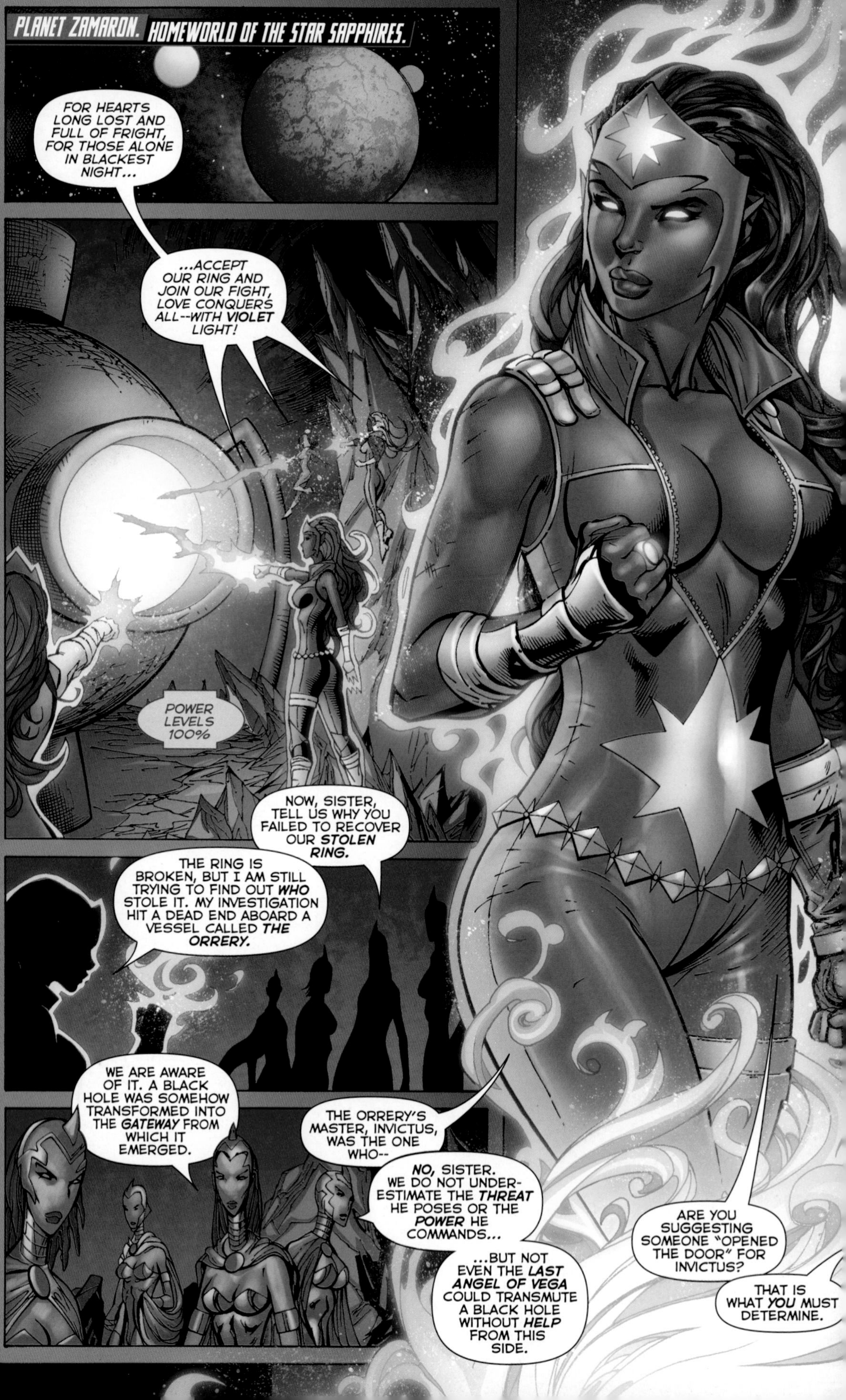
PLANET ZAMARON. HOMEWORLD OF THE STAR SAPPHIRES.
FOR HEARTS LONG LOST AND FULL OF FRIGHT, FOR THOSE ALONE IN BLACKEST NIGHT...
...ACCEPT OUR RING AND JOIN OUR FIGHT, LOVE CONQUERS ALL--WITH VIOLET LIGHT!
POWER LEVELS 100%
NOW, SISTER, TELL US WHY YOU FAILED TO RECOVER OUR STOLEN RING.
THE RING IS BROKEN, BUT I AM STILL TRYING TO FIND OUT WHO STOLE IT. MY INVESTIGATION HIT A DEAD END ABOARD A VESSEL CALLED THE ORRERY.
WE ARE AWARE OF IT. A BLACK HOLE WAS SOMEHOW TRANSFORMED INTO THE GATEWAY FROM WHICH IT EMERGED.
THE ORRERY'S MASTER, INVICTUS, WAS THE ONE WHO--
NO, SISTER. WE DO NOT UNDER-ESTIMATE THE THREAT HE POSES OR THE POWER HE COMMANDS...
...BUT NOT EVEN THE LAST ANGEL OF VEGA COULD TRANSMUTE A BLACK HOLE WITHOUT HELP FROM THIS SIDE.
ARE YOU SUGGESTING SOMEONE "OPENED THE DOOR" FOR INVICTUS?
THAT IS WHAT YOU MUST DETERMINE.

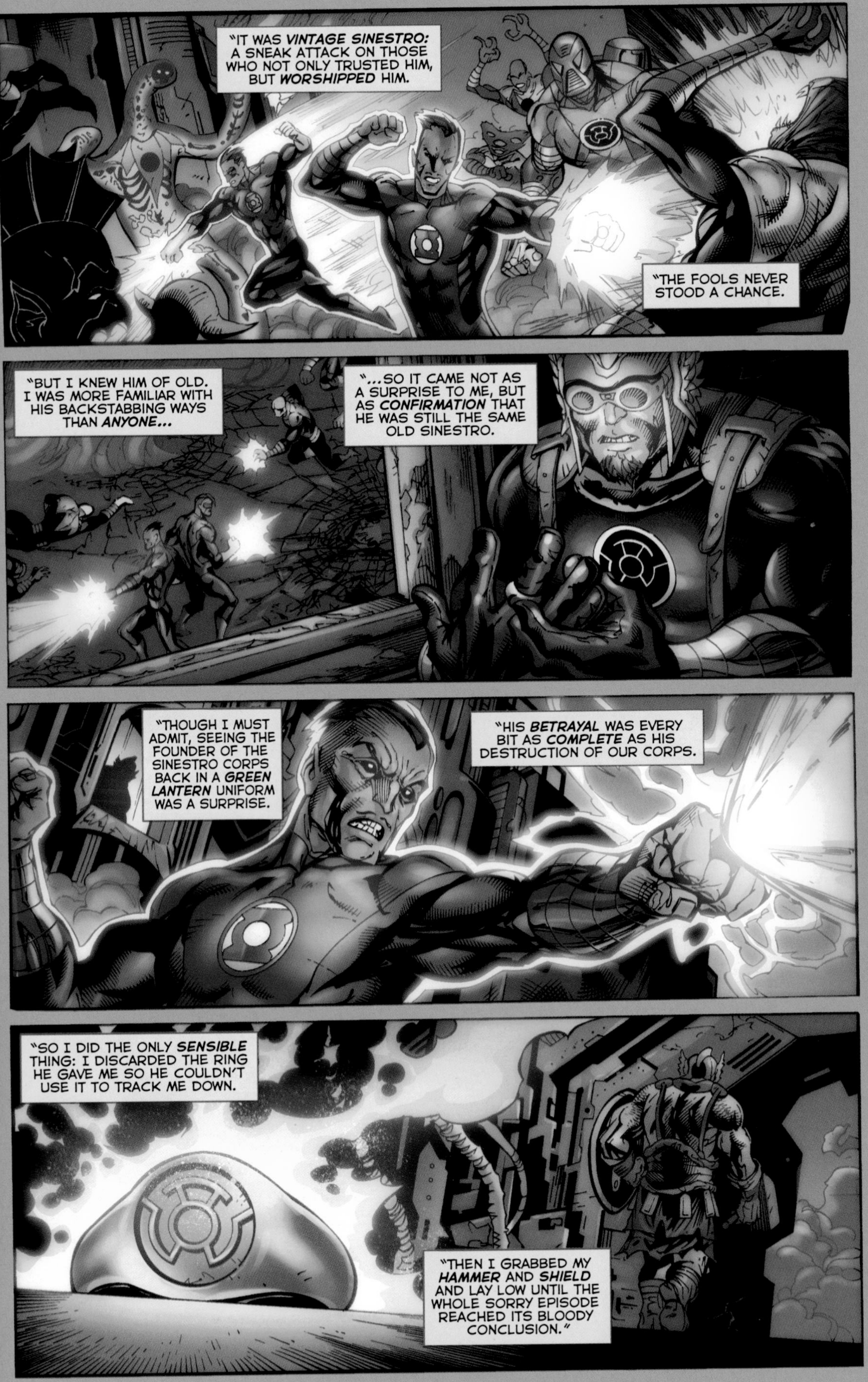
"IT WAS VINTAGE SINESTRO: A SNEAK ATTACK ON THOSE WHO NOT ONLY TRUSTED HIM, BUT WORSHIPPED HIM.
"THE FOOLS NEVER STOOD A CHANCE.
"BUT I KNEW HIM OF OLD. I WAS MORE FAMILIAR WITH HIS BACKSTABBING WAYS THAN ANYONE...
"...SO IT CAME NOT AS A SURPRISE TO ME, BUT AS CONFIRMATION THAT HE WAS STILL THE SAME OLD SINESTRO.
"THOUGH I MUST ADMIT, SEEING THE FOUNDER OF THE SINESTRO CORPS BACK IN A GREEN LANTERN UNIFORM WAS A SURPRISE.
"HIS BETRAYAL WAS EVERY BIT AS COMPLETE AS HIS DESTRUCTION OF OUR CORPS.
"SO I DID THE ONLY SENSIBLE THING: I DISCARDED THE RING HE GAVE ME SO HE COULDN'T USE IT TO TRACK ME DOWN.
"THEN I GRABBED MY HAMMER AND SHIELD AND LAY LOW UNTIL THE WHOLE SORRY EPISODE REACHED ITS BLOODY CONCLUSION."

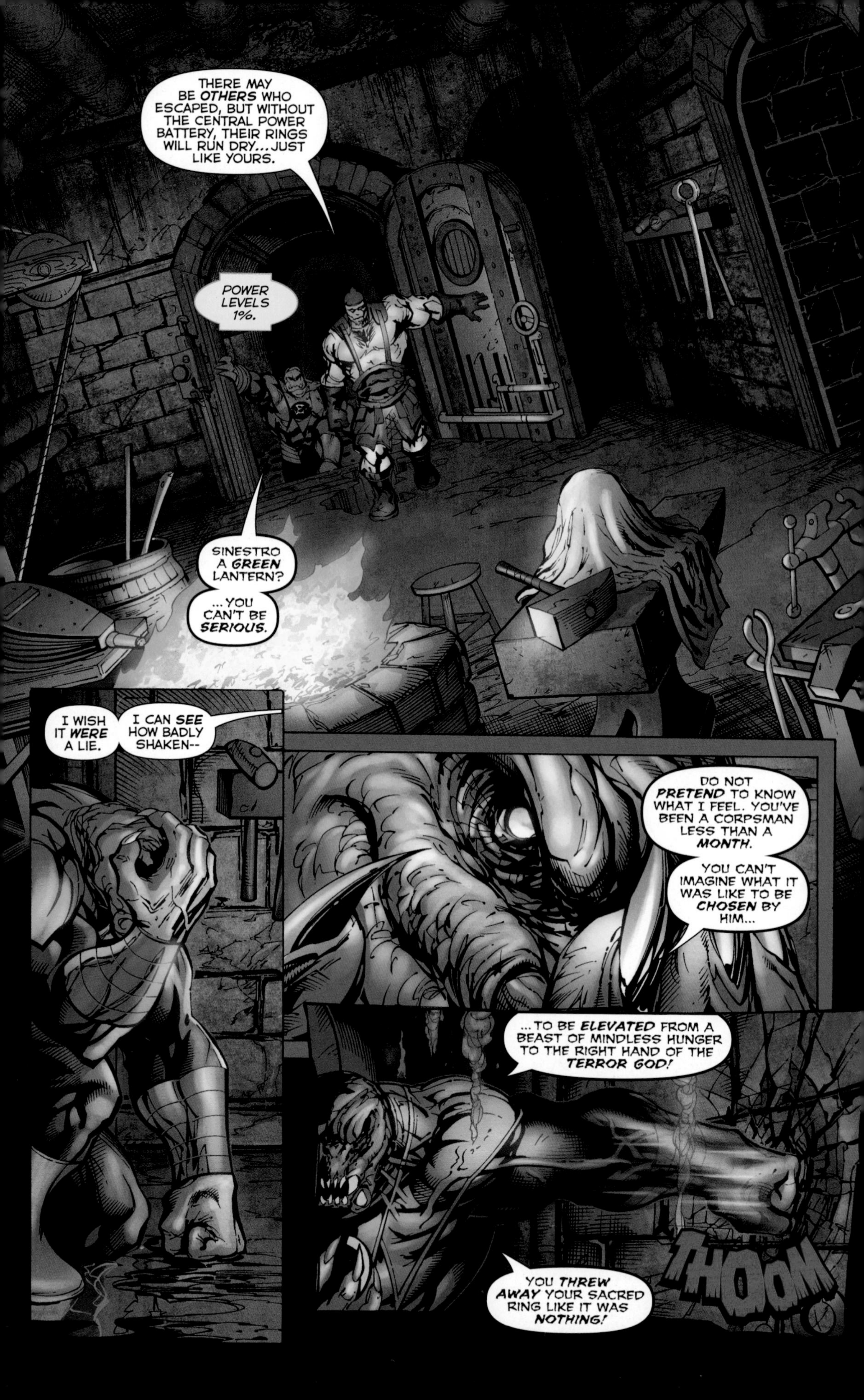

THERE MAY BE OTHERS WHO ESCAPED, BUT WITHOUT THE CENTRAL POWER BATTERY, THEIR RINGS WILL RUN DRY... JUST LIKE YOURS.
POWER LEVELS 1%.
SINESTRO A GREEN LANTERN?
...YOU CAN'T BE SERIOUS.
I WISH IT WERE A LIE.
I CAN SEE HOW BADLY SHAKEN--
DO NOT PRETEND TO KNOW WHAT I FEEL. YOU'VE BEEN A CORPSMAN LESS THAN A MONTH.
YOU CAN'T IMAGINE WHAT IT WAS LIKE TO BE CHOSEN BY HIM...
...TO BE ELEVATED FROM A BEAST OF MINDLESS HUNGER TO THE RIGHT HAND OF THE TERROR GOD!
THOOM
YOU THREW AWAY YOUR SACRED RING LIKE IT WAS NOTHING!

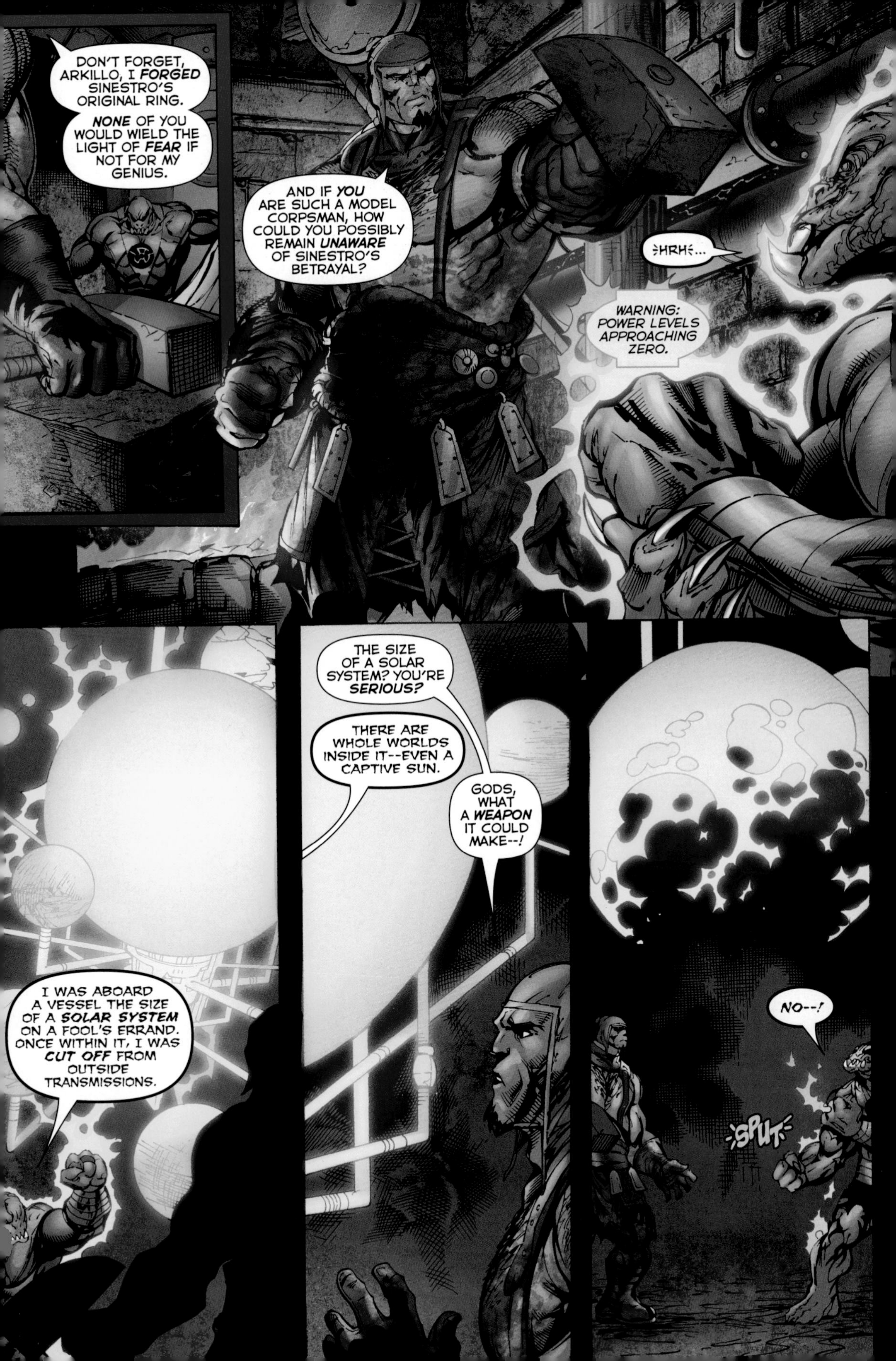
DON'T FORGET, ARKILLO, I FORGED SINESTRO'S ORIGINAL RING.
NONE OF YOU WOULD WIELD THE LIGHT OF FEAR IF NOT FOR MY GENIUS.
AND IF YOU ARE SUCH A MODEL CORPSMAN, HOW COULD YOU POSSIBLY REMAIN UNAWARE OF SINESTRO'S BETRAYAL?
HRH...
WARNING: POWER LEVELS APPROACHING ZERO.
I WAS ABOARD A VESSEL THE SIZE OF A SOLAR SYSTEM ON A FOOL'S ERRAND. ONCE WITHIN IT, I WAS CUT OFF FROM OUTSIDE TRANSMISSIONS.
THE SIZE OF A SOLAR SYSTEM? YOU'RE SERIOUS?
THERE ARE WHOLE WORLDS INSIDE IT--EVEN A CAPTIVE SUN.
GODS, WHAT A WEAPON IT COULD MAKE--!
NO--!
SPUT

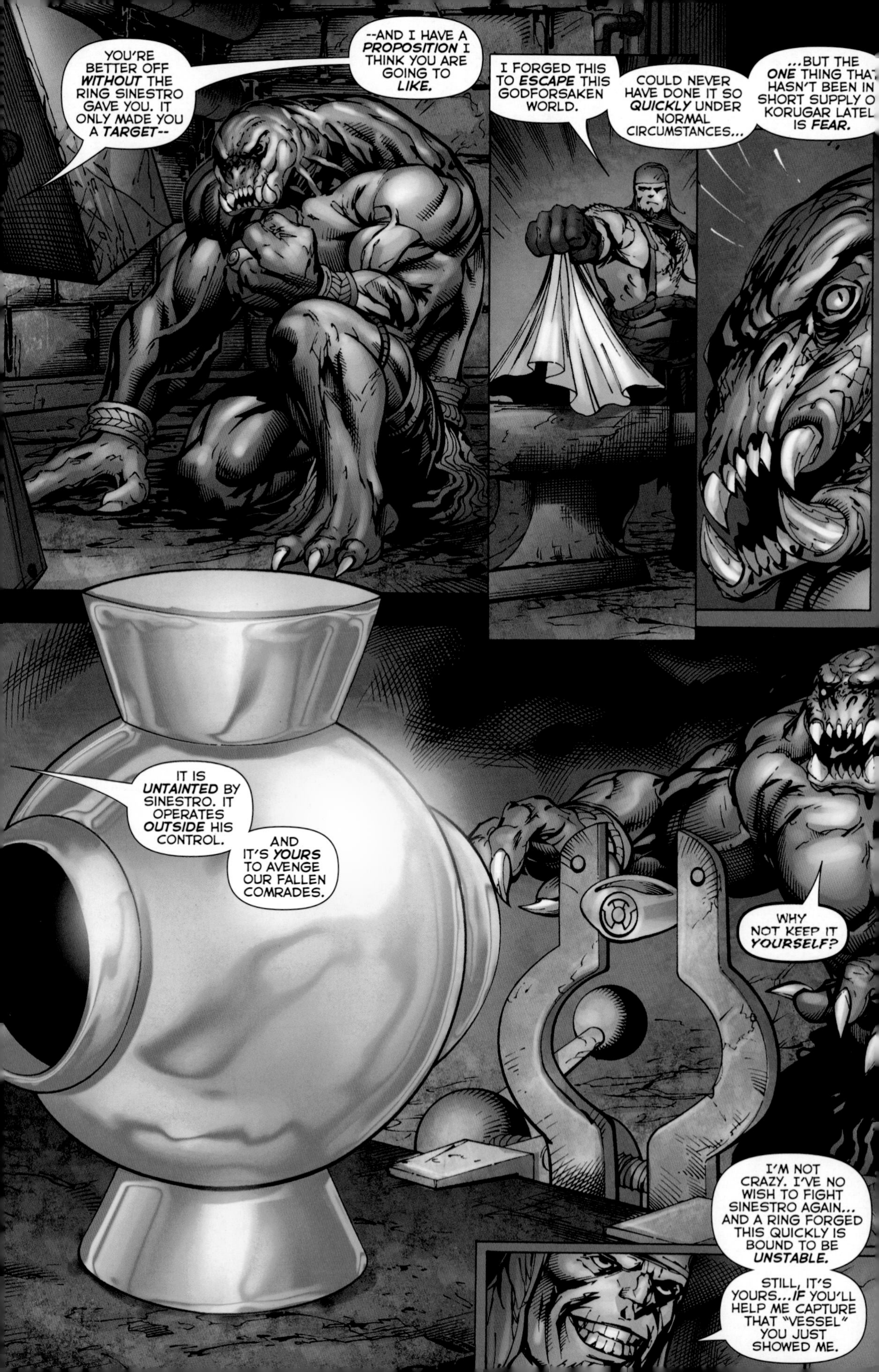

YOU'RE BETTER OFF WITHOUT THE RING SINESTRO GAVE YOU. IT ONLY MADE YOU A TARGET--
--AND I HAVE A PROPOSITION I THINK YOU ARE GOING TO LIKE.
I FORGED THIS TO ESCAPE THIS GODFORSAKEN WORLD.
COULD NEVER HAVE DONE IT SO QUICKLY UNDER NORMAL CIRCUMSTANCES...
...BUT THE ONE THING THAT HASN'T BEEN IN SHORT SUPPLY ON KORUGAR LATELY IS FEAR.
IT IS UNTAINTED BY SINESTRO. IT OPERATES OUTSIDE HIS CONTROL.
AND IT'S YOURS TO AVENGE OUR FALLEN COMRADES.
WHY NOT KEEP IT YOURSELF?
I'M NOT CRAZY. I'VE NO WISH TO FIGHT SINESTRO AGAIN... AND A RING FORGED THIS QUICKLY IS BOUND TO BE UNSTABLE.
STILL, IT'S YOURS...IF YOU'LL HELP ME CAPTURE THAT "VESSEL" YOU JUST SHOWED ME.

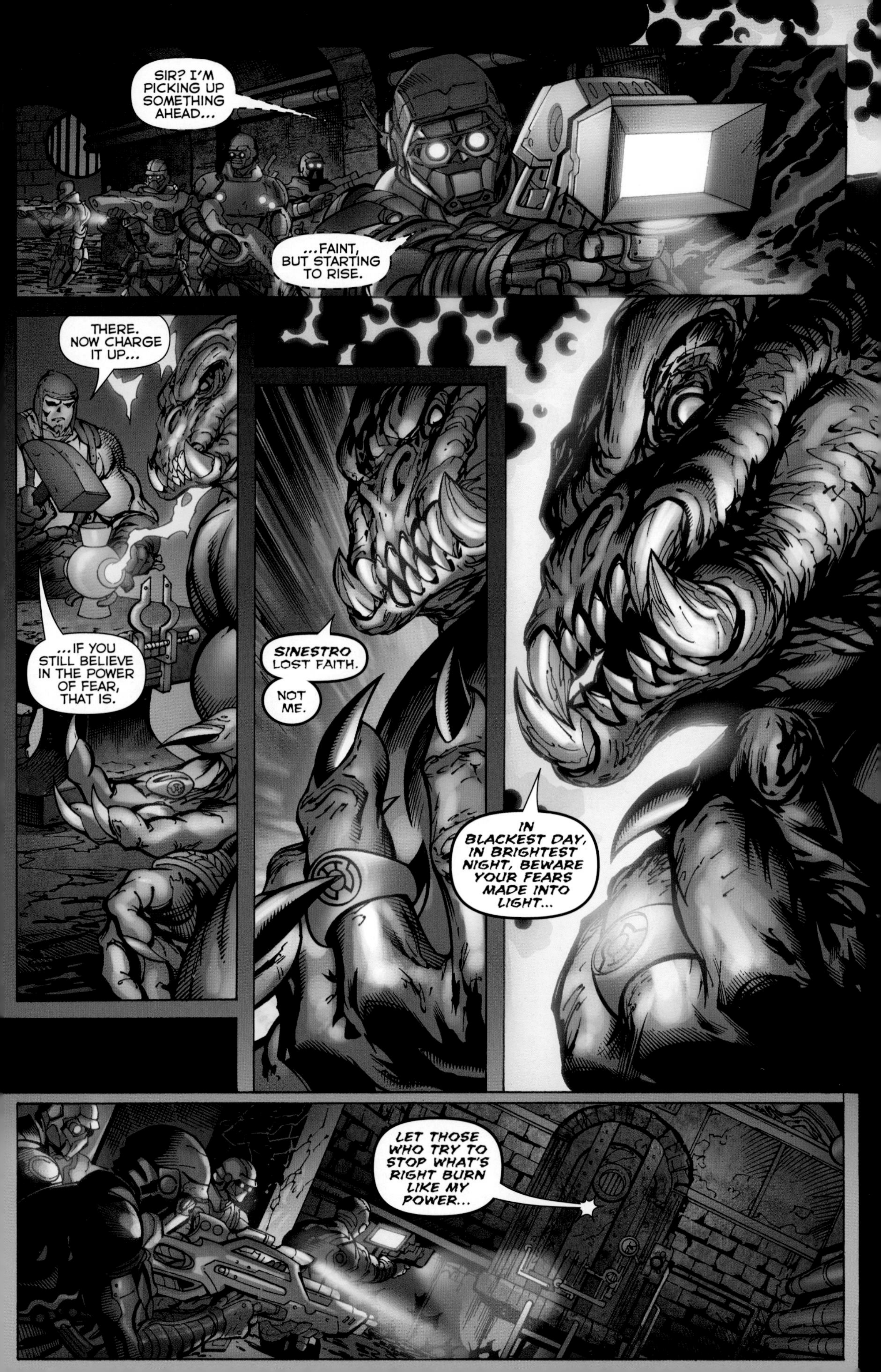
SIR? I'M PICKING UP SOMETHING AHEAD...
...FAINT, BUT STARTING TO RISE.
THERE. NOW CHARGE IT UP...
...IF YOU STILL BELIEVE IN THE POWER OF FEAR, THAT IS.
SINESTRO LOST FAITH.
NOT ME.
IN BLACKEST DAY, IN BRIGHTEST NIGHT, BEWARE YOUR FEARS MADE INTO LIGHT...
LET THOSE WHO TRY TO STOP WHAT'S RIGHT BURN LIKE MY POWER...

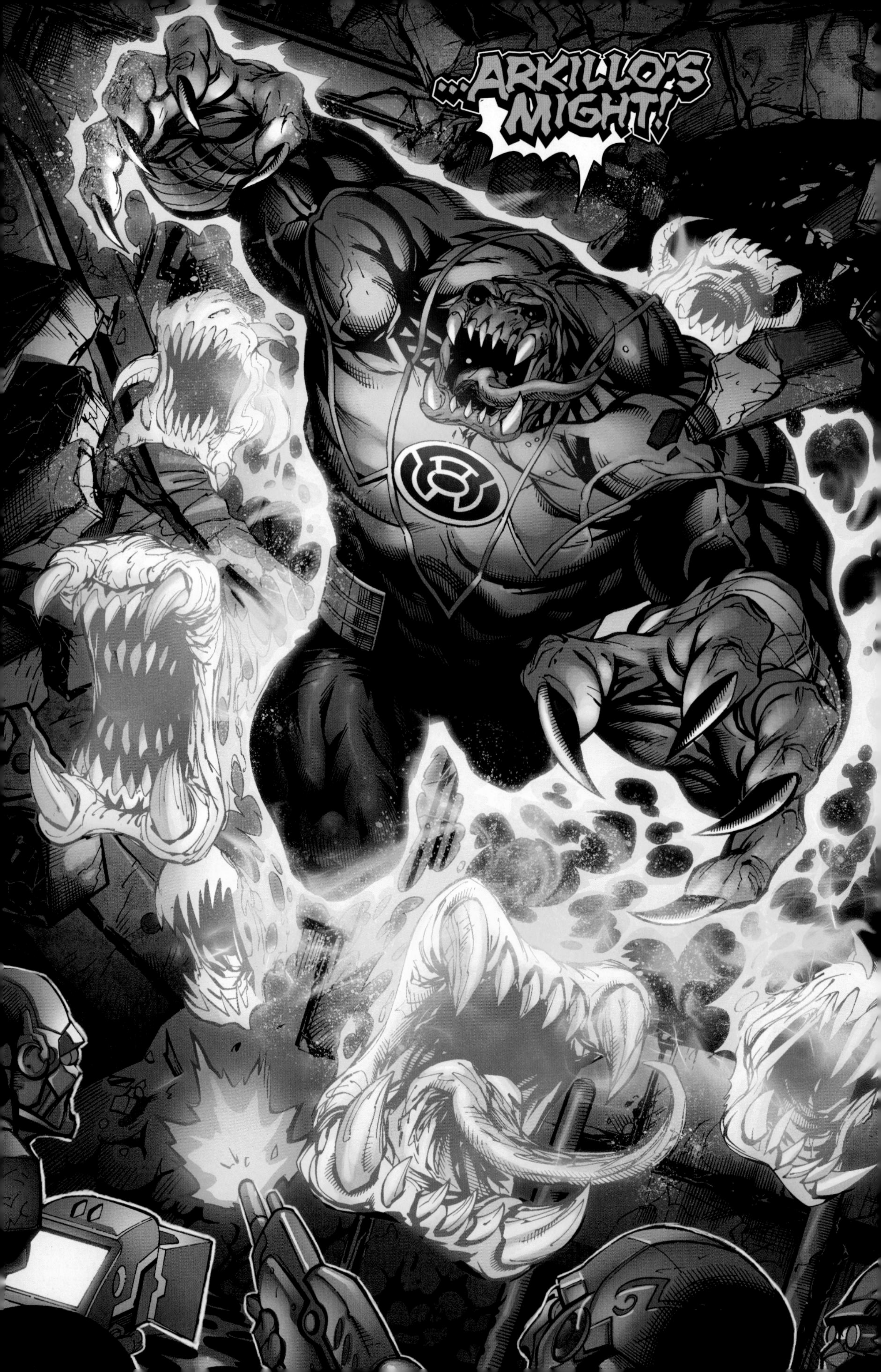
...ARKILLO'S MIGHT!

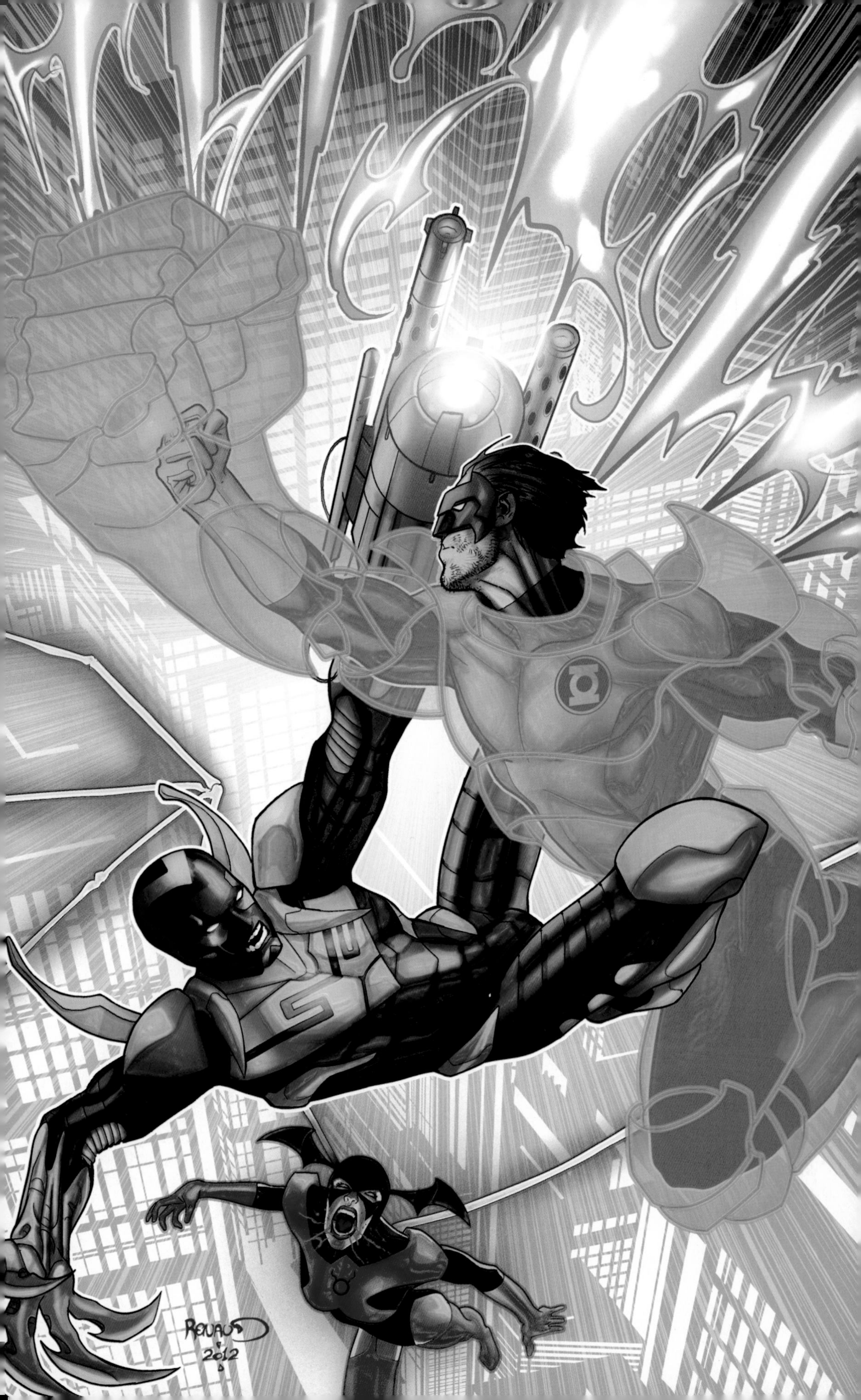
RENAUD
2012

THE ENEMY OF MY ENEMY

TONY BEDARD writer **MARCIO TAKARA** artist cover by **PAUL RENAUD**

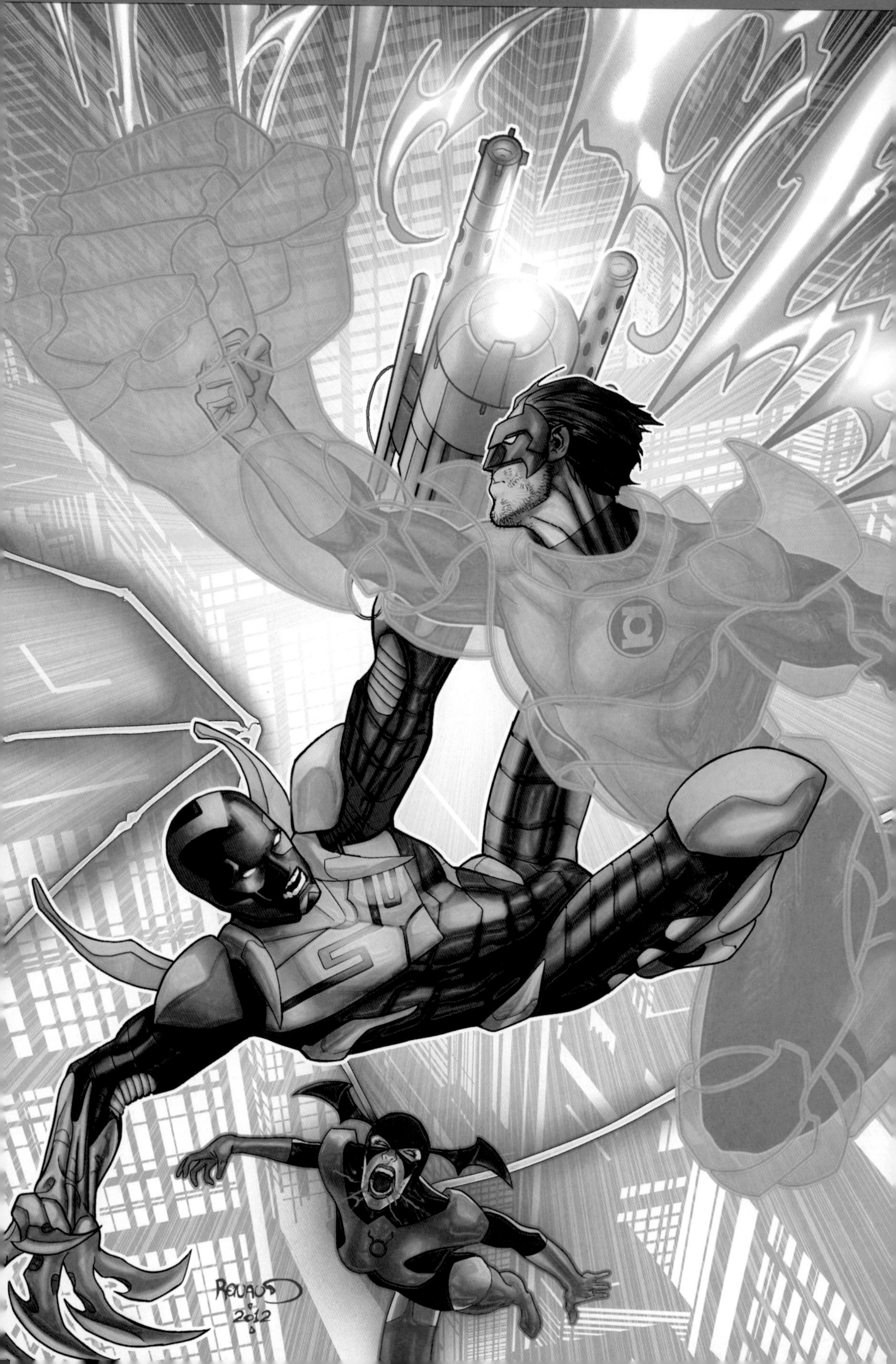
RENAUD
2012

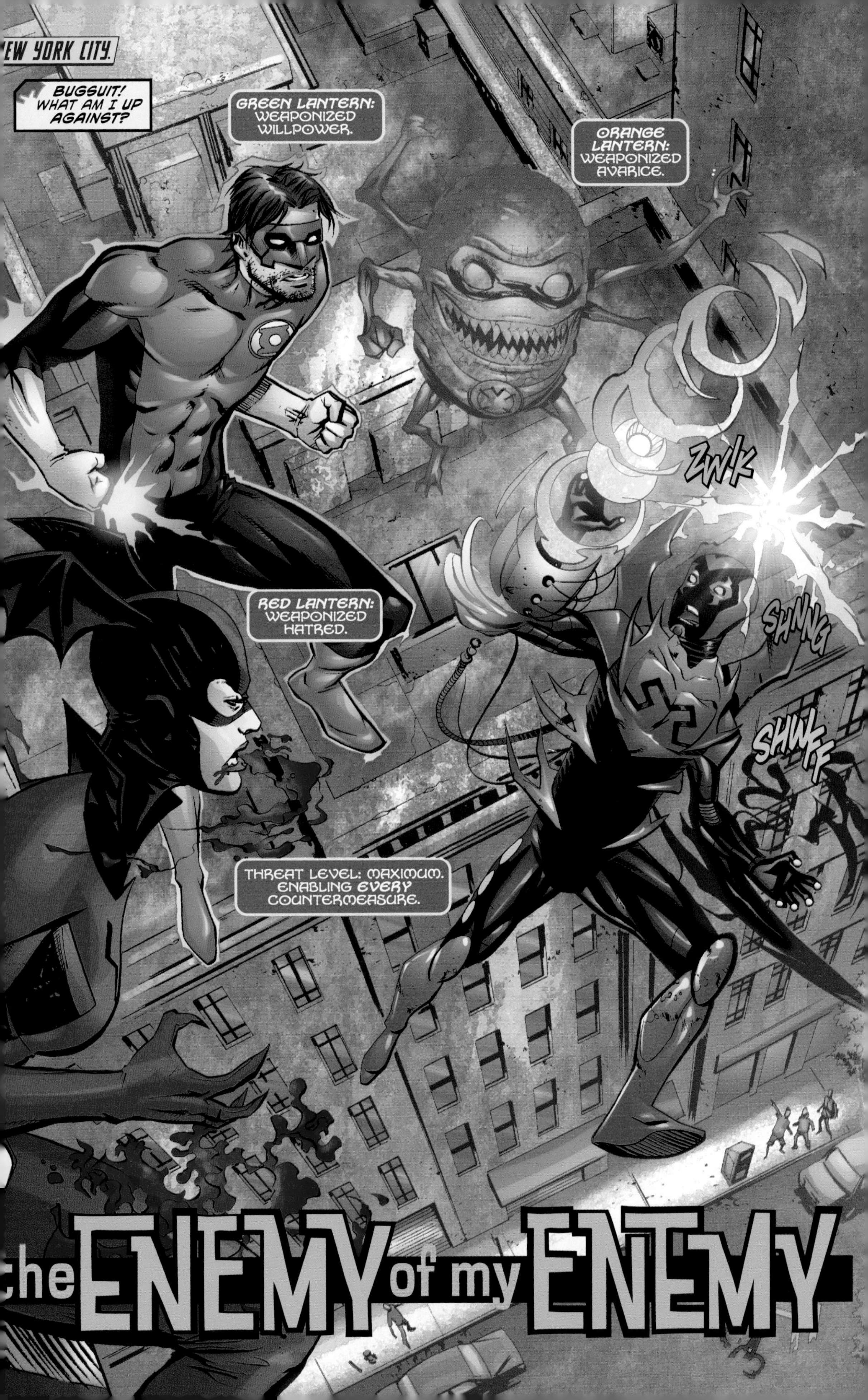
EW YORK CITY.
BUGSUIT! WHAT AM I UP AGAINST?
GREEN LANTERN: WEAPONIZED WILLPOWER.
ORANGE LANTERN: WEAPONIZED AVARICE.
ZWIK
RED LANTERN: WEAPONIZED HATRED.
SHNNG
SHWFF
THREAT LEVEL: MAXIMUM. ENABLING EVERY COUNTERMEASURE.
the ENEMY of my ENEMY

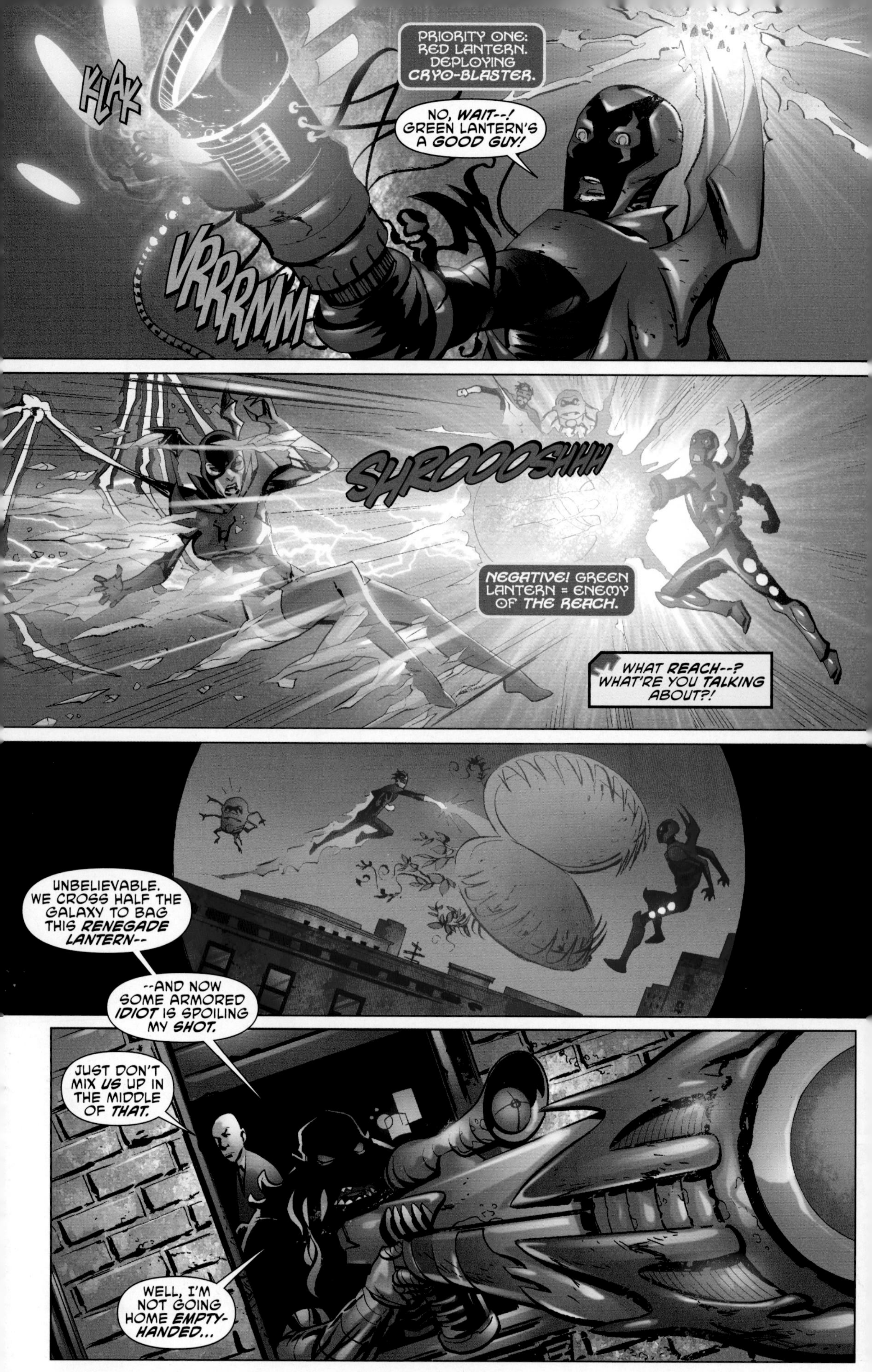
KLAK
PRIORITY ONE: RED LANTERN. DEPLOYING CRYO-BLASTER.
NO, WAIT--! GREEN LANTERN'S A GOOD GUY!
VRRRMM
SHROOOOSHHH
NEGATIVE! GREEN LANTERN = ENEMY OF THE REACH.
WHAT REACH--? WHAT'RE YOU TALKING ABOUT?!
UNBELIEVABLE. WE CROSS HALF THE GALAXY TO BAG THIS RENEGADE LANTERN--
--AND NOW SOME ARMORED IDIOT IS SPOILING MY SHOT.
JUST DON'T MIX US UP IN THE MIDDLE OF THAT.
WELL, I'M NOT GOING HOME EMPTY-HANDED...

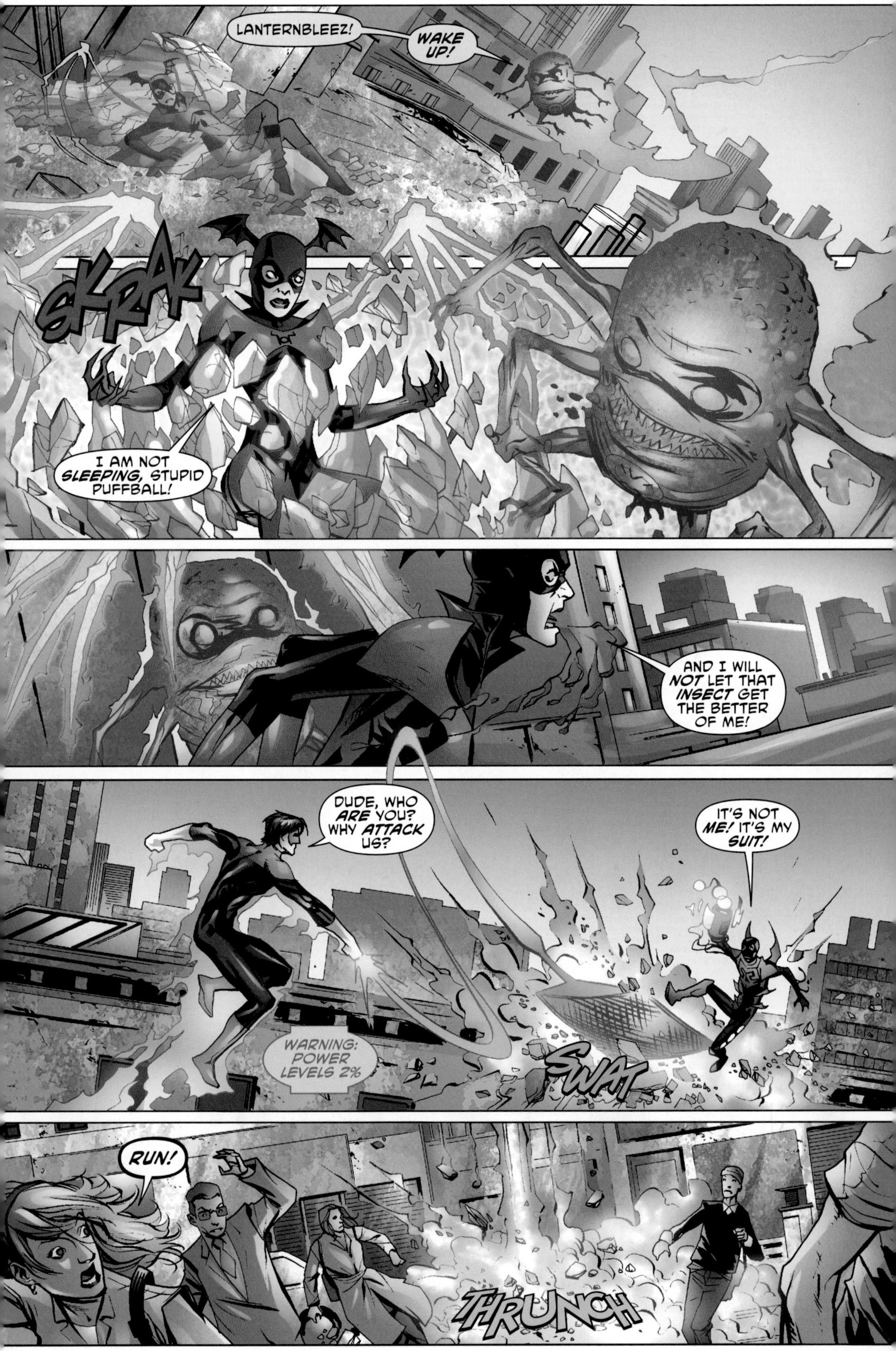

LANTERNBLEEZ!
WAKE UP!
SKRAK
I AM NOT SLEEPING, STUPID PUFFBALL!
AND I WILL NOT LET THAT INSECT GET THE BETTER OF ME!
DUDE, WHO ARE YOU? WHY ATTACK US?
IT'S NOT ME! IT'S MY SUIT!
WARNING: POWER LEVELS 2%
SWAT
RUN!
THRUNCH

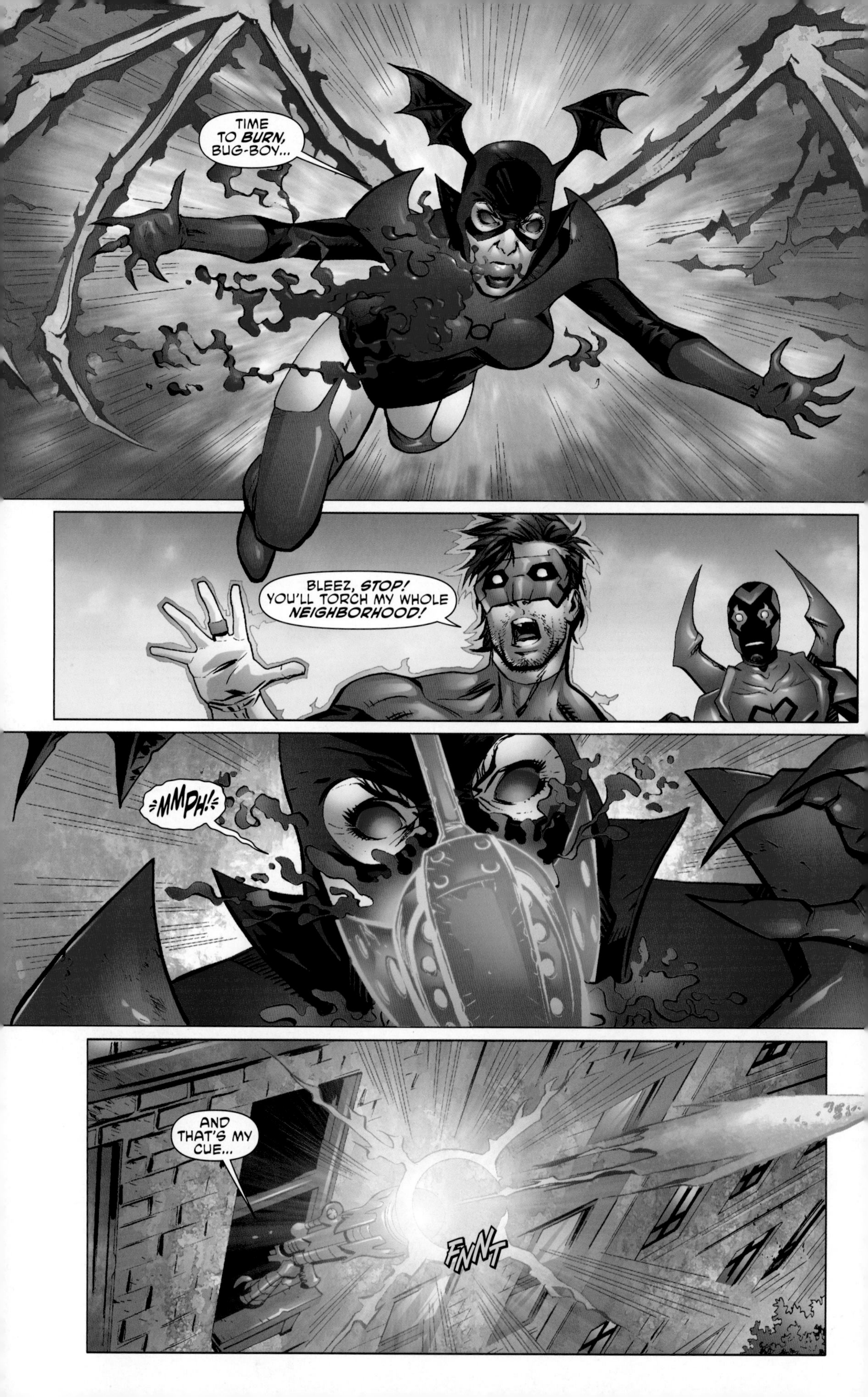
TIME TO *BURN,* BUG-BOY...
BLEEZ, *STOP!* YOU'LL TORCH MY WHOLE *NEIGHBORHOOD!*
MMPH!
AND THAT'S MY CUE...
FNNT

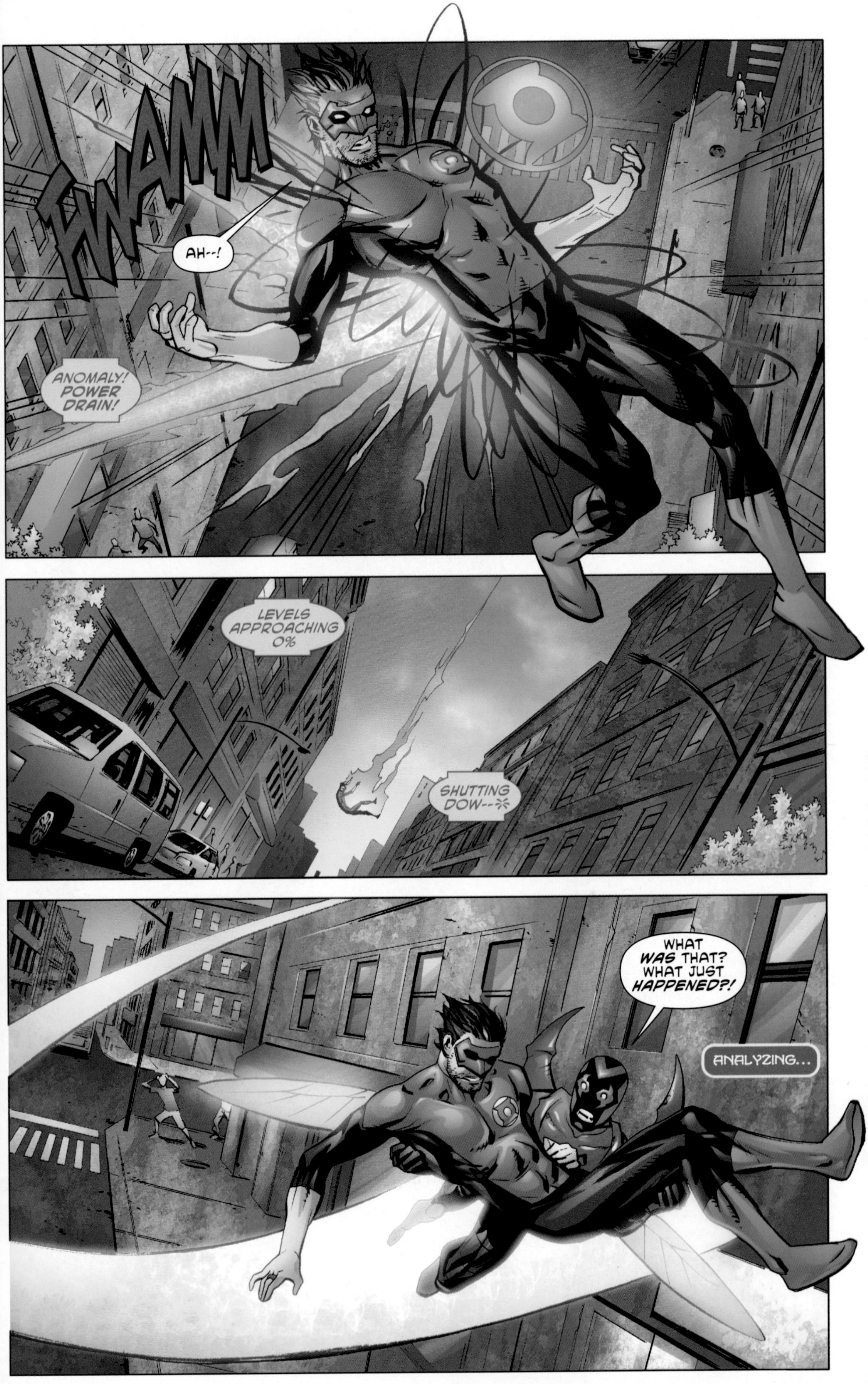
FWAMM
AH--!
ANOMALY! POWER DRAIN!
LEVELS APPROACHING 0%
SHUTTING DOW--
WHAT WAS THAT? WHAT JUST HAPPENED?!
ANALYZING...

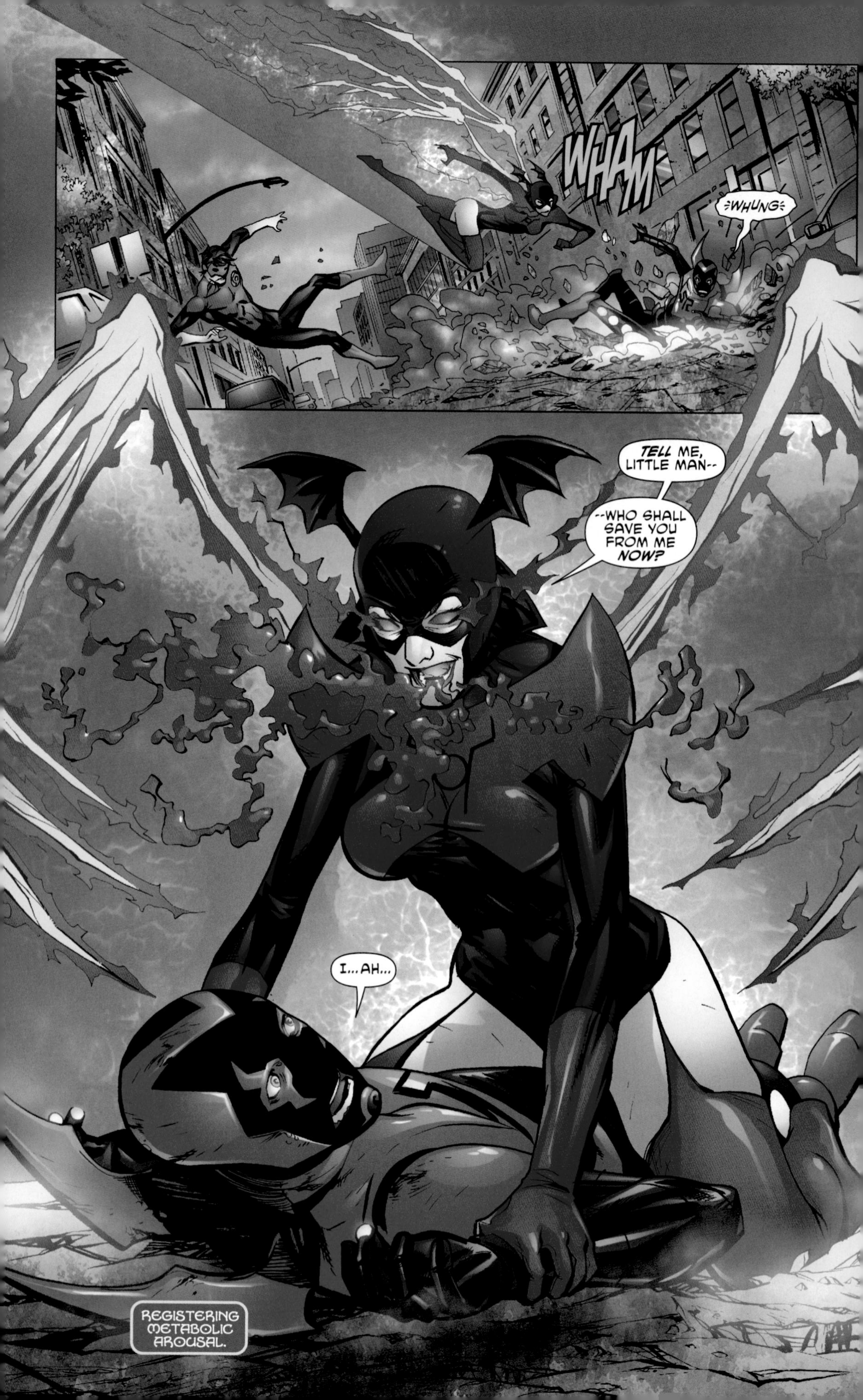
WHAM
WHUNG
TELL ME, LITTLE MAN--
--WHO SHALL SAVE YOU FROM ME NOW?
I...AH...
REGISTERING METABOLIC AROUSAL.

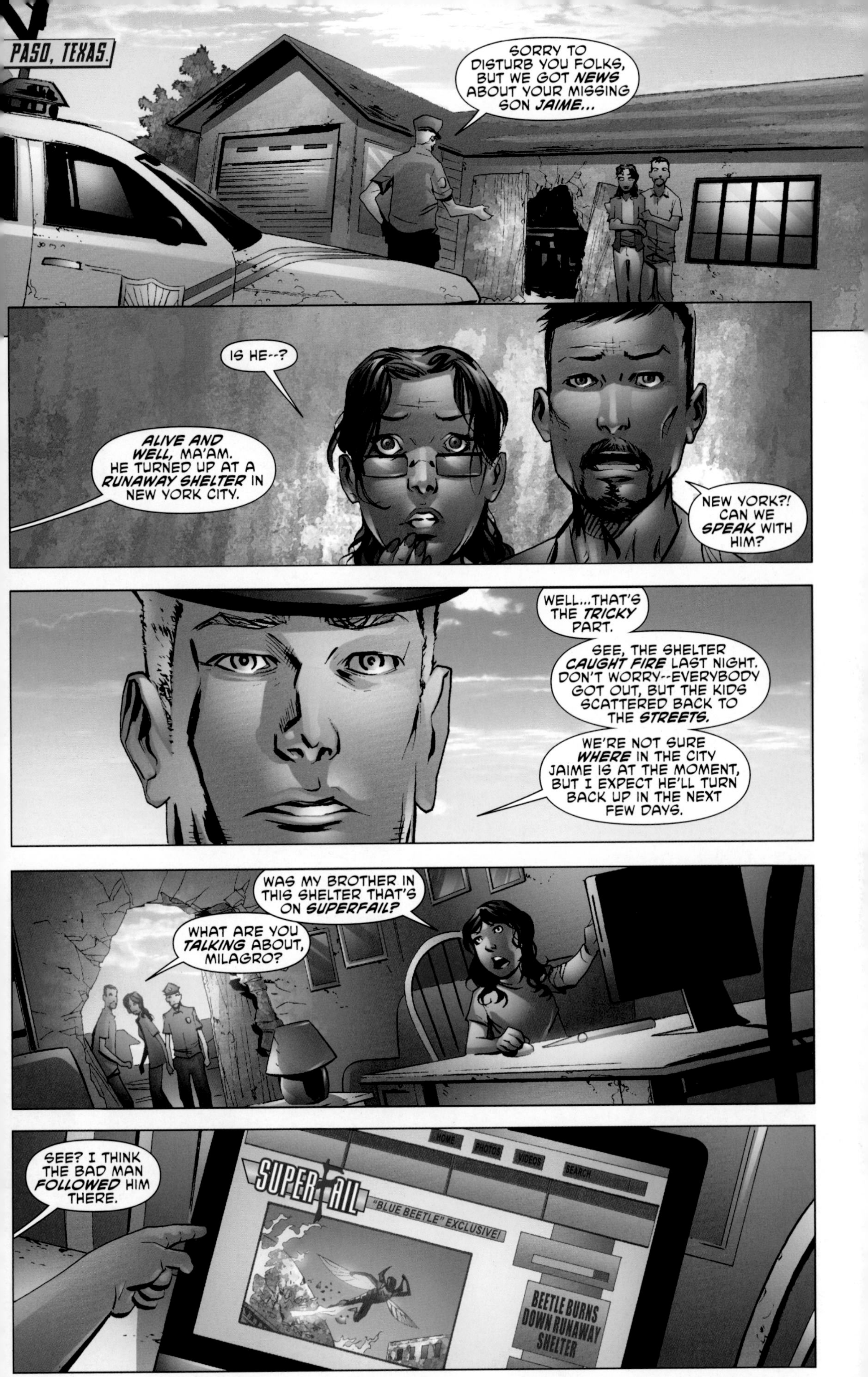
PASO, TEXAS.
SORRY TO DISTURB YOU FOLKS, BUT WE GOT NEWS ABOUT YOUR MISSING SON JAIME...
IS HE--?
ALIVE AND WELL, MA'AM. HE TURNED UP AT A RUNAWAY SHELTER IN NEW YORK CITY.
NEW YORK?! CAN WE SPEAK WITH HIM?
WELL...THAT'S THE TRICKY PART.
SEE, THE SHELTER CAUGHT FIRE LAST NIGHT. DON'T WORRY--EVERYBODY GOT OUT, BUT THE KIDS SCATTERED BACK TO THE STREETS.
WE'RE NOT SURE WHERE IN THE CITY JAIME IS AT THE MOMENT, BUT I EXPECT HE'LL TURN BACK UP IN THE NEXT FEW DAYS.
WAS MY BROTHER IN THIS SHELTER THAT'S ON SUPERFAIL?
WHAT ARE YOU TALKING ABOUT, MILAGRO?
SEE? I THINK THE BAD MAN FOLLOWED HIM THERE.
HOME
PHOTOS
VIDEOS
SEARCH
SUPERFAIL
"BLUE BEETLE" EXCLUSIVE!
BEETLE BURNS DOWN RUNAWAY SHELTER

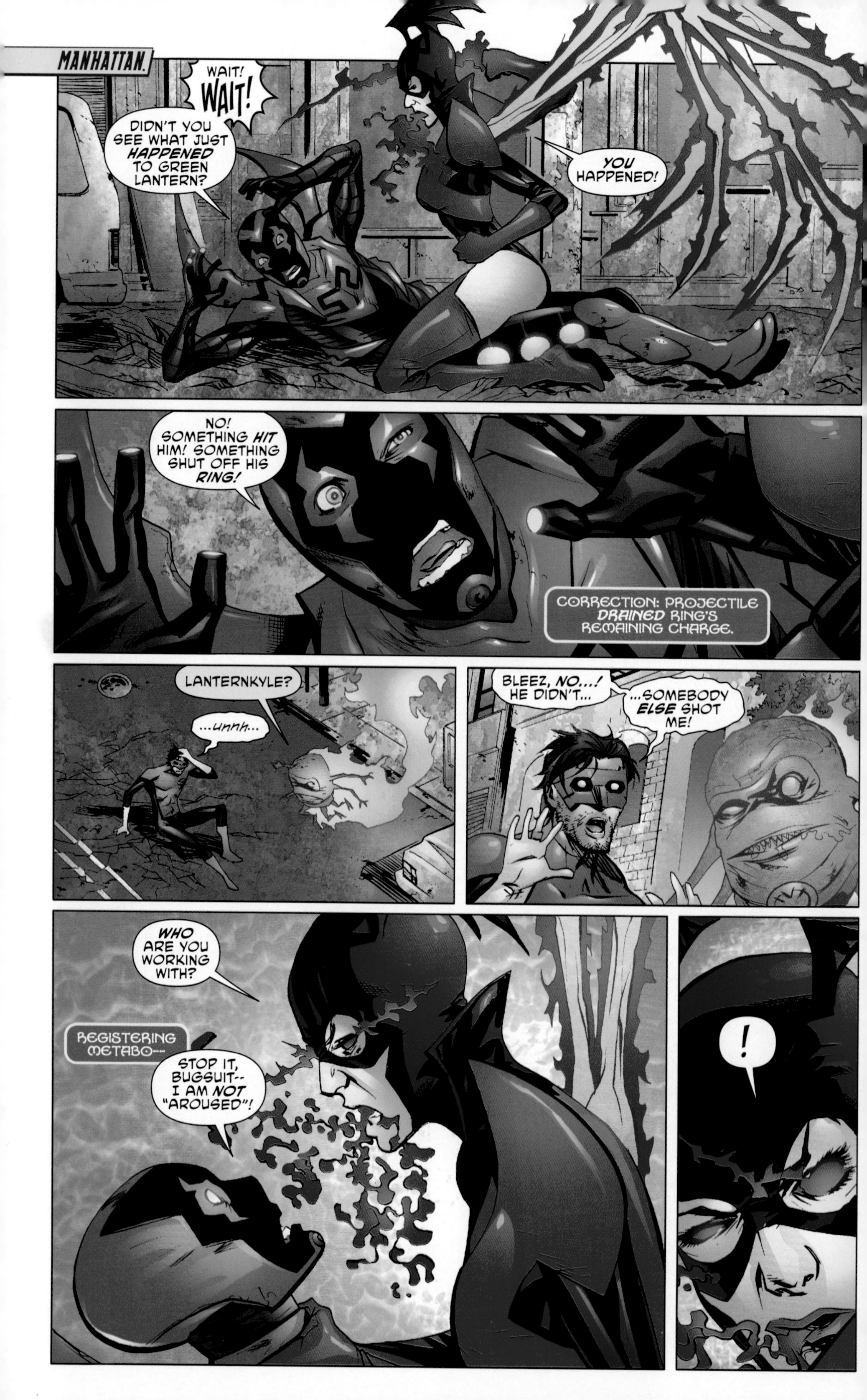
MANHATTAN.
WAIT! WAIT!
DIDN'T YOU SEE WHAT JUST HAPPENED TO GREEN LANTERN?
YOU HAPPENED!
NO! SOMETHING HIT HIM! SOMETHING SHUT OFF HIS RING!
CORRECTION: PROJECTILE DRAINED RING'S REMAINING CHARGE.
LANTERNKYLE?
...unnh...
BLEEZ, NO...! HE DIDN'T...
...SOMEBODY ELSE SHOT ME!
WHO ARE YOU WORKING WITH?
REGISTERING METABO--
STOP IT, BUGSUIT-- I AM NOT "AROUSED"!
!

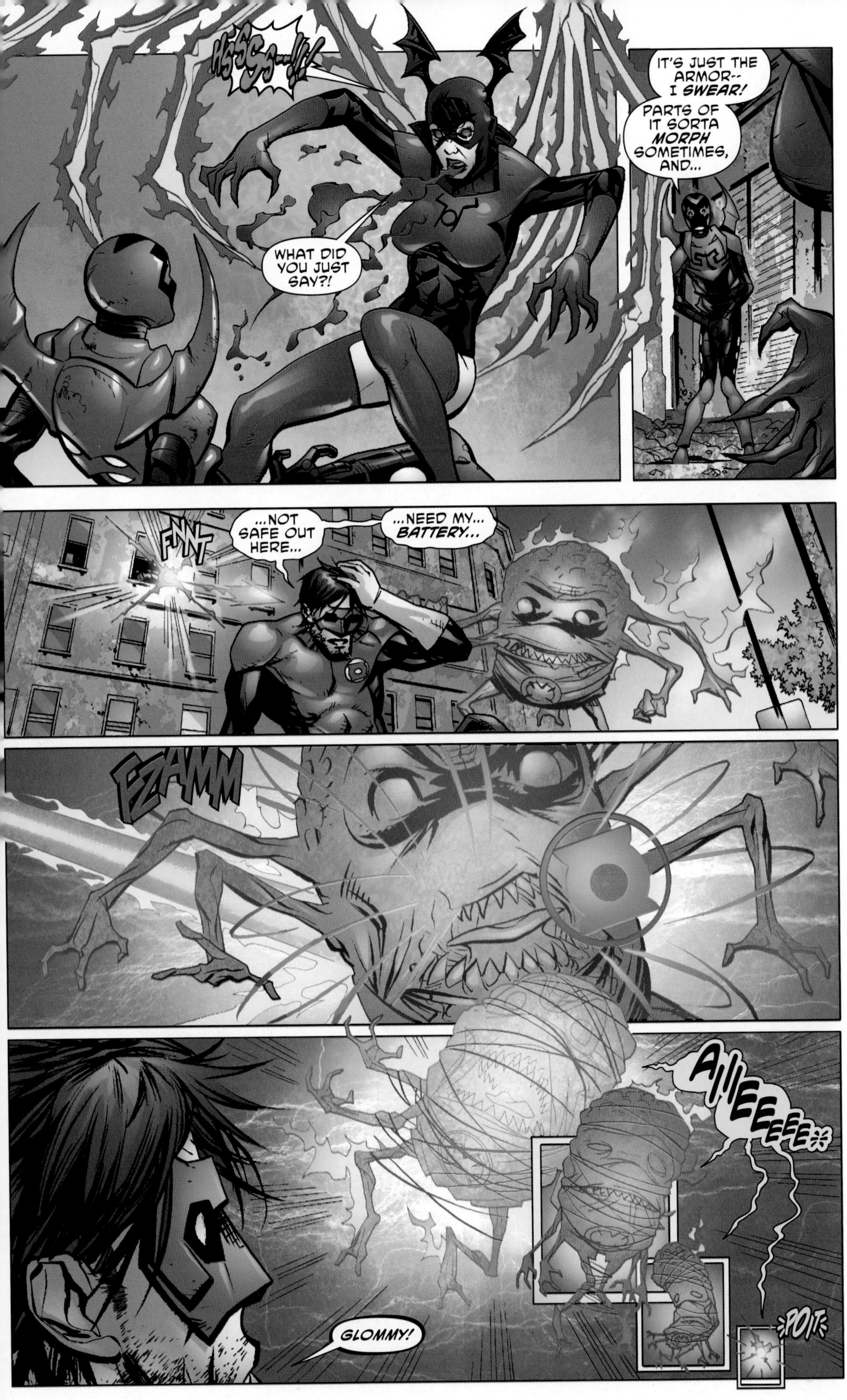
HSSSS--!!!
WHAT DID YOU JUST SAY?!
IT'S JUST THE ARMOR-- I SWEAR!
PARTS OF IT SORTA MORPH SOMETIMES, AND...
FNNT
...NOT SAFE OUT HERE...
...NEED MY... BATTERY...
FZAMM
AIIEEEEEE!!
GLOMMY!
POIT

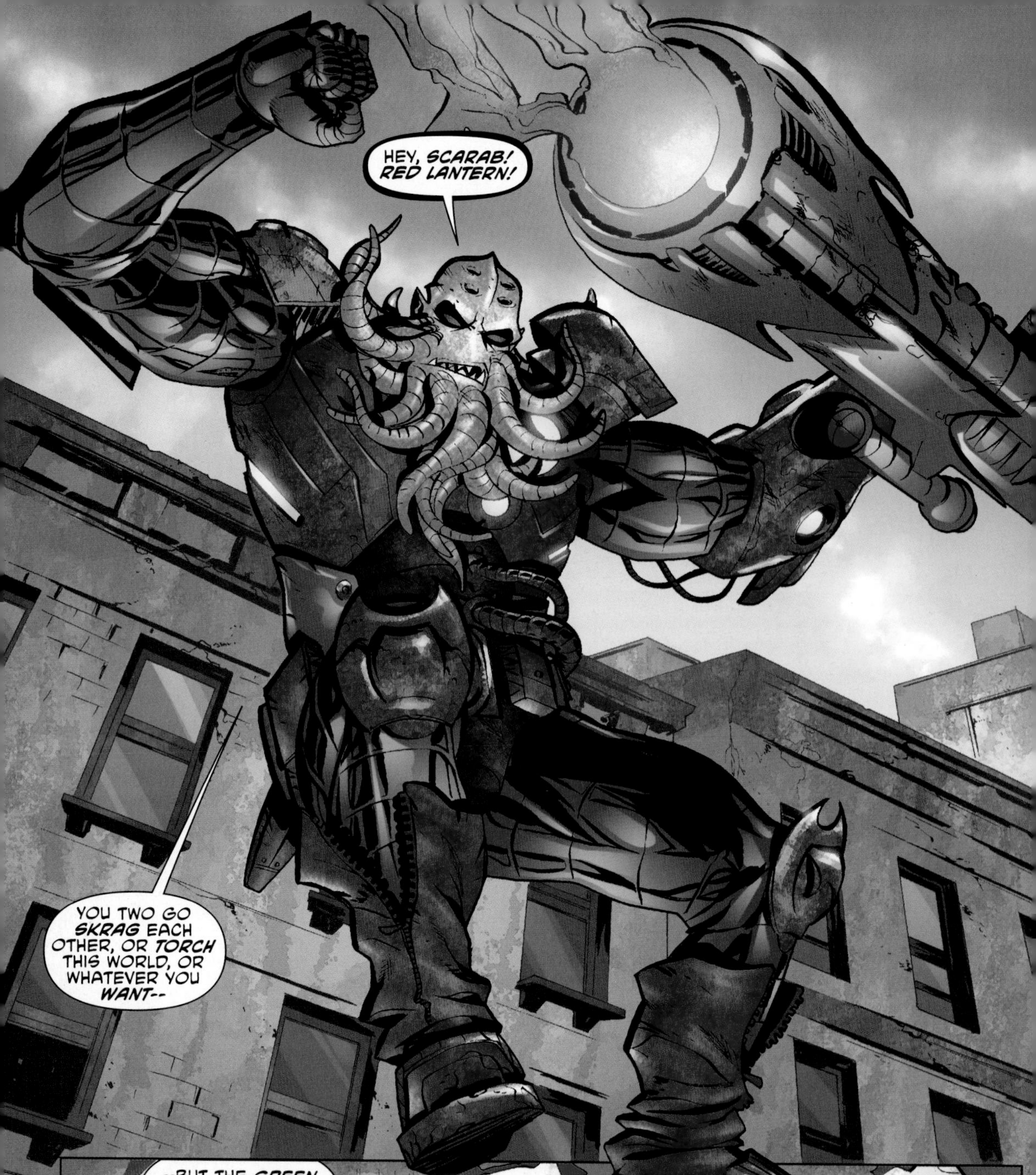
HEY, SCARAB! RED LANTERN!
YOU TWO GO SKRAG EACH OTHER, OR TORCH THIS WORLD, OR WHATEVER YOU WANT--

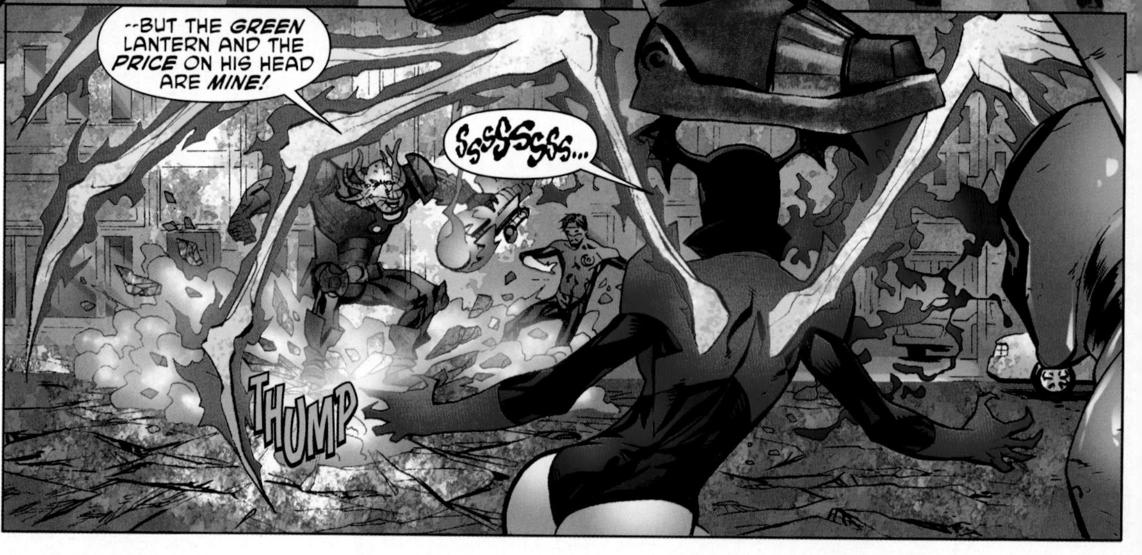
--BUT THE GREEN LANTERN AND THE PRICE ON HIS HEAD ARE MINE!
SsSSSSS...
THUMP

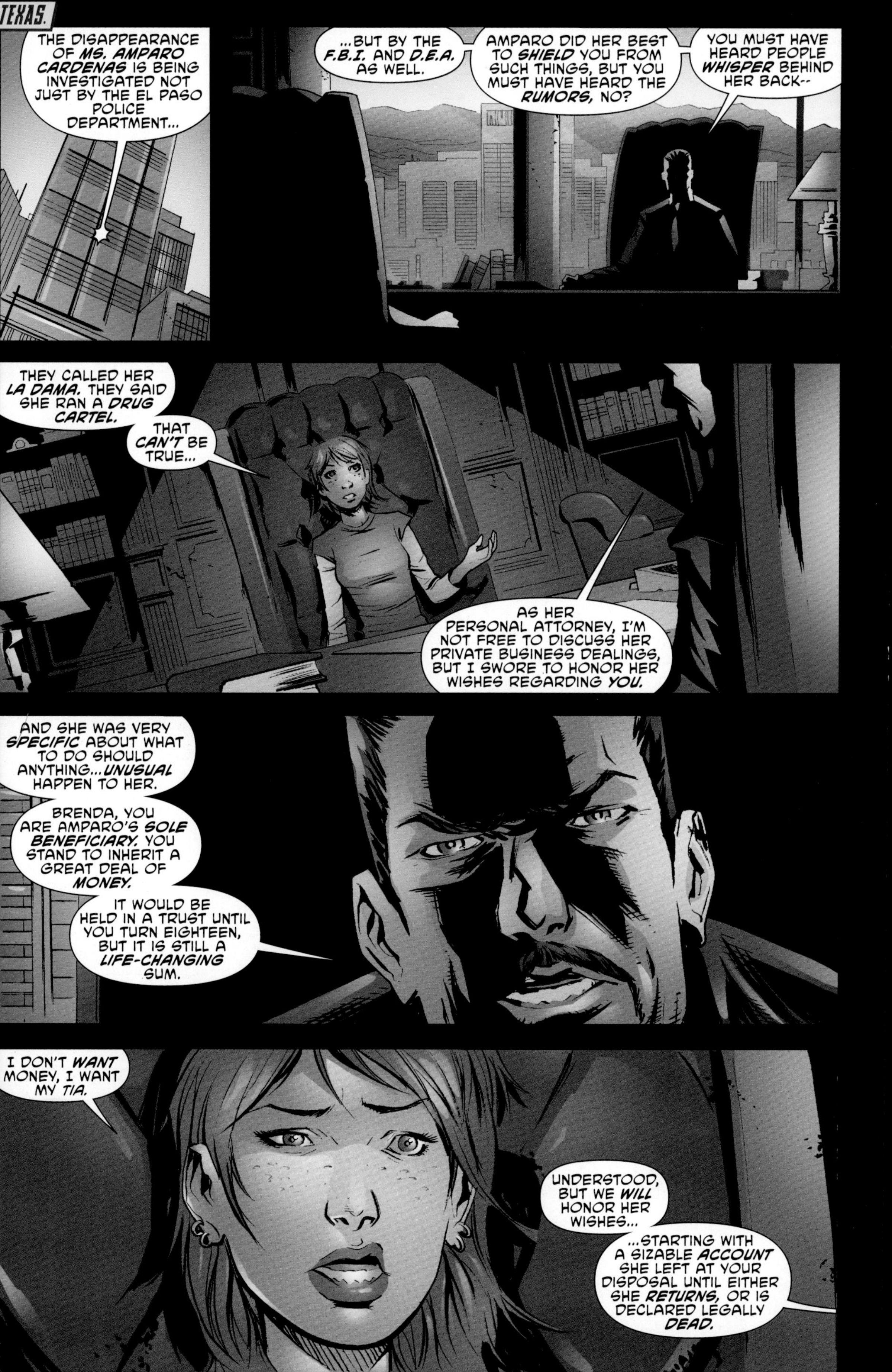
TEXAS.
THE DISAPPEARANCE OF MS. AMPARO CARDENAS IS BEING INVESTIGATED NOT JUST BY THE EL PASO POLICE DEPARTMENT...
...BUT BY THE F.B.I. AND D.E.A. AS WELL.
AMPARO DID HER BEST TO SHIELD YOU FROM SUCH THINGS, BUT YOU MUST HAVE HEARD THE RUMORS, NO?
YOU MUST HAVE HEARD PEOPLE WHISPER BEHIND HER BACK--
THEY CALLED HER LA DAMA. THEY SAID SHE RAN A DRUG CARTEL.
THAT CAN'T BE TRUE...
AS HER PERSONAL ATTORNEY, I'M NOT FREE TO DISCUSS HER PRIVATE BUSINESS DEALINGS, BUT I SWORE TO HONOR HER WISHES REGARDING YOU.
AND SHE WAS VERY SPECIFIC ABOUT WHAT TO DO SHOULD ANYTHING...UNUSUAL HAPPEN TO HER.
BRENDA, YOU ARE AMPARO'S SOLE BENEFICIARY. YOU STAND TO INHERIT A GREAT DEAL OF MONEY.
IT WOULD BE HELD IN A TRUST UNTIL YOU TURN EIGHTEEN, BUT IT IS STILL A LIFE-CHANGING SUM.
I DON'T WANT MONEY, I WANT MY TIA.
UNDERSTOOD, BUT WE WILL HONOR HER WISHES...
...STARTING WITH A SIZABLE ACCOUNT SHE LEFT AT YOUR DISPOSAL UNTIL EITHER SHE RETURNS, OR IS DECLARED LEGALLY DEAD.

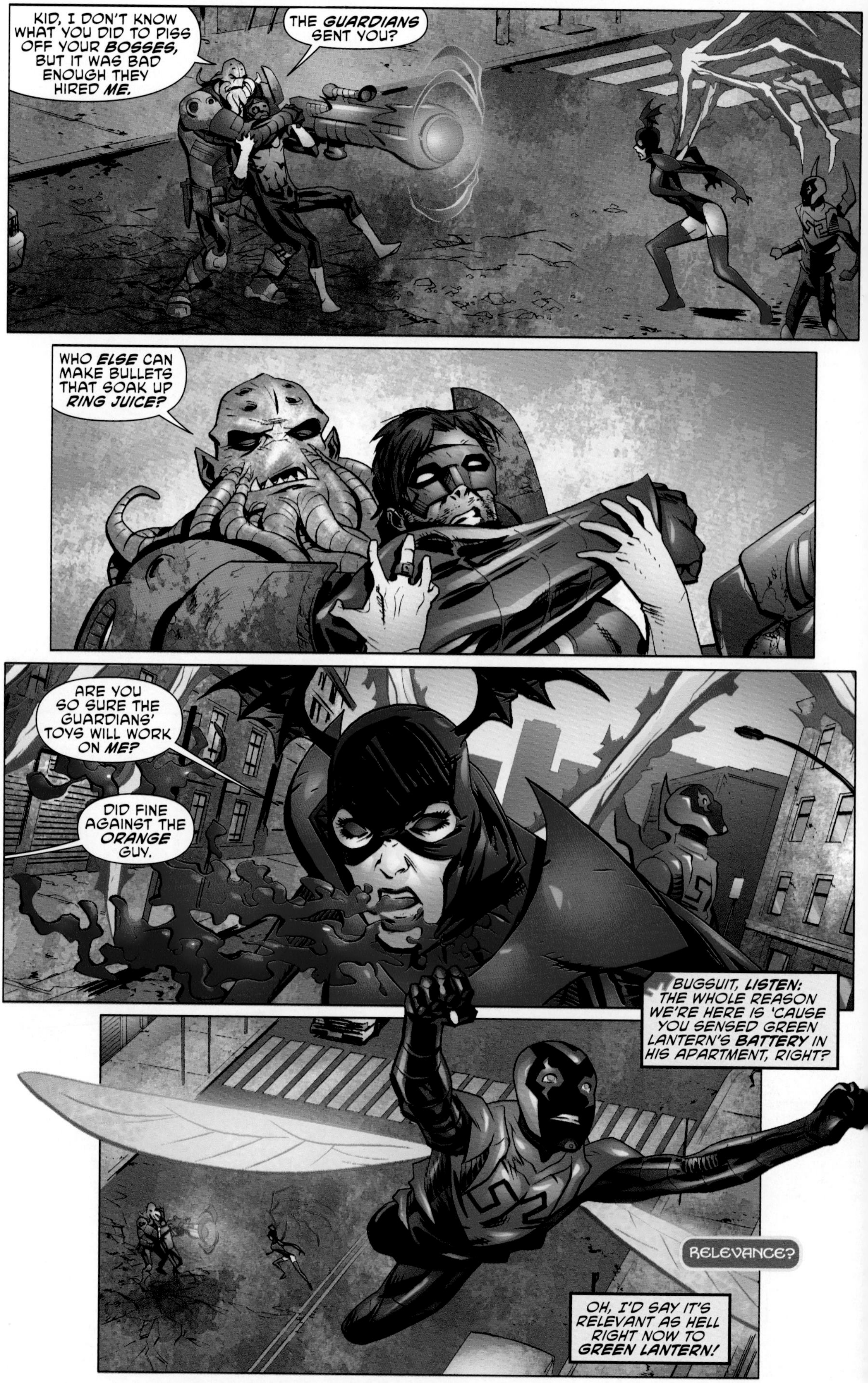
KID, I DON'T KNOW WHAT YOU DID TO PISS OFF YOUR BOSSES, BUT IT WAS BAD ENOUGH THEY HIRED ME.
THE GUARDIANS SENT YOU?
WHO ELSE CAN MAKE BULLETS THAT SOAK UP RING JUICE?
ARE YOU SO SURE THE GUARDIANS' TOYS WILL WORK ON ME?
DID FINE AGAINST THE ORANGE GUY.
BUGSUIT, LISTEN: THE WHOLE REASON WE'RE HERE IS 'CAUSE YOU SENSED GREEN LANTERN'S BATTERY IN HIS APARTMENT, RIGHT?
RELEVANCE?
OH, I'D SAY IT'S RELEVANT AS HELL RIGHT NOW TO GREEN LANTERN!

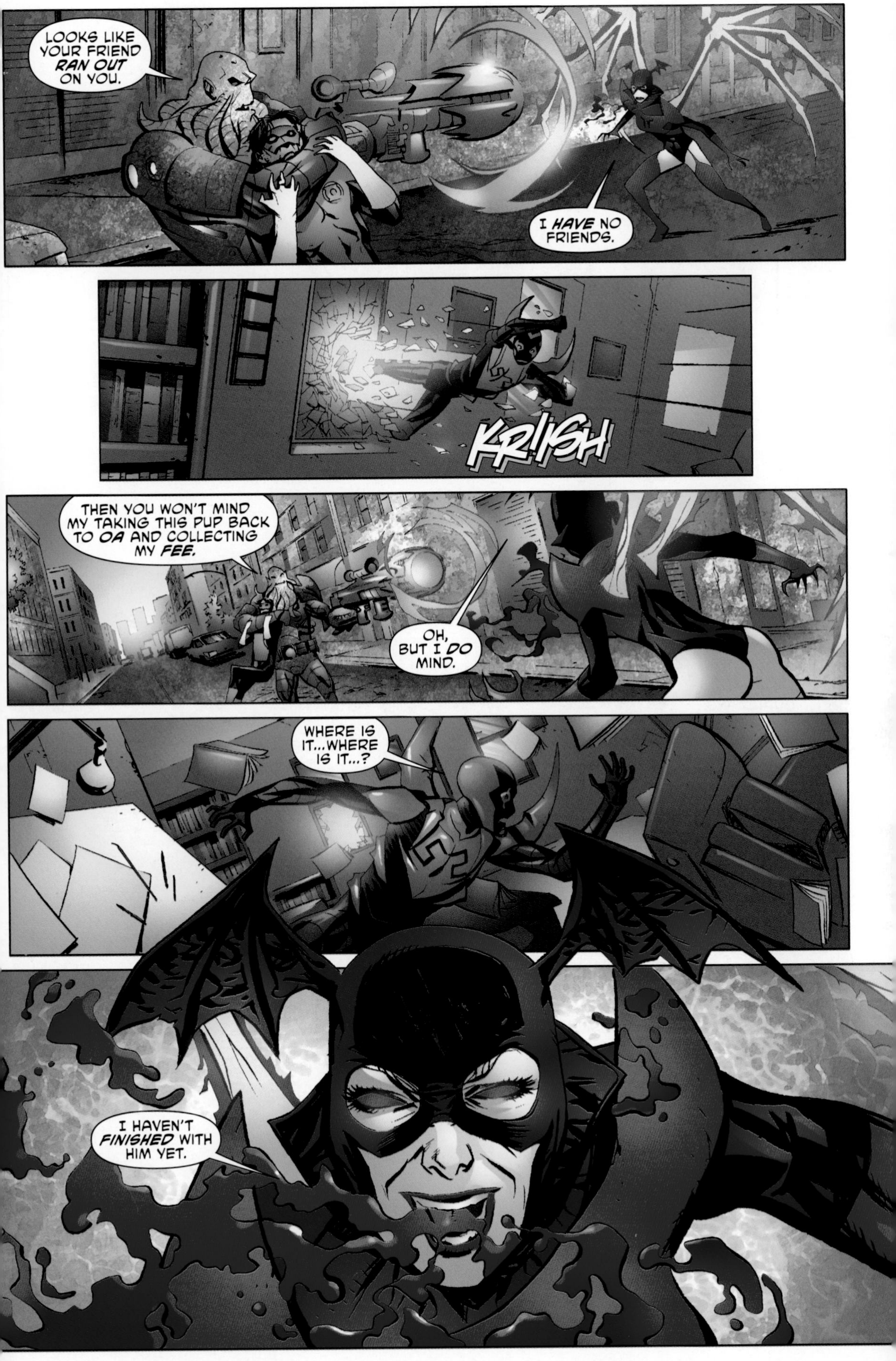
LOOKS LIKE YOUR FRIEND RAN OUT ON YOU.
I HAVE NO FRIENDS.
KRIISH
THEN YOU WON'T MIND MY TAKING THIS PUP BACK TO OA AND COLLECTING MY FEE.
OH, BUT I DO MIND.
WHERE IS IT...WHERE IS IT...?
I HAVEN'T FINISHED WITH HIM YET.

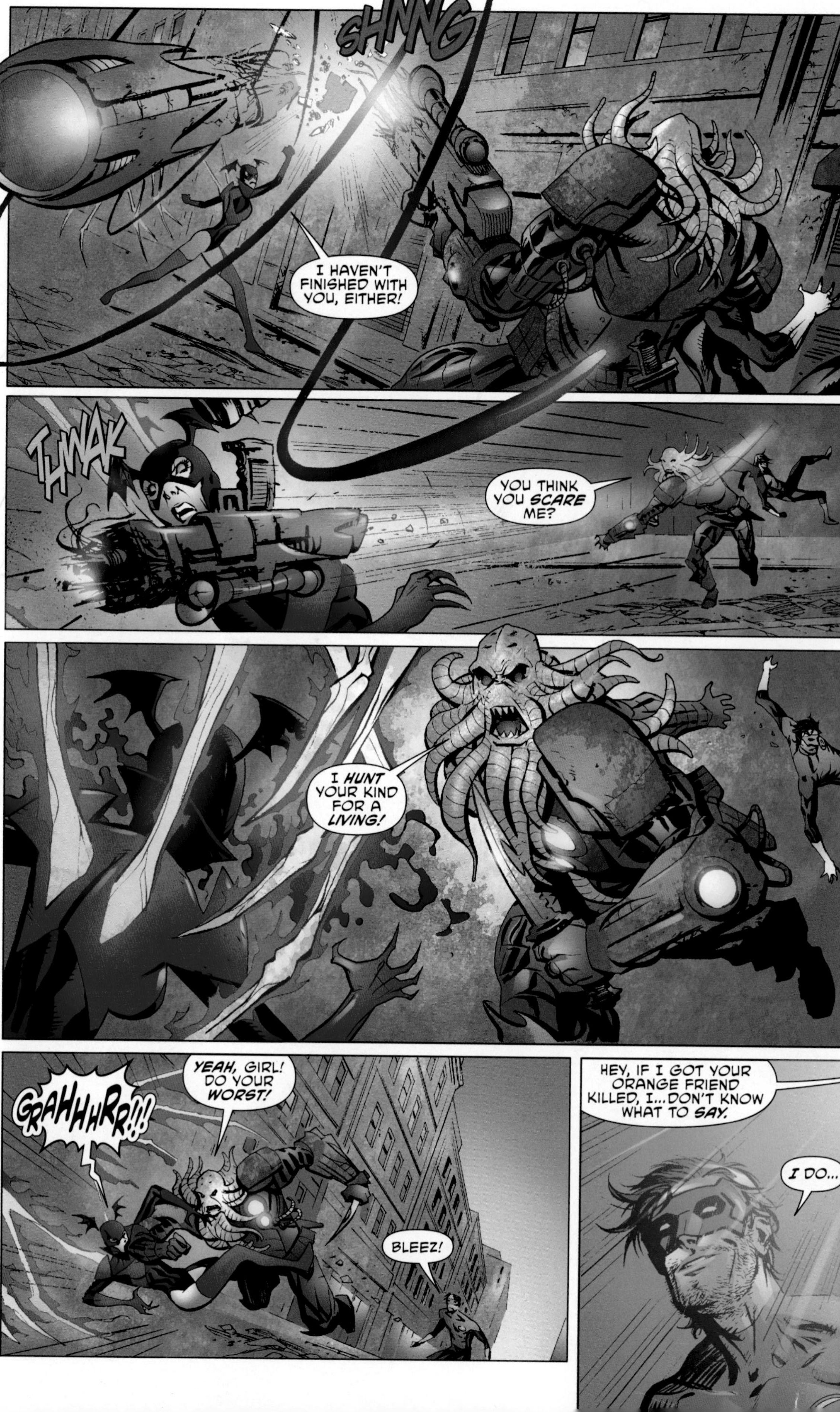
SHNNG
I HAVEN'T FINISHED WITH YOU, EITHER!
THWAK
YOU THINK YOU SCARE ME?
I HUNT YOUR KIND FOR A LIVING!
GRAHHHRR!!!
YEAH, GIRL! DO YOUR WORST!
BLEEZ!
HEY, IF I GOT YOUR ORANGE FRIEND KILLED, I...DON'T KNOW WHAT TO SAY.
I DO...

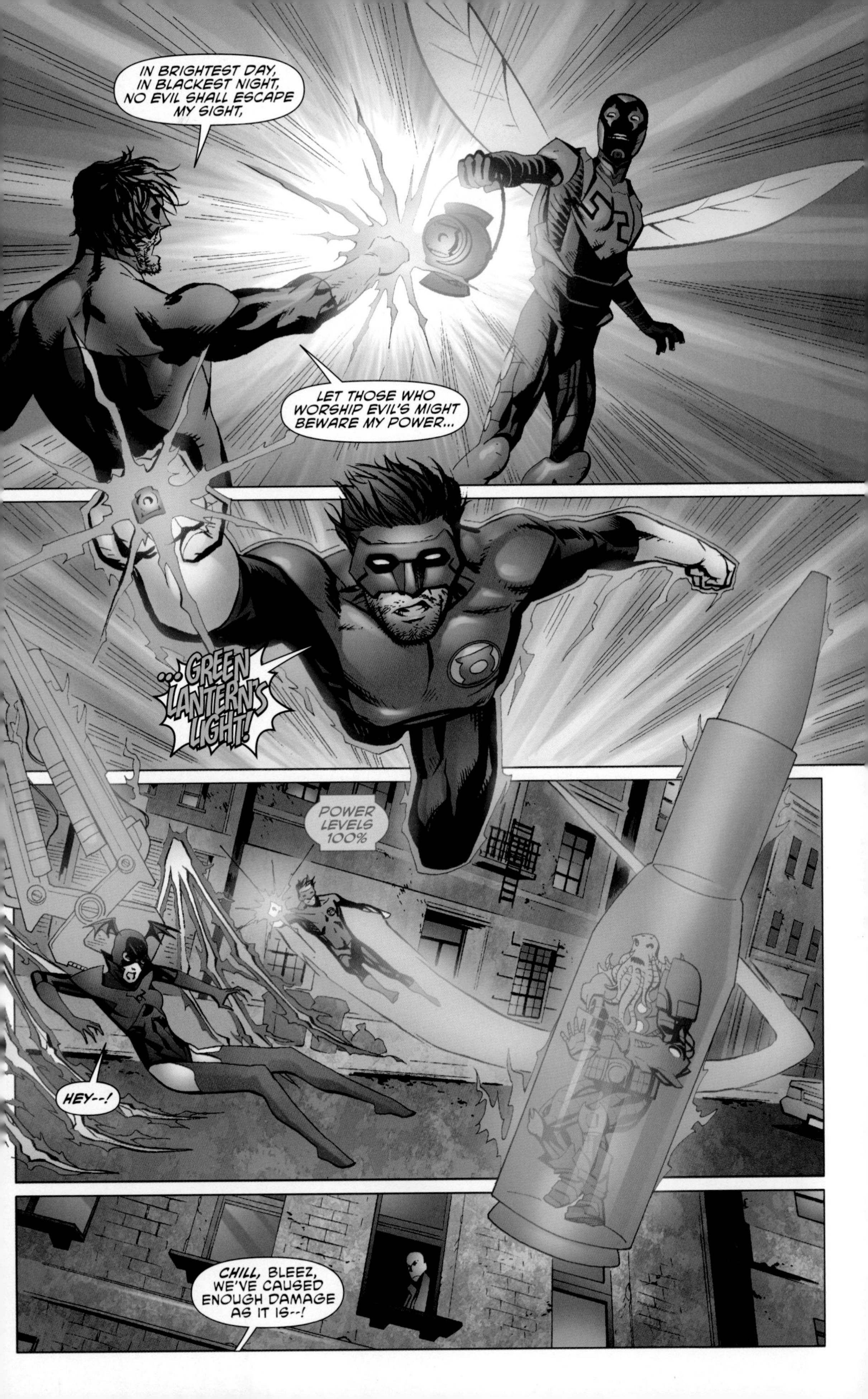
IN BRIGHTEST DAY, IN BLACKEST NIGHT, NO EVIL SHALL ESCAPE MY SIGHT,
LET THOSE WHO WORSHIP EVIL'S MIGHT BEWARE MY POWER...
...GREEN LANTERN'S LIGHT!
POWER LEVELS 100%
HEY--!
CHILL, BLEEZ, WE'VE CAUSED ENOUGH DAMAGE AS IT IS--!

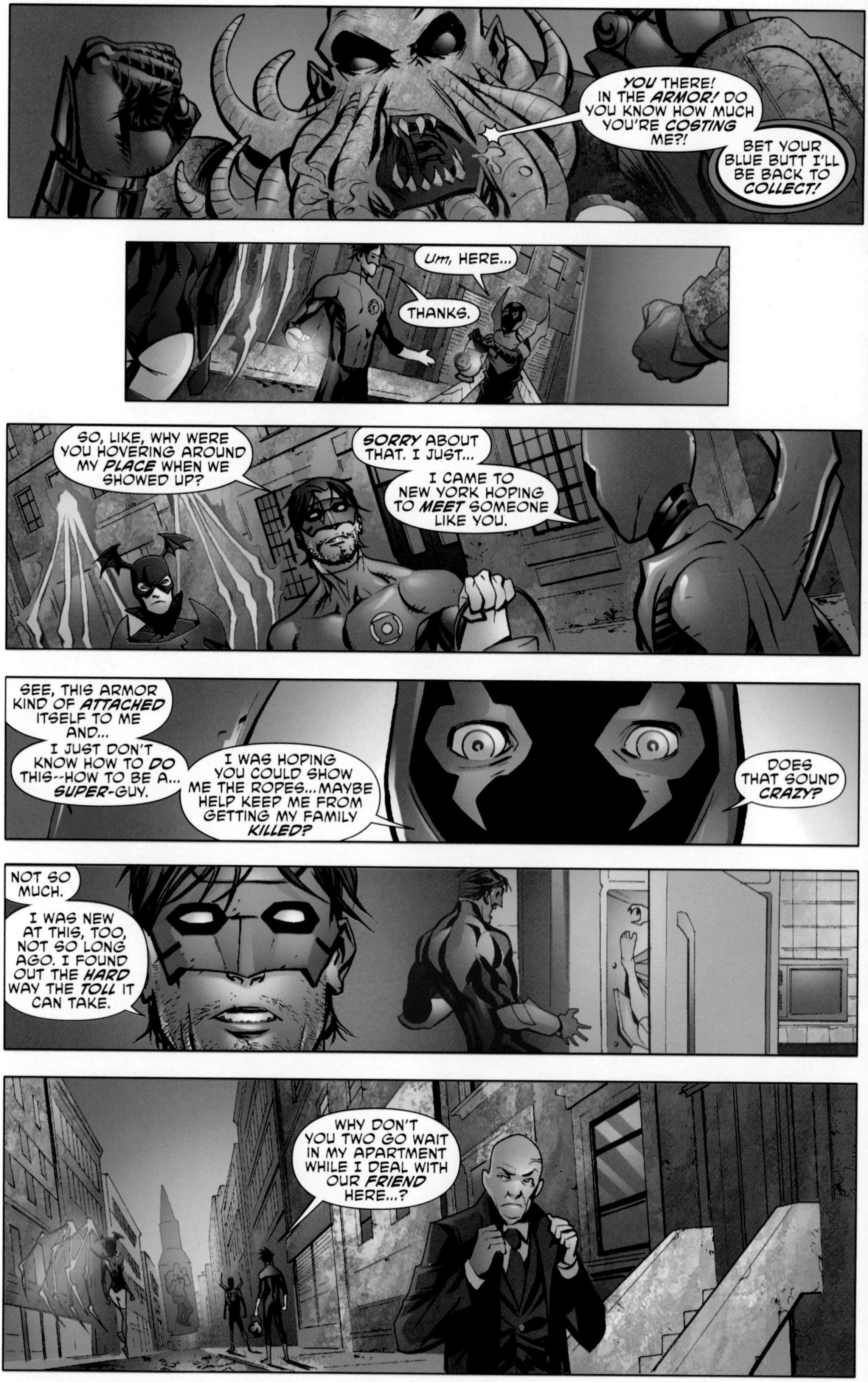
YOU THERE! IN THE ARMOR! DO YOU KNOW HOW MUCH YOU'RE COSTING ME?!
BET YOUR BLUE BUTT I'LL BE BACK TO COLLECT!
Um, HERE...
THANKS.
SO, LIKE, WHY WERE YOU HOVERING AROUND MY PLACE WHEN WE SHOWED UP?
SORRY ABOUT THAT. I JUST...
I CAME TO NEW YORK HOPING TO MEET SOMEONE LIKE YOU.
SEE, THIS ARMOR KIND OF ATTACHED ITSELF TO ME AND...
I JUST DON'T KNOW HOW TO DO THIS--HOW TO BE A... SUPER-GUY.
I WAS HOPING YOU COULD SHOW ME THE ROPES... MAYBE HELP KEEP ME FROM GETTING MY FAMILY KILLED?
DOES THAT SOUND CRAZY?
NOT SO MUCH.
I WAS NEW AT THIS, TOO, NOT SO LONG AGO. I FOUND OUT THE HARD WAY THE TOLL IT CAN TAKE.
WHY DON'T YOU TWO GO WAIT IN MY APARTMENT WHILE I DEAL WITH OUR FRIEND HERE...?

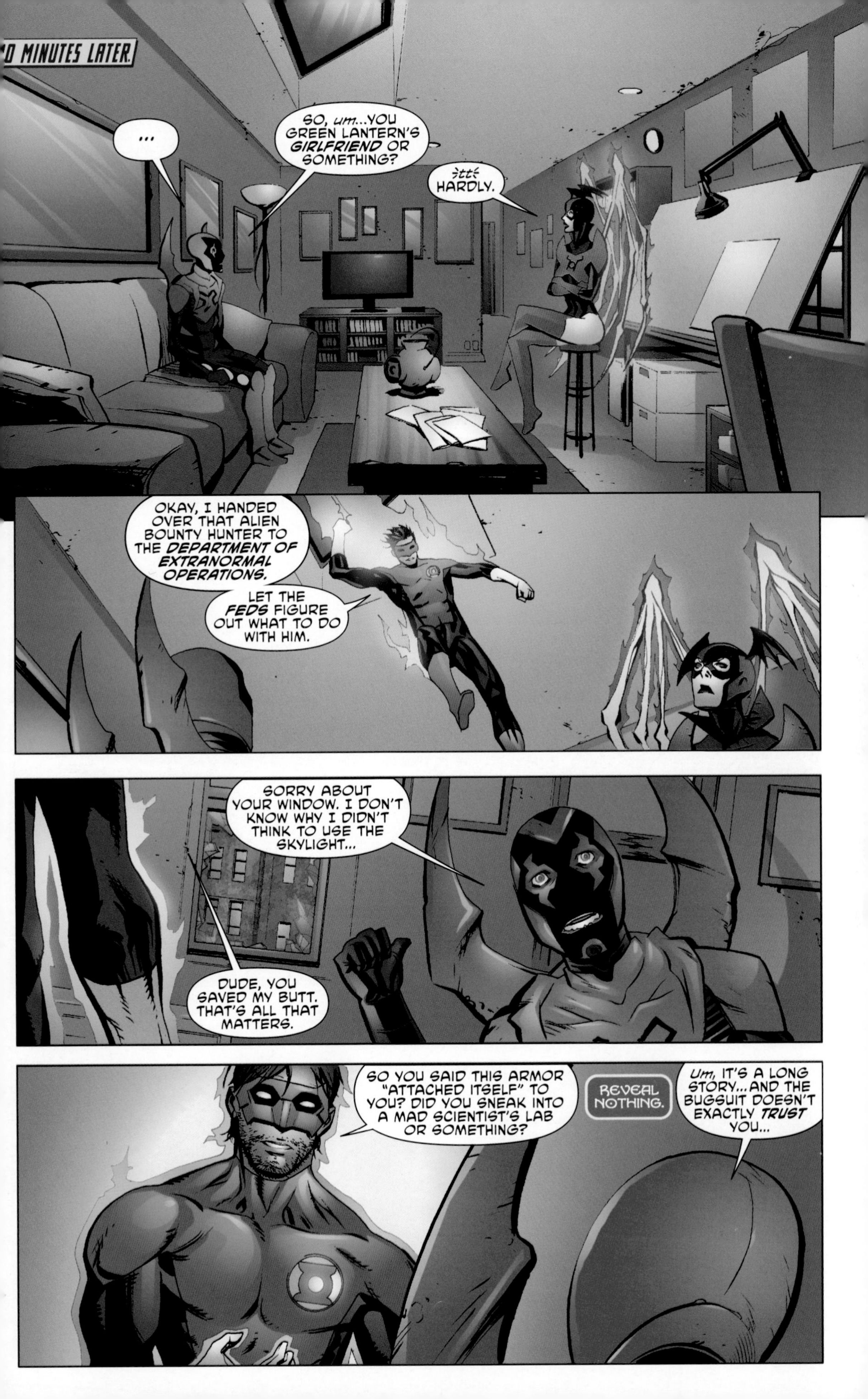
O MINUTES LATER.
...
SO, *um*...YOU GREEN LANTERN'S *GIRLFRIEND* OR SOMETHING?
HARDLY.
OKAY, I HANDED OVER THAT ALIEN BOUNTY HUNTER TO THE *DEPARTMENT OF EXTRANORMAL OPERATIONS.*
LET THE *FEDS* FIGURE OUT WHAT TO DO WITH HIM.
SORRY ABOUT YOUR WINDOW. I DON'T KNOW WHY I DIDN'T THINK TO USE THE SKYLIGHT...
DUDE, YOU SAVED MY BUTT. THAT'S ALL THAT MATTERS.
SO YOU SAID THIS ARMOR "ATTACHED ITSELF" TO YOU? DID YOU SNEAK INTO A MAD SCIENTIST'S LAB OR SOMETHING?
REVEAL NOTHING.
Um, IT'S A LONG STORY...AND THE BUGSUIT DOESN'T EXACTLY *TRUST* YOU...

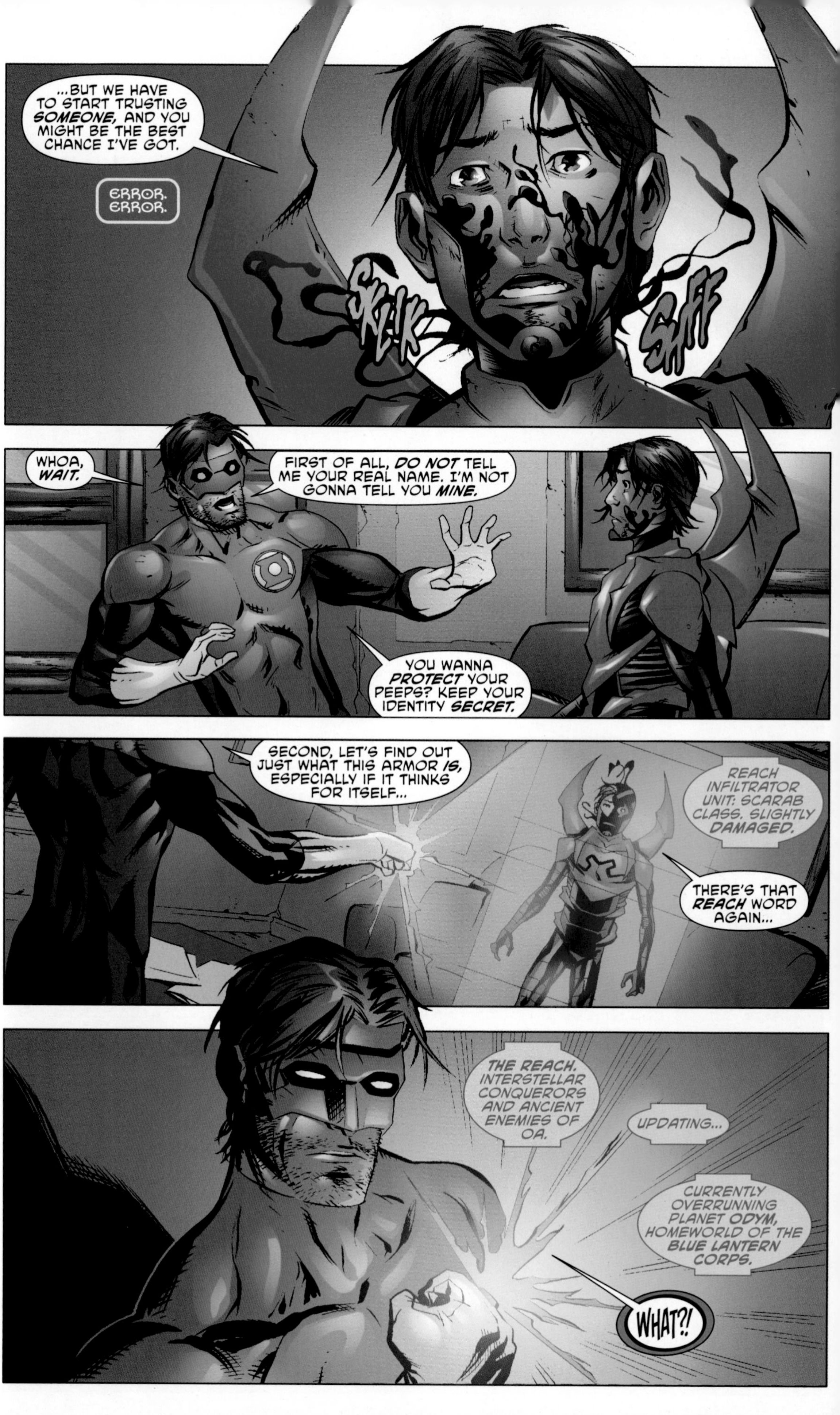

...BUT WE HAVE TO START TRUSTING SOMEONE, AND YOU MIGHT BE THE BEST CHANCE I'VE GOT.
ERROR. ERROR.
SKLIK
SHFF
WHOA, WAIT.
FIRST OF ALL, DO NOT TELL ME YOUR REAL NAME. I'M NOT GONNA TELL YOU MINE.
YOU WANNA PROTECT YOUR PEEPS? KEEP YOUR IDENTITY SECRET.
SECOND, LET'S FIND OUT JUST WHAT THIS ARMOR IS, ESPECIALLY IF IT THINKS FOR ITSELF...
REACH INFILTRATOR UNIT: SCARAB CLASS. SLIGHTLY DAMAGED.
THERE'S THAT REACH WORD AGAIN...
THE REACH. INTERSTELLAR CONQUERORS AND ANCIENT ENEMIES OF OA.
UPDATING...
CURRENTLY OVERRUNNING PLANET ODYM, HOMEWORLD OF THE BLUE LANTERN CORPS.
WHAT?!

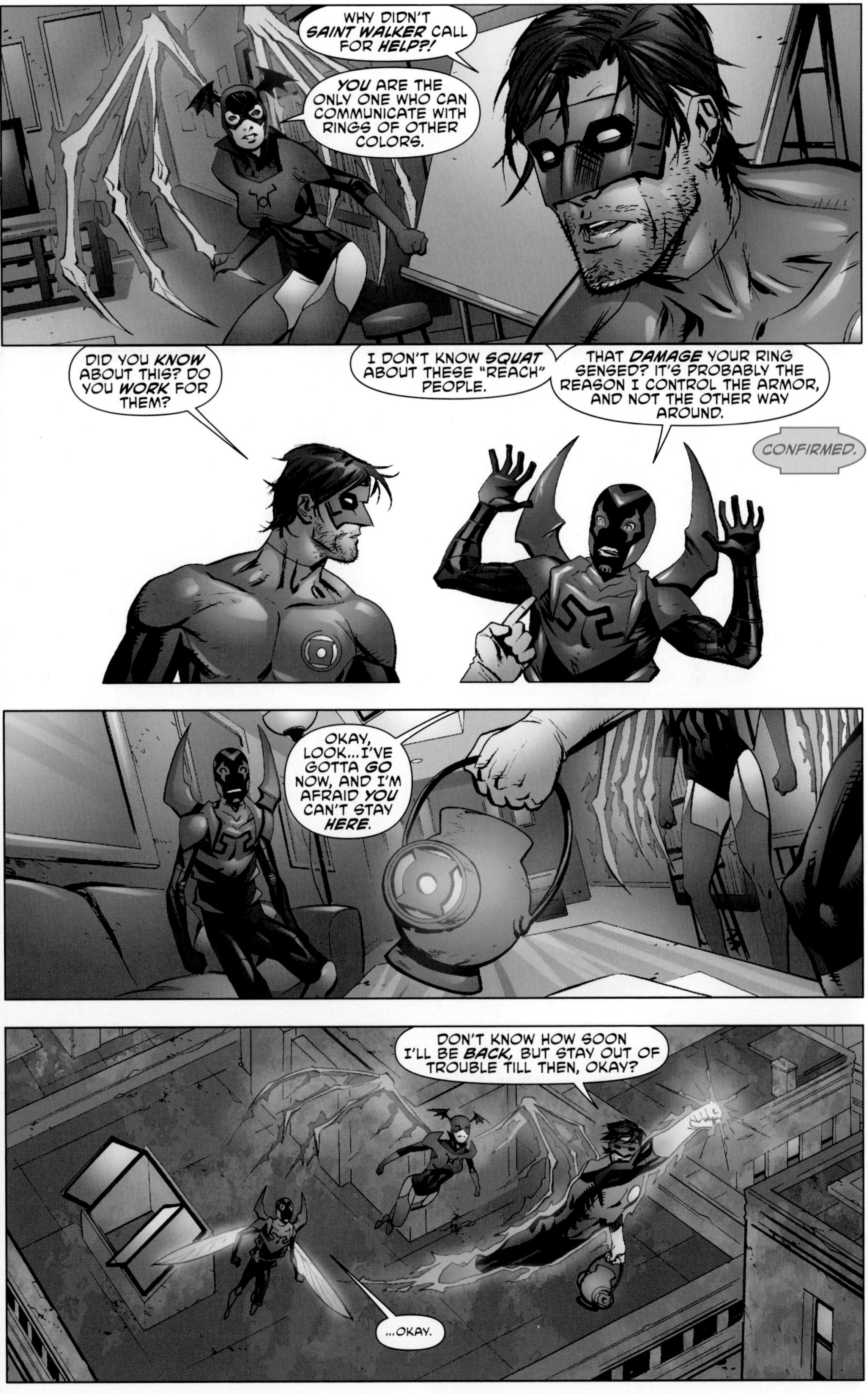
WHY DIDN'T SAINT WALKER CALL FOR HELP?!
YOU ARE THE ONLY ONE WHO CAN COMMUNICATE WITH RINGS OF OTHER COLORS.
DID YOU KNOW ABOUT THIS? DO YOU WORK FOR THEM?
I DON'T KNOW SQUAT ABOUT THESE "REACH" PEOPLE.
THAT DAMAGE YOUR RING SENSED? IT'S PROBABLY THE REASON I CONTROL THE ARMOR, AND NOT THE OTHER WAY AROUND.
CONFIRMED.
OKAY, LOOK...I'VE GOTTA GO NOW, AND I'M AFRAID YOU CAN'T STAY HERE.
DON'T KNOW HOW SOON I'LL BE BACK, BUT STAY OUT OF TROUBLE TILL THEN, OKAY?
...OKAY.

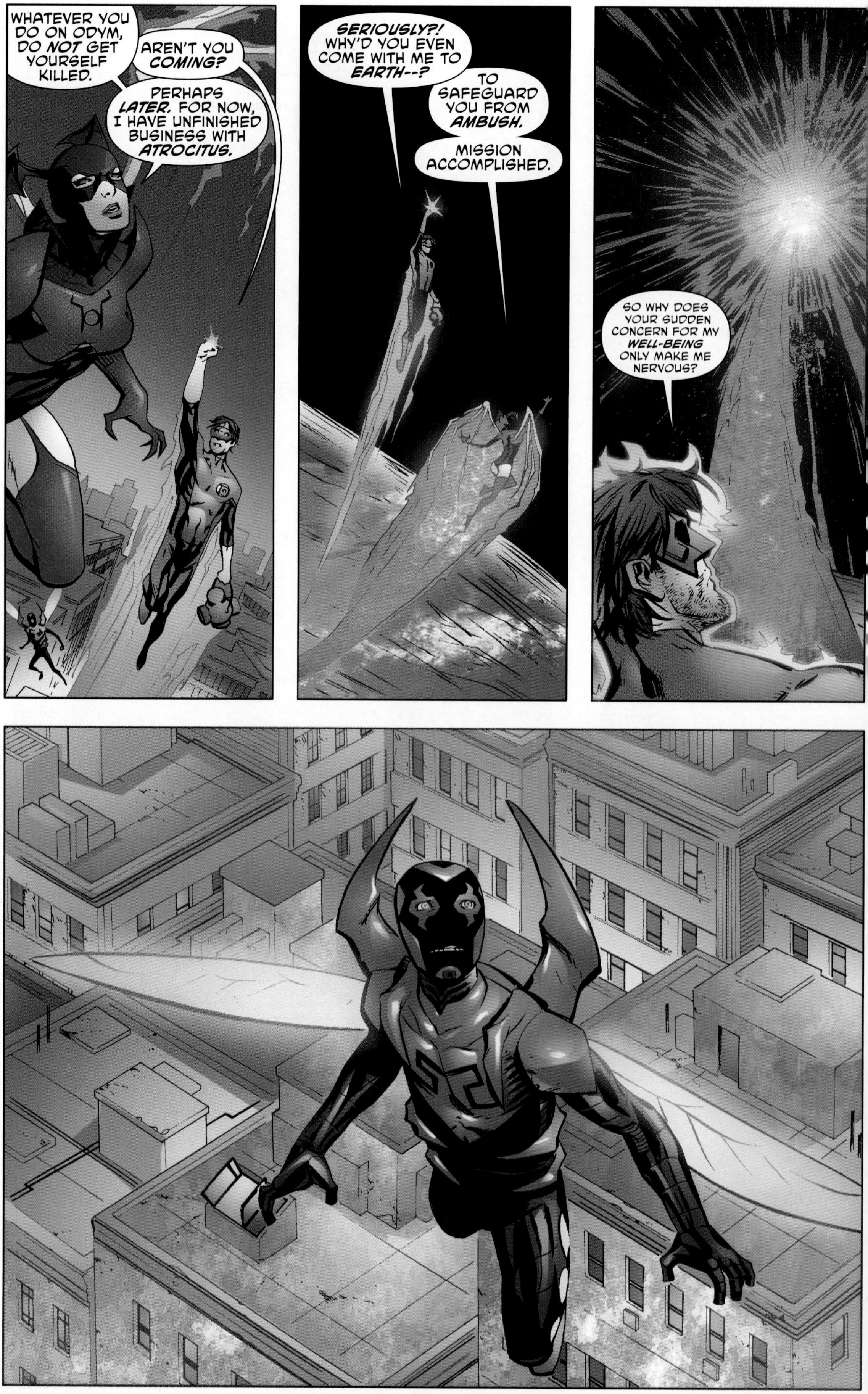
WHATEVER YOU DO ON ODYM, DO NOT GET YOURSELF KILLED.
AREN'T YOU COMING?
PERHAPS LATER. FOR NOW, I HAVE UNFINISHED BUSINESS WITH ATROCITUS.
SERIOUSLY?! WHY'D YOU EVEN COME WITH ME TO EARTH--?
TO SAFEGUARD YOU FROM AMBUSH.
MISSION ACCOMPLISHED.
SO WHY DOES YOUR SUDDEN CONCERN FOR MY WELL-BEING ONLY MAKE ME NERVOUS?

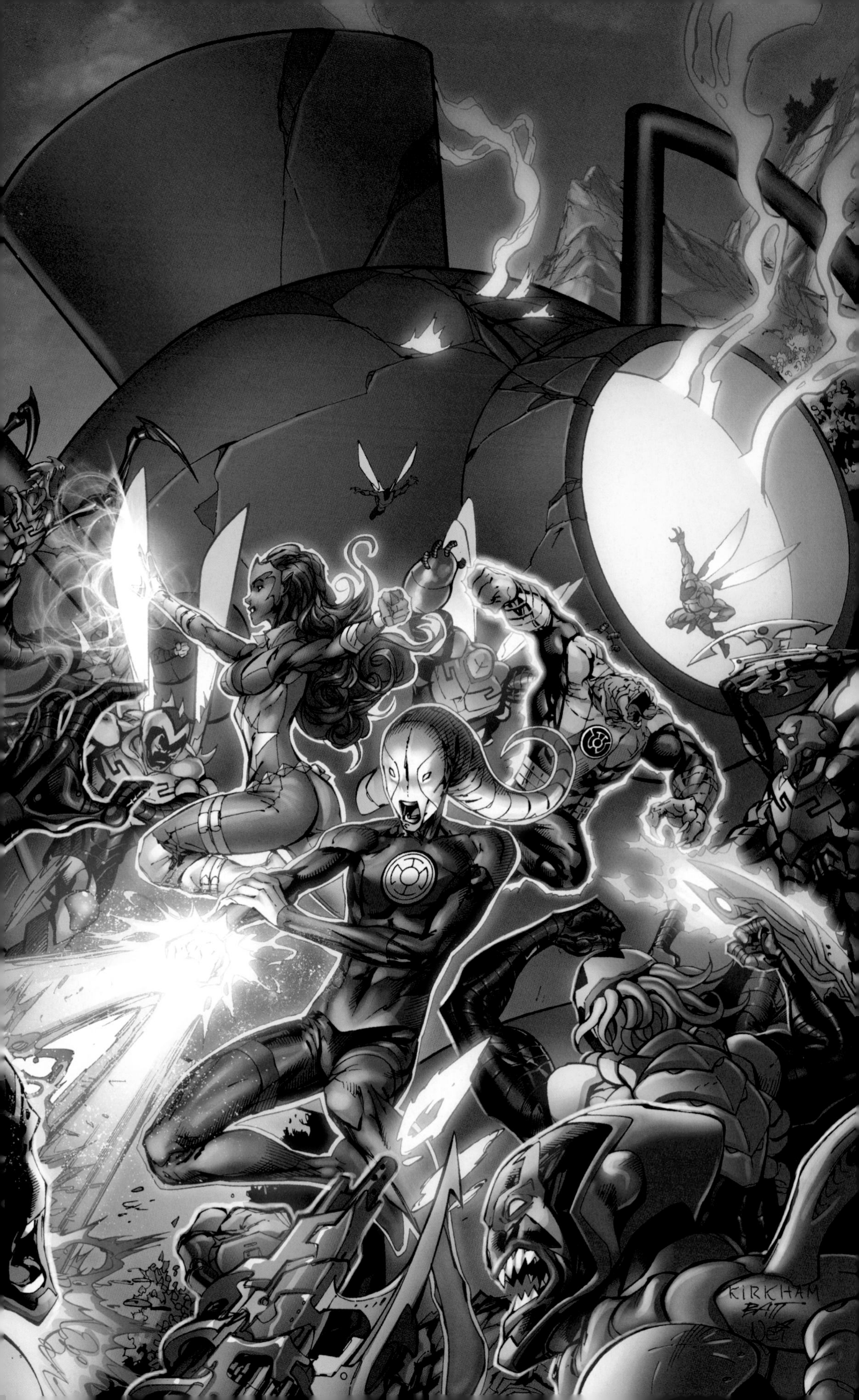
KIRKHAM
BATT

BEYOND HOPE

TONY BEDARD writer TYLER KIRKHAM – pgs 1-9, 12-15, 17-20 TOMAS GIORELLO – pgs 10, 11 & 16 pencillers BATT inker cover by TYLER KIRKHAM, BATT & NEI RUFFI

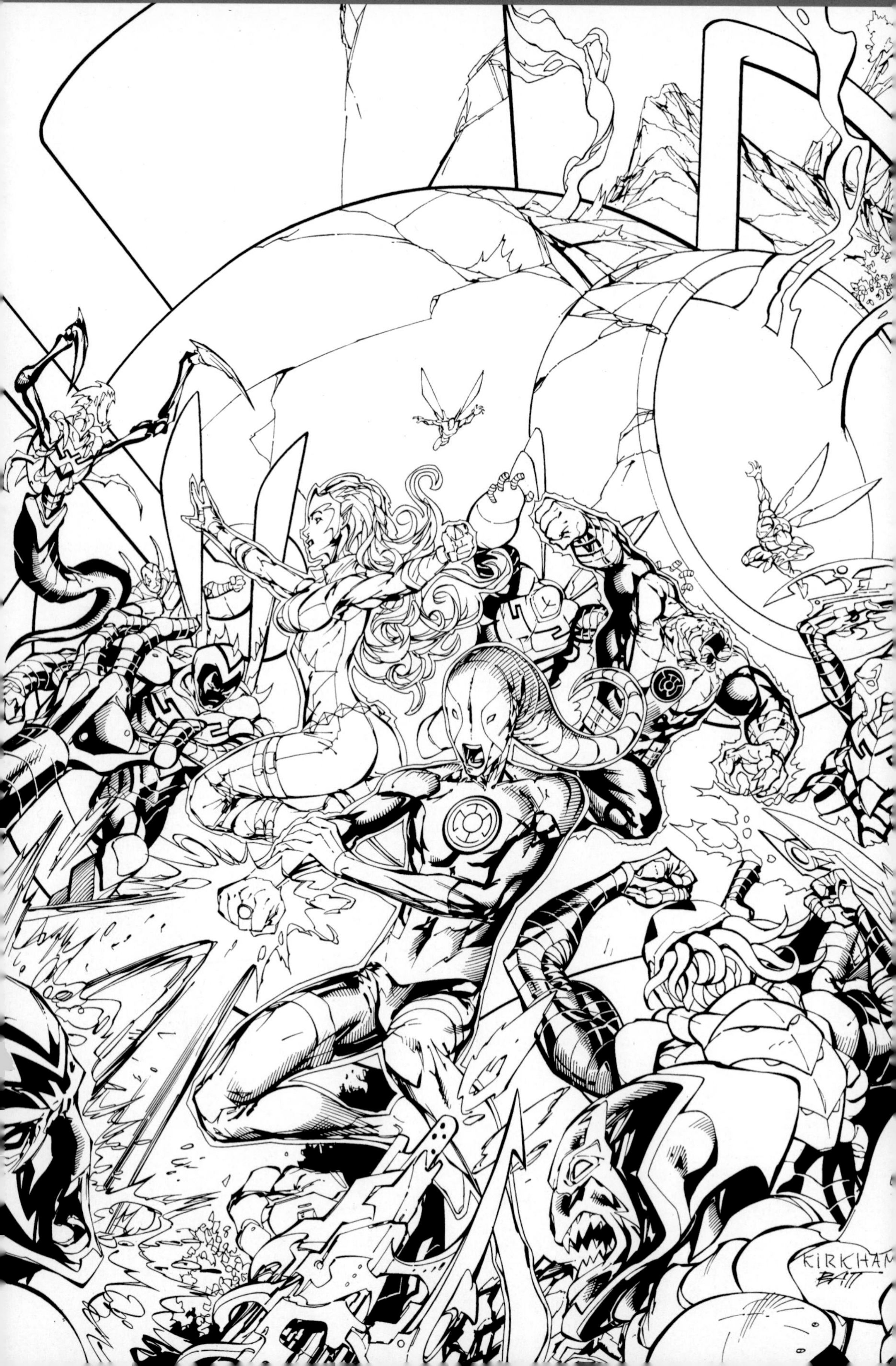

KIRKHAM
BATT

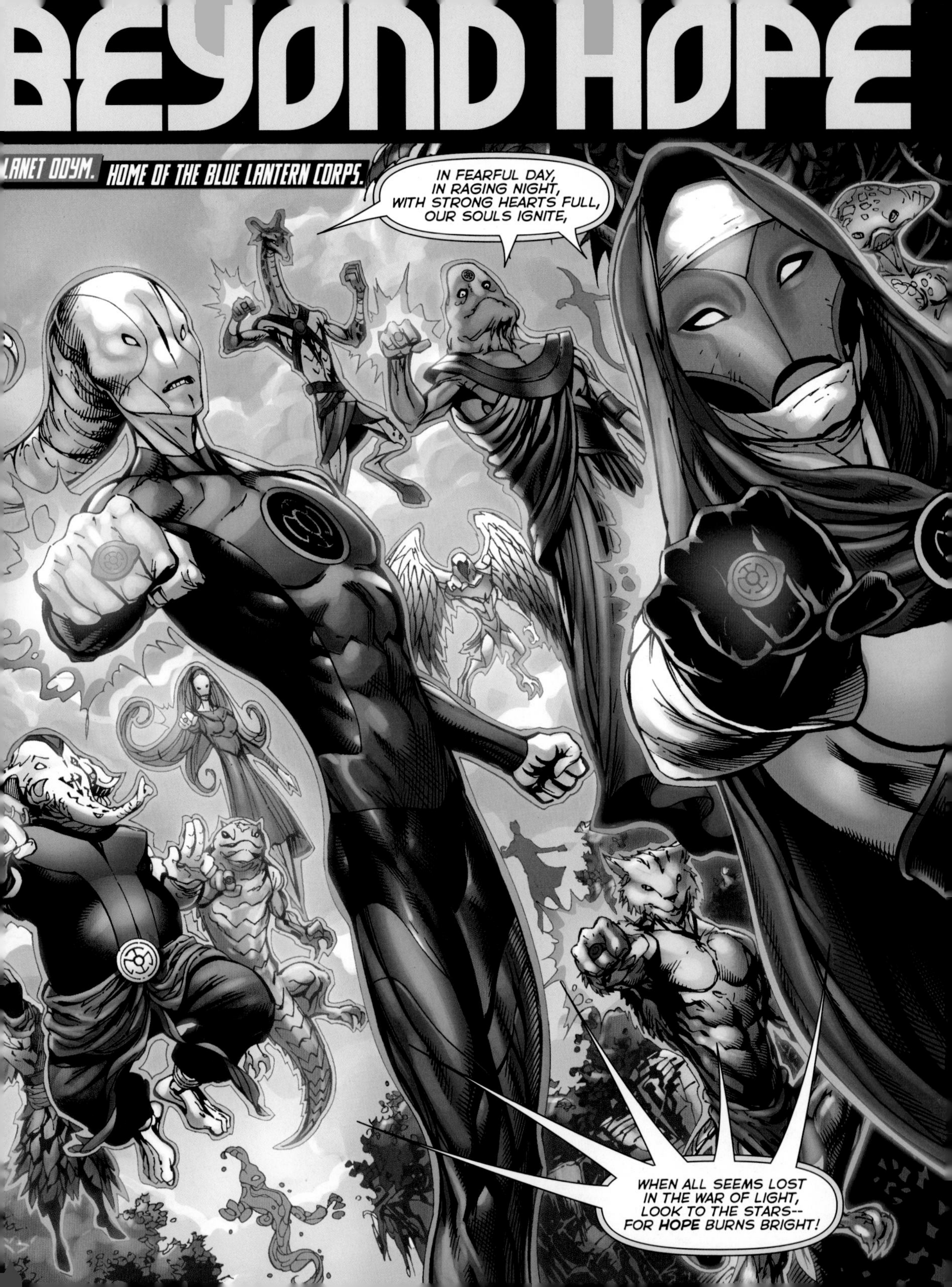
BEYOND HOPE
LANET ODYM.
HOME OF THE BLUE LANTERN CORPS.
IN FEARFUL DAY, IN RAGING NIGHT, WITH STRONG HEARTS FULL, OUR SOULS IGNITE,
WHEN ALL SEEMS LOST IN THE WAR OF LIGHT, LOOK TO THE STARS-- FOR HOPE BURNS BRIGHT!

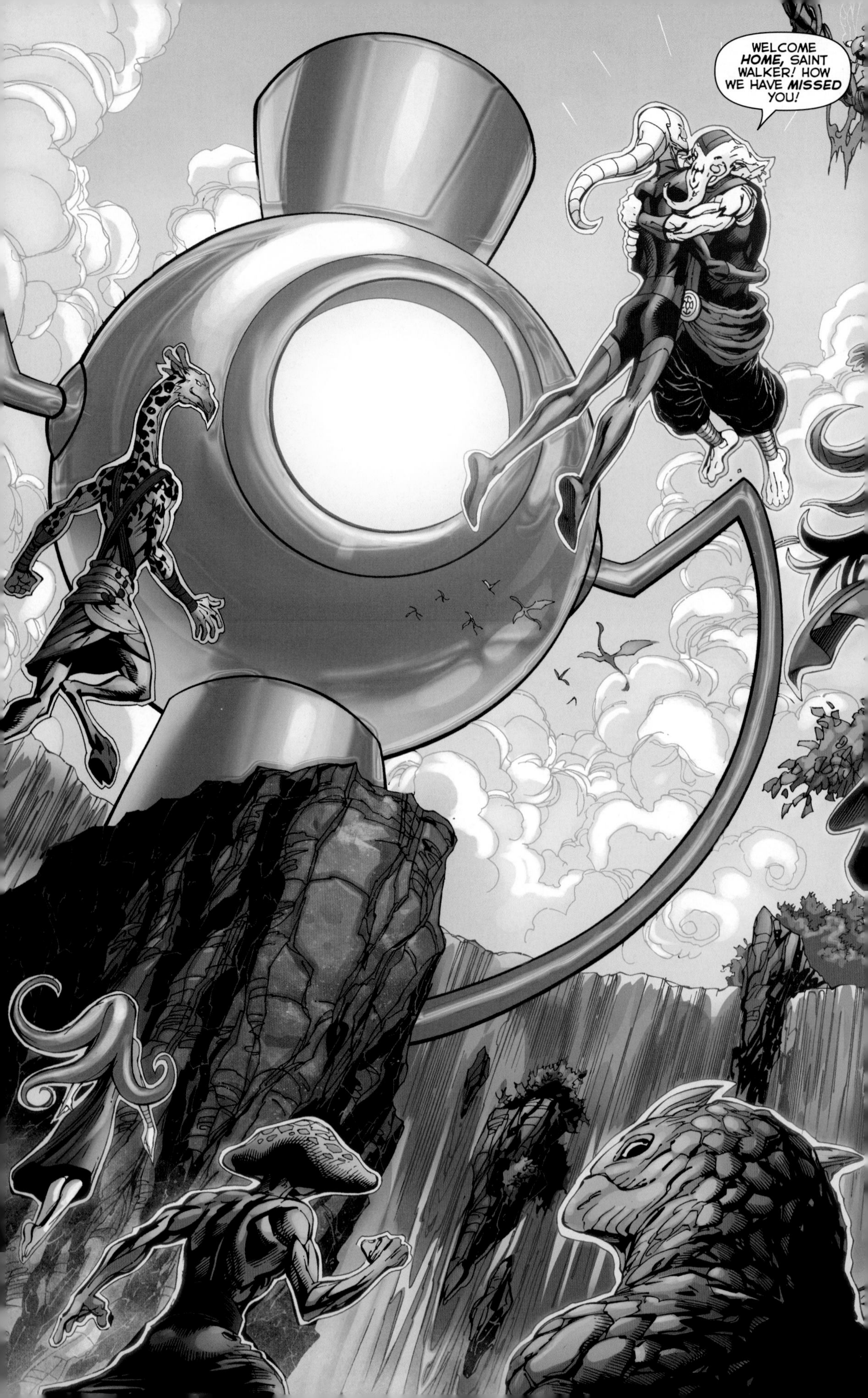
WELCOME **HOME,** SAINT WALKER! HOW WE HAVE **MISSED** YOU!

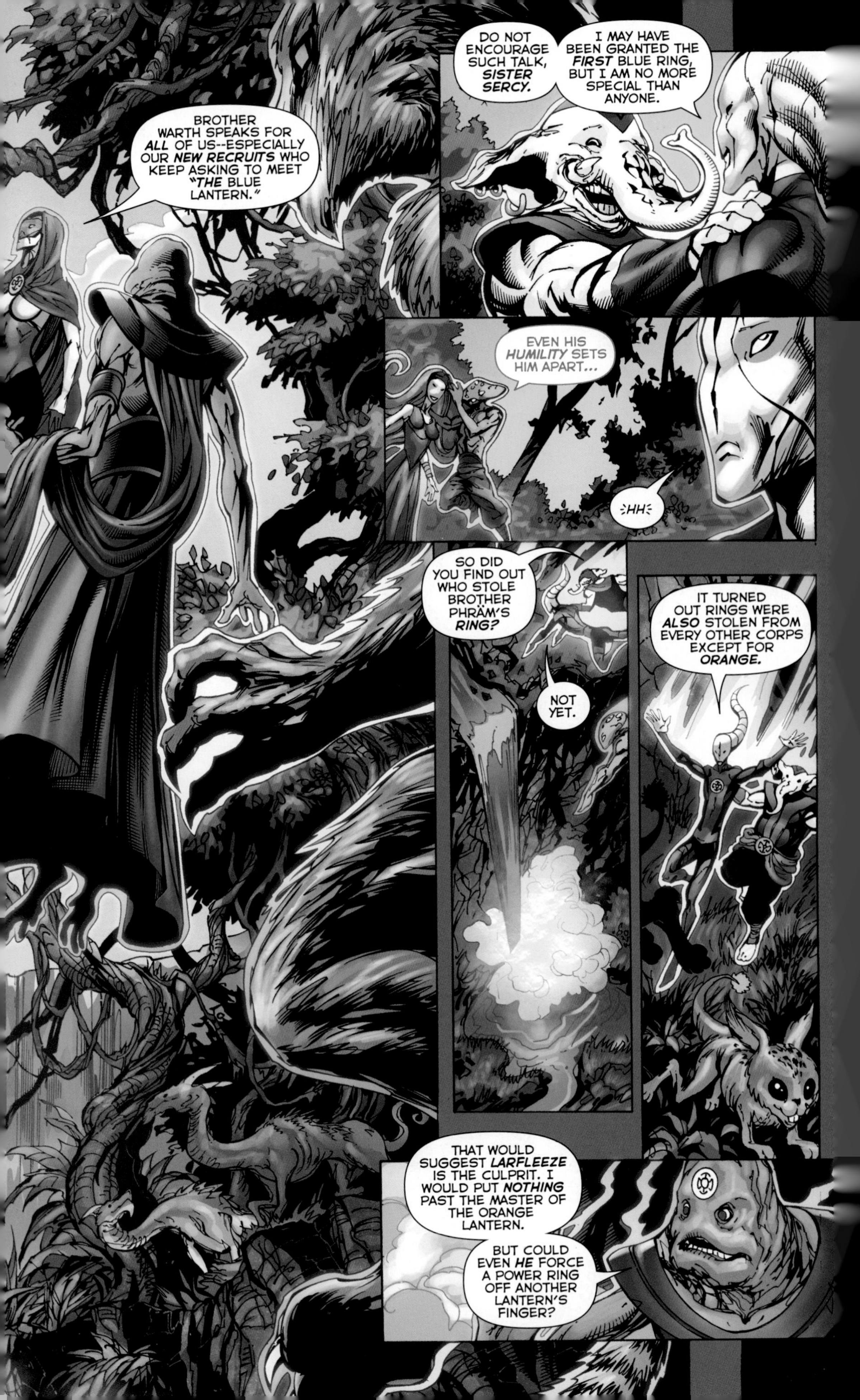
BROTHER WARTH SPEAKS FOR ALL OF US--ESPECIALLY OUR NEW RECRUITS WHO KEEP ASKING TO MEET "THE BLUE LANTERN."
DO NOT ENCOURAGE SUCH TALK, SISTER SERCY.
I MAY HAVE BEEN GRANTED THE FIRST BLUE RING, BUT I AM NO MORE SPECIAL THAN ANYONE.
EVEN HIS HUMILITY SETS HIM APART...
HH
SO DID YOU FIND OUT WHO STOLE BROTHER PHRÄM'S RING?
NOT YET.
IT TURNED OUT RINGS WERE ALSO STOLEN FROM EVERY OTHER CORPS EXCEPT FOR ORANGE.
THAT WOULD SUGGEST LARFLEEZE IS THE CULPRIT. I WOULD PUT NOTHING PAST THE MASTER OF THE ORANGE LANTERN.
BUT COULD EVEN HE FORCE A POWER RING OFF ANOTHER LANTERN'S FINGER?

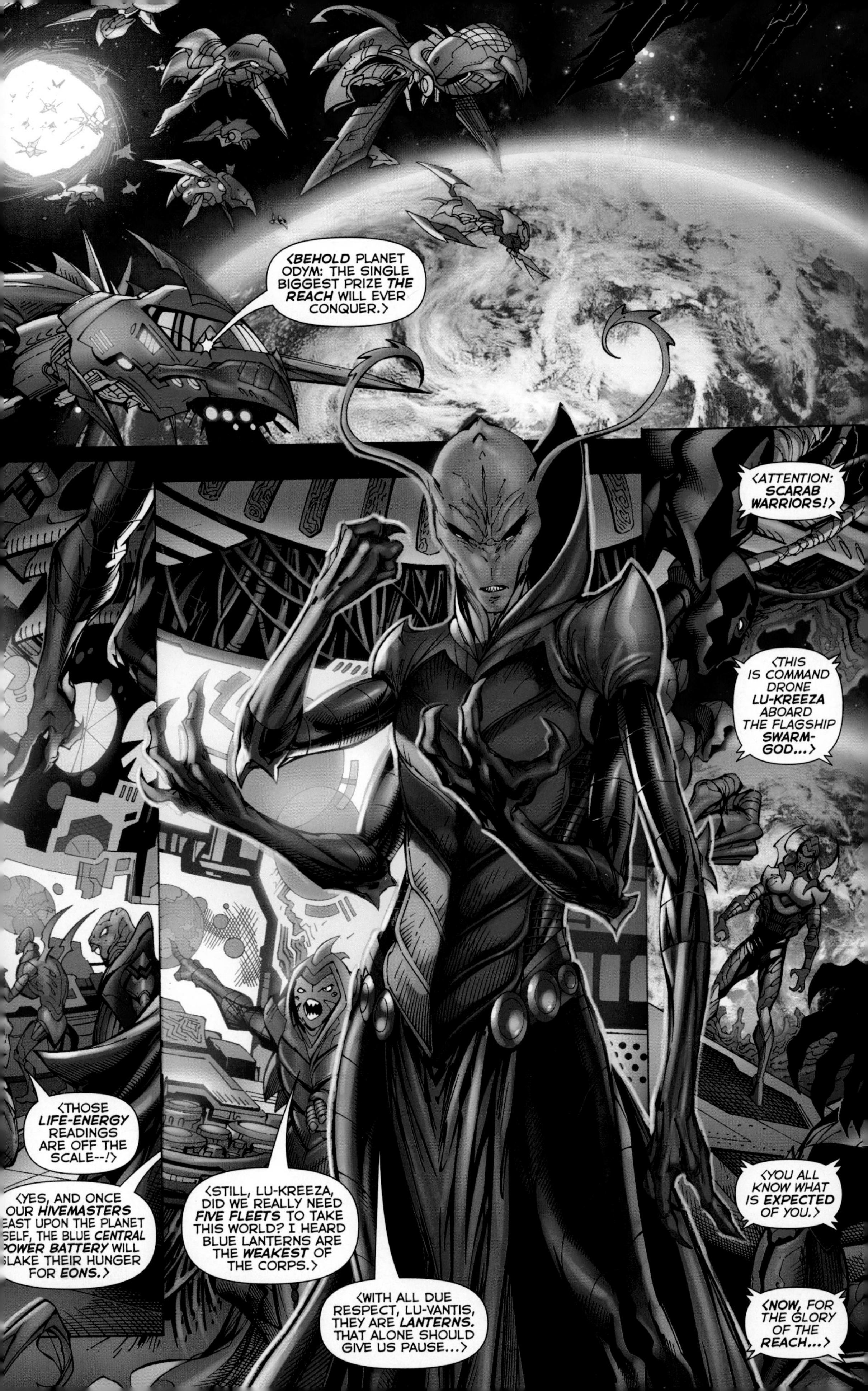
<BEHOLD PLANET ODYM: THE SINGLE BIGGEST PRIZE THE REACH WILL EVER CONQUER.>
<ATTENTION: SCARAB WARRIORS!>
<THIS IS COMMAND DRONE LU-KREEZA ABOARD THE FLAGSHIP SWARM-GOD...>
<THOSE LIFE-ENERGY READINGS ARE OFF THE SCALE--!>
<YES, AND ONCE OUR HIVEMASTERS FEAST UPON THE PLANET ITSELF, THE BLUE CENTRAL POWER BATTERY WILL SLAKE THEIR HUNGER FOR EONS.>
<STILL, LU-KREEZA, DID WE REALLY NEED FIVE FLEETS TO TAKE THIS WORLD? I HEARD BLUE LANTERNS ARE THE WEAKEST OF THE CORPS.>
<WITH ALL DUE RESPECT, LU-VANTIS, THEY ARE LANTERNS. THAT ALONE SHOULD GIVE US PAUSE...>
<YOU ALL KNOW WHAT IS EXPECTED OF YOU.>
<NOW, FOR THE GLORY OF THE REACH...>

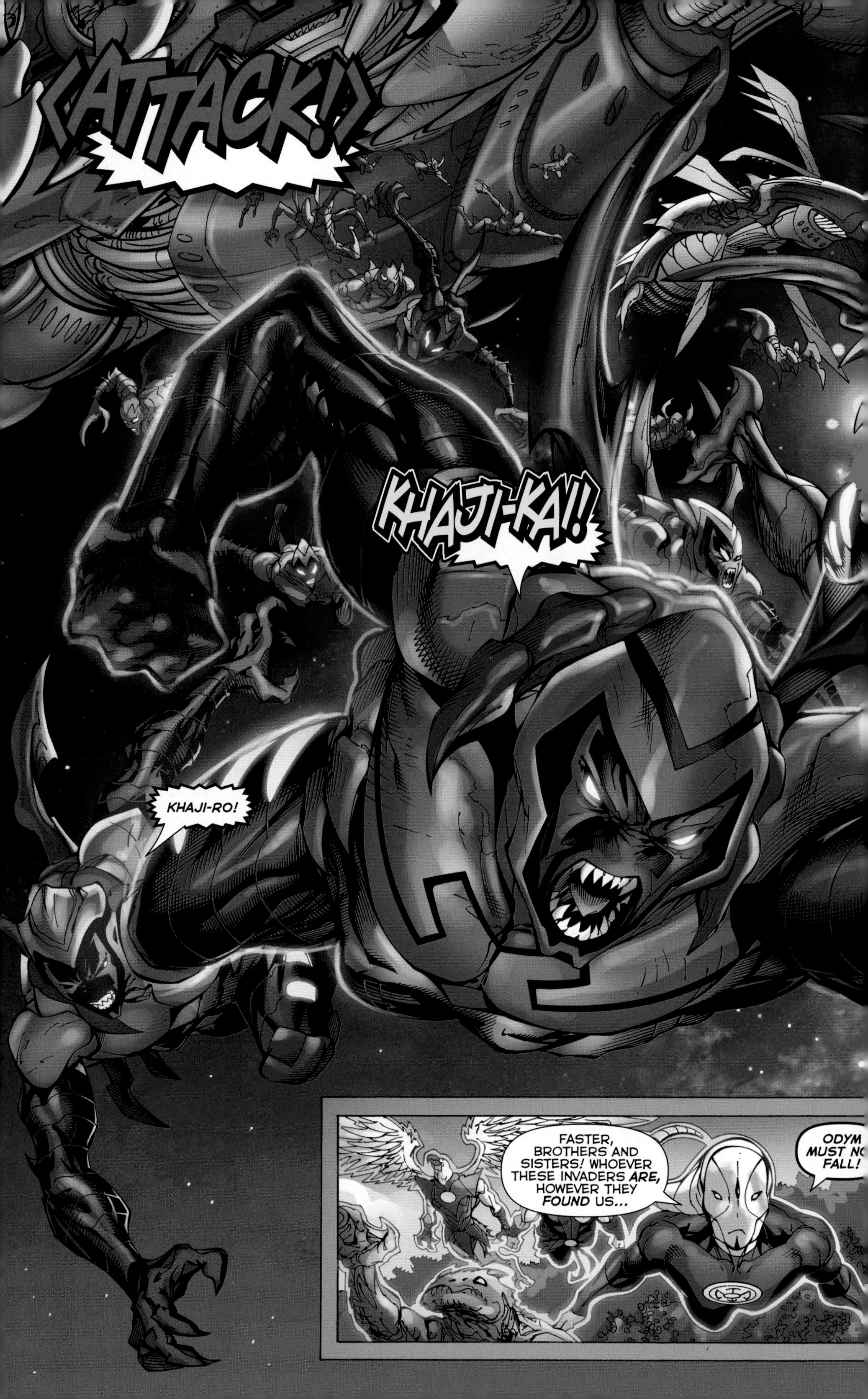

‹ATTACK!›
KHAJI-KA!!
KHAJI-RO!
FASTER, BROTHERS AND SISTERS! WHOEVER THESE INVADERS *ARE*, HOWEVER THEY *FOUND* US...
ODYM MUST NO FALL!

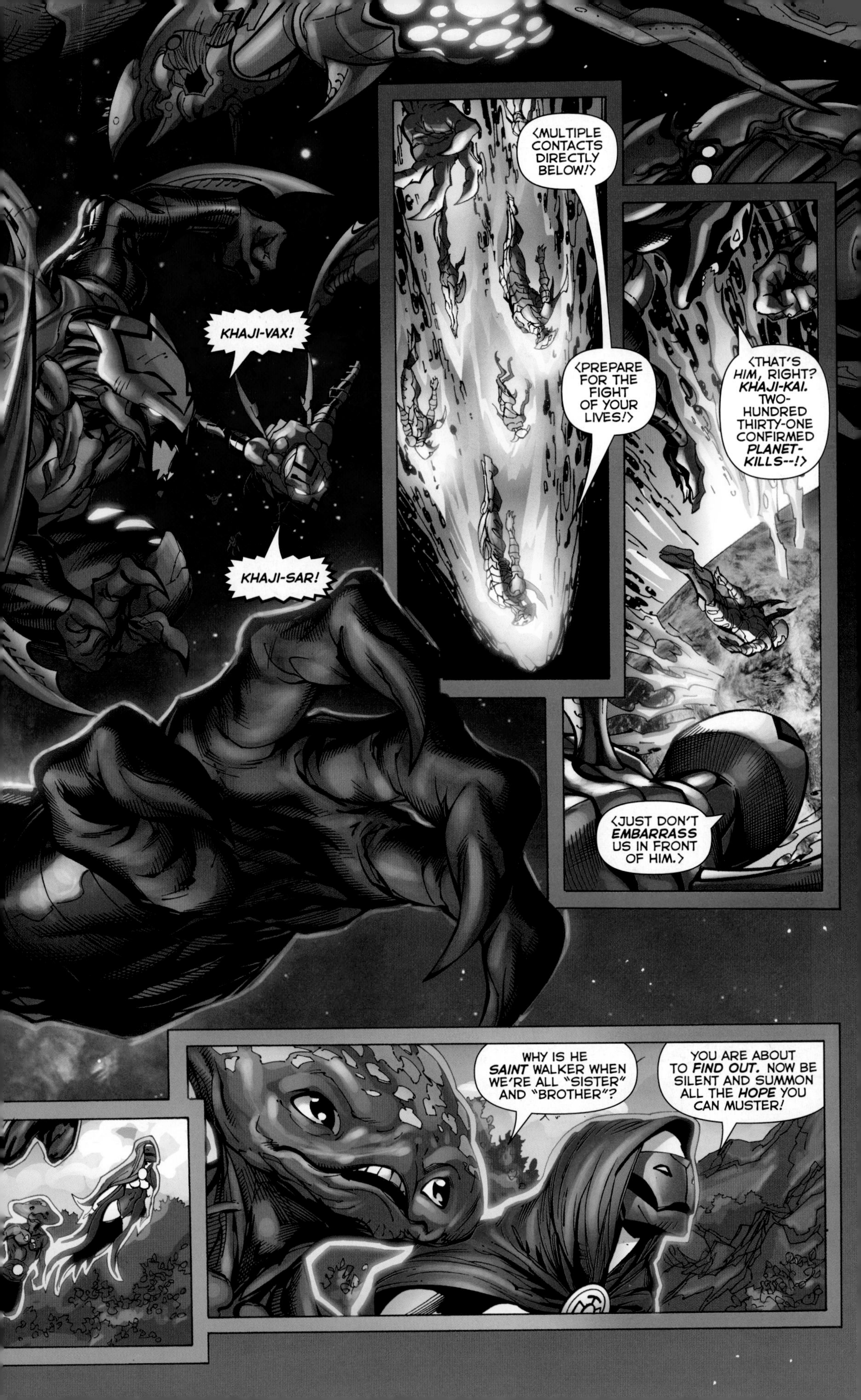
KHAJI-VAX!
KHAJI-SAR!
<MULTIPLE CONTACTS DIRECTLY BELOW!>
<PREPARE FOR THE FIGHT OF YOUR LIVES!>
<THAT'S HIM, RIGHT? KHAJI-KAI. TWO-HUNDRED THIRTY-ONE CONFIRMED PLANET-KILLS--!>
<JUST DON'T EMBARRASS US IN FRONT OF HIM.>
WHY IS HE SAINT WALKER WHEN WE'RE ALL "SISTER" AND "BROTHER"?
YOU ARE ABOUT TO FIND OUT. NOW BE SILENT AND SUMMON ALL THE HOPE YOU CAN MUSTER!

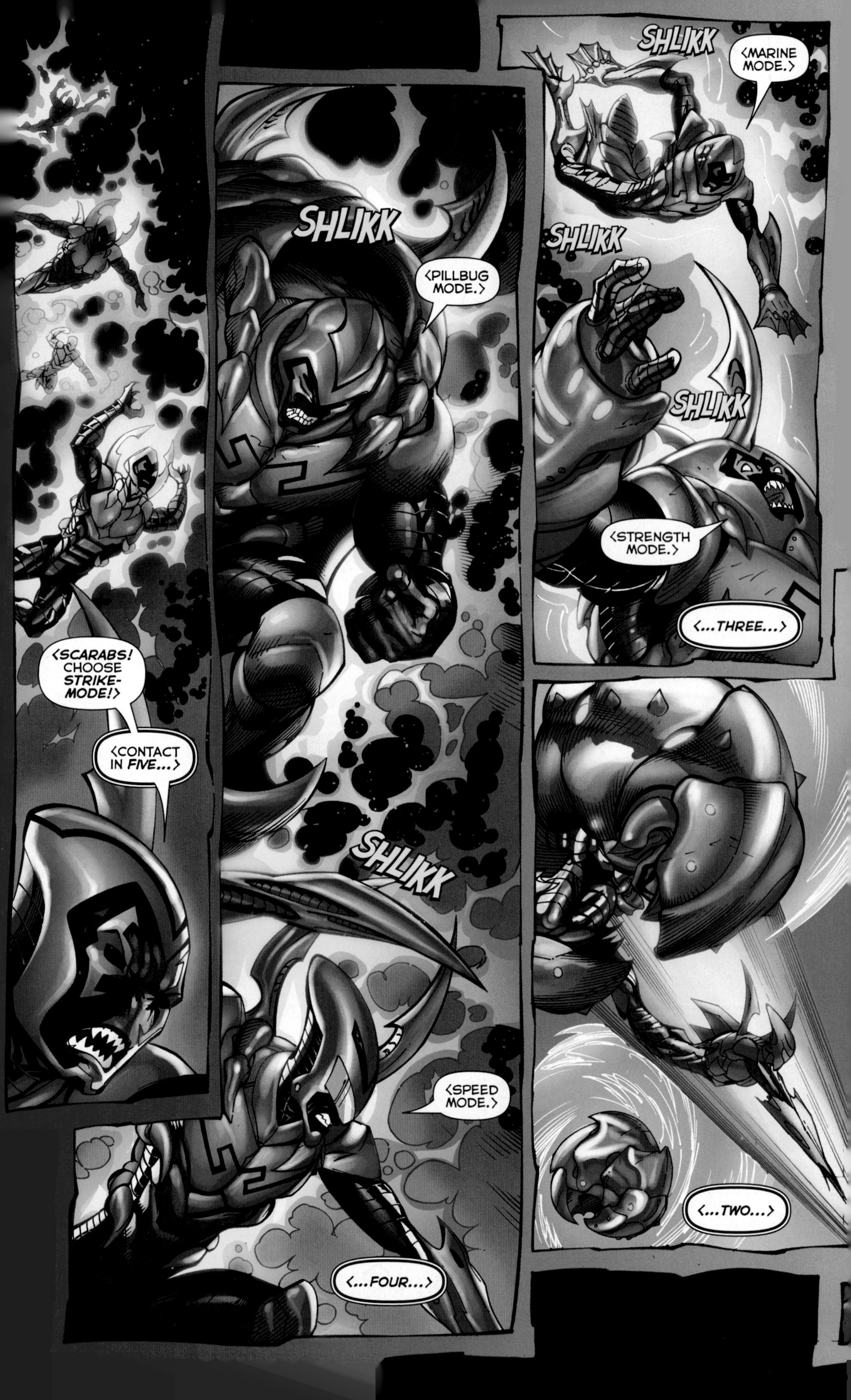
<SCARABS! CHOOSE STRIKE-MODE!>
<CONTACT IN FIVE...>
SHLIKK
<PILLBUG MODE.>
SHLIKK
<SPEED MODE.>
<...FOUR...>
SHLIKK
<MARINE MODE.>
SHLIKK
SHLIKK
<STRENGTH MODE.>
<...THREE...>
<...TWO...>

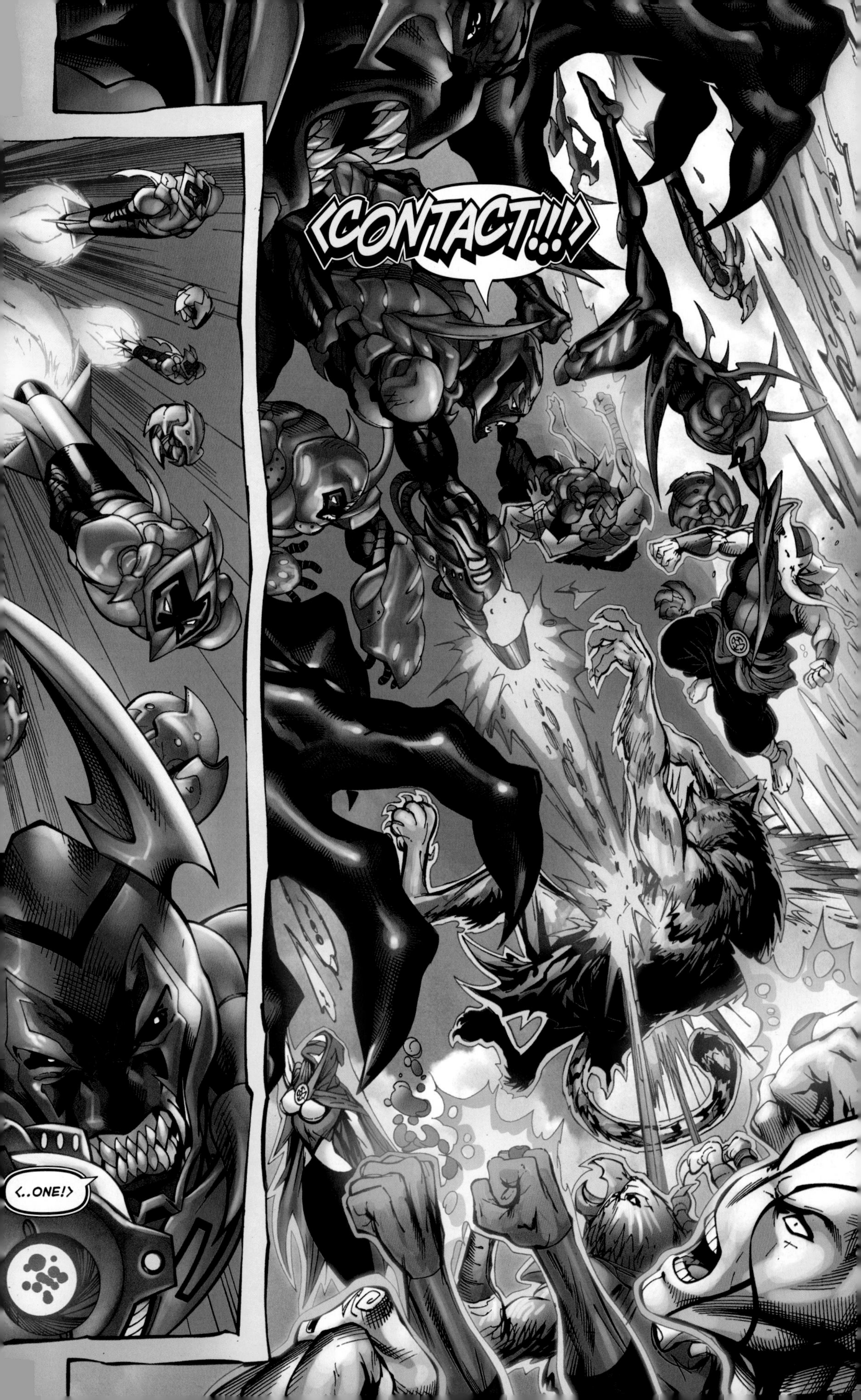

<CONTACT!!!>
<..ONE!>

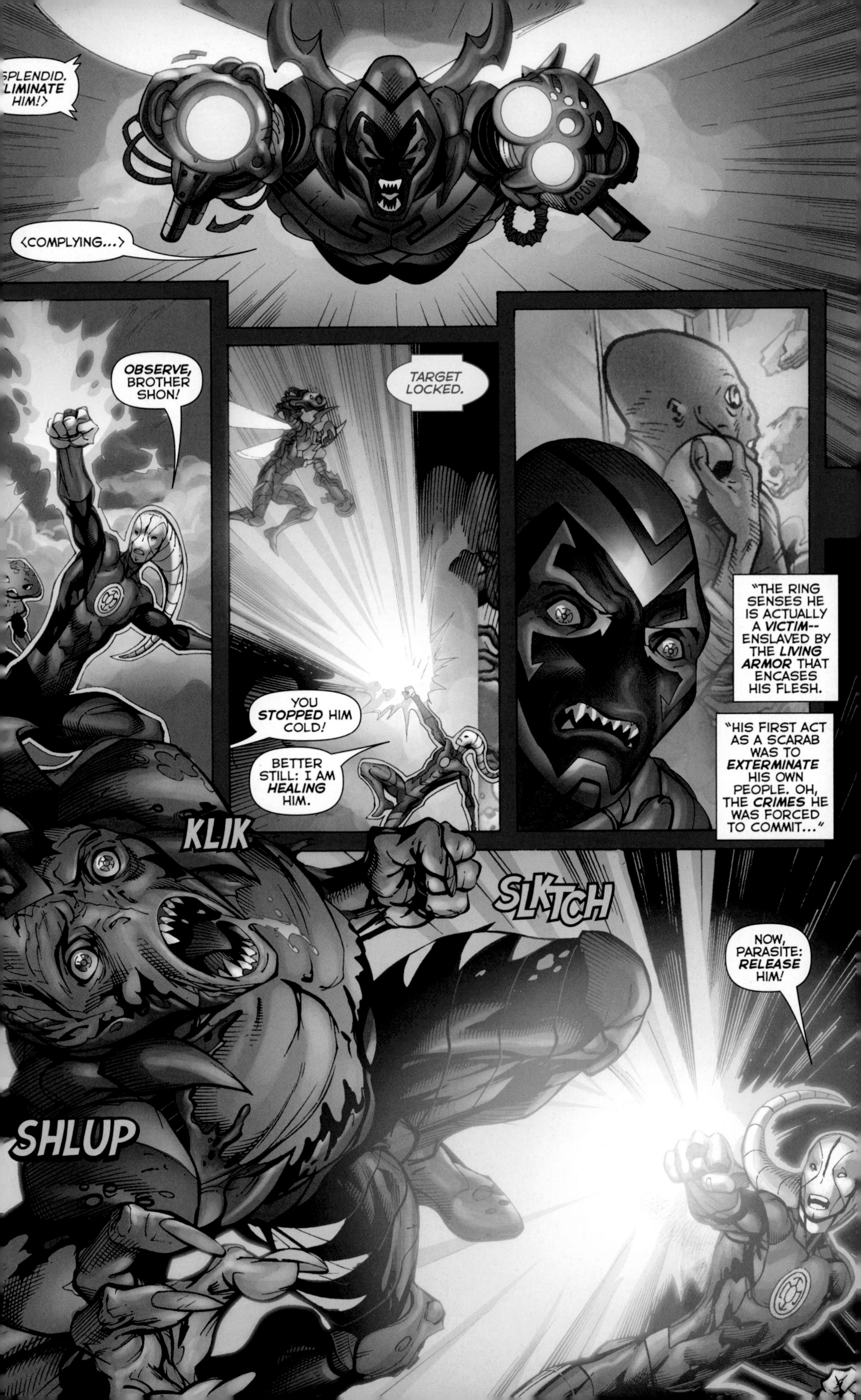

SPLENDID. ELIMINATE HIM!>
<COMPLYING...>
OBSERVE, BROTHER SHON!
TARGET LOCKED.
YOU STOPPED HIM COLD!
BETTER STILL: I AM HEALING HIM.
"THE RING SENSES HE IS ACTUALLY A VICTIM-- ENSLAVED BY THE LIVING ARMOR THAT ENCASES HIS FLESH.
"HIS FIRST ACT AS A SCARAB WAS TO EXTERMINATE HIS OWN PEOPLE. OH, THE CRIMES HE WAS FORCED TO COMMIT..."
KLIK
SLKTCH
NOW, PARASITE: RELEASE HIM!
SHLUP

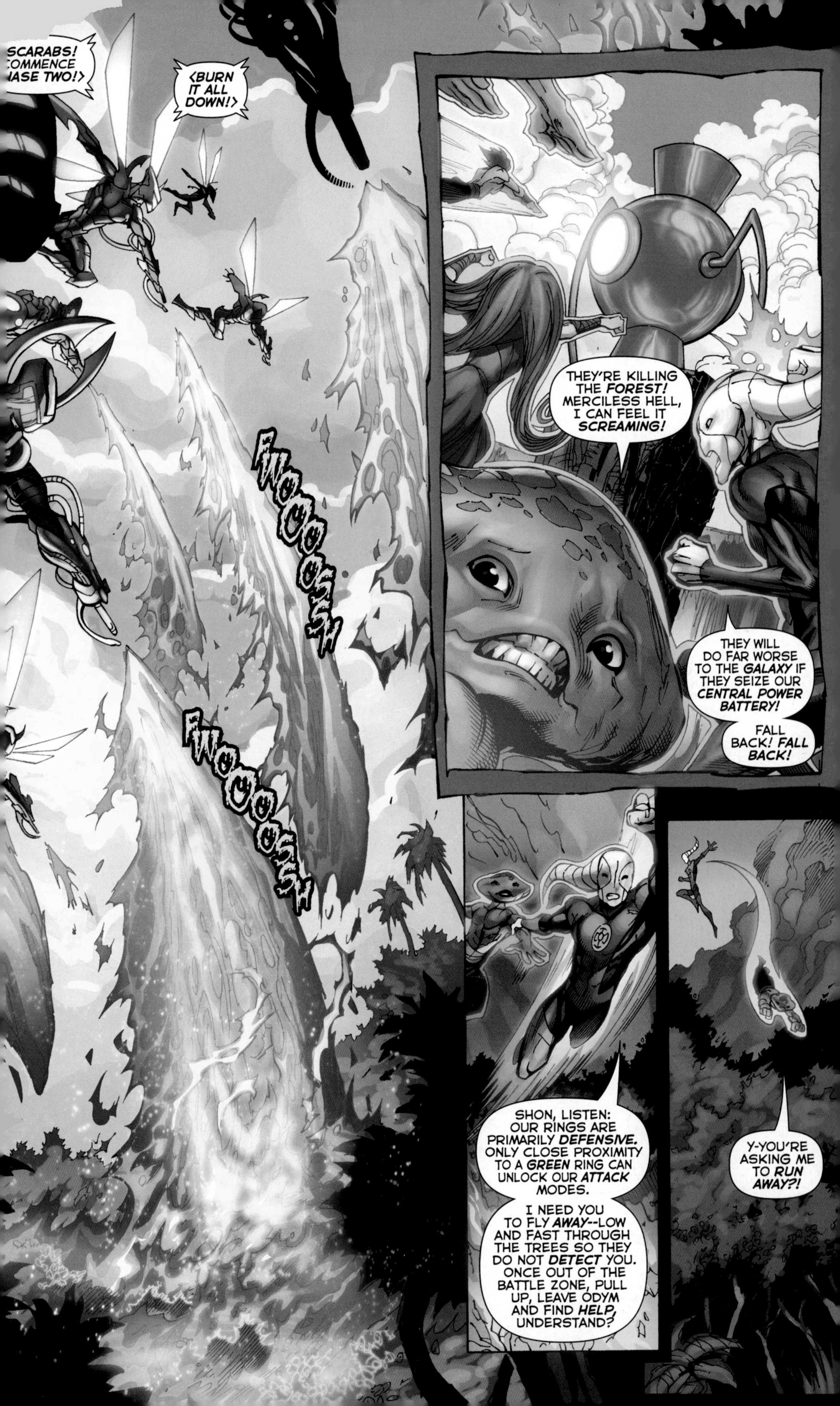
SCARABS! COMMENCE HASE TWO!>
<BURN IT ALL DOWN!>
FWOOOOSSH
FWOOOOSSH
THEY'RE KILLING THE FOREST! MERCILESS HELL, I CAN FEEL IT SCREAMING!
THEY WILL DO FAR WORSE TO THE GALAXY IF THEY SEIZE OUR CENTRAL POWER BATTERY!
FALL BACK! FALL BACK!
SHON, LISTEN: OUR RINGS ARE PRIMARILY DEFENSIVE. ONLY CLOSE PROXIMITY TO A GREEN RING CAN UNLOCK OUR ATTACK MODES.
I NEED YOU TO FLY AWAY--LOW AND FAST THROUGH THE TREES SO THEY DO NOT DETECT YOU. ONCE OUT OF THE BATTLE ZONE, PULL UP, LEAVE ODYM AND FIND HELP, UNDERSTAND?
Y-YOU'RE ASKING ME TO RUN AWAY?!

DYM.

YOU ALL HEARD MY RING: A *GREEN LANTERN* IS ON HIS WAY--PERHAPS *MORE* IF BROTHER SHON IS SUCCESSFUL.

NOW GET IN POSITION AND *EXTEND* YOUR AURAS!

THAT'S IT! *LINK* THEM SO NO PART OF THE BATTERY IS UNSHIELDED!

WALKER, I *RECOGNIZE* THESE CREATURES. *THE REACH* ARE THE SCOURGE OF MY HOME SECTOR!

WHAT DO THEY *WANT* FROM US? WILL THEY LISTEN TO *REASON?*

"IF THEY DID, IT WOULD BE A *FIRST.*"

PLEASE, MOTHERGOD... PLEASE LET ME BE FAR ENOUGH...

HOPE

OH, NO... NO...!

"YOU SEE, THE REACH ARE LIKE *LOCUSTS*, MOVING FROM ONE WORLD TO THE NEXT, CONSUMING ALL LIFE.

"FIRST THEIR *SCARABS* DESTROY YOUR PLANET'S DEFENSES..."

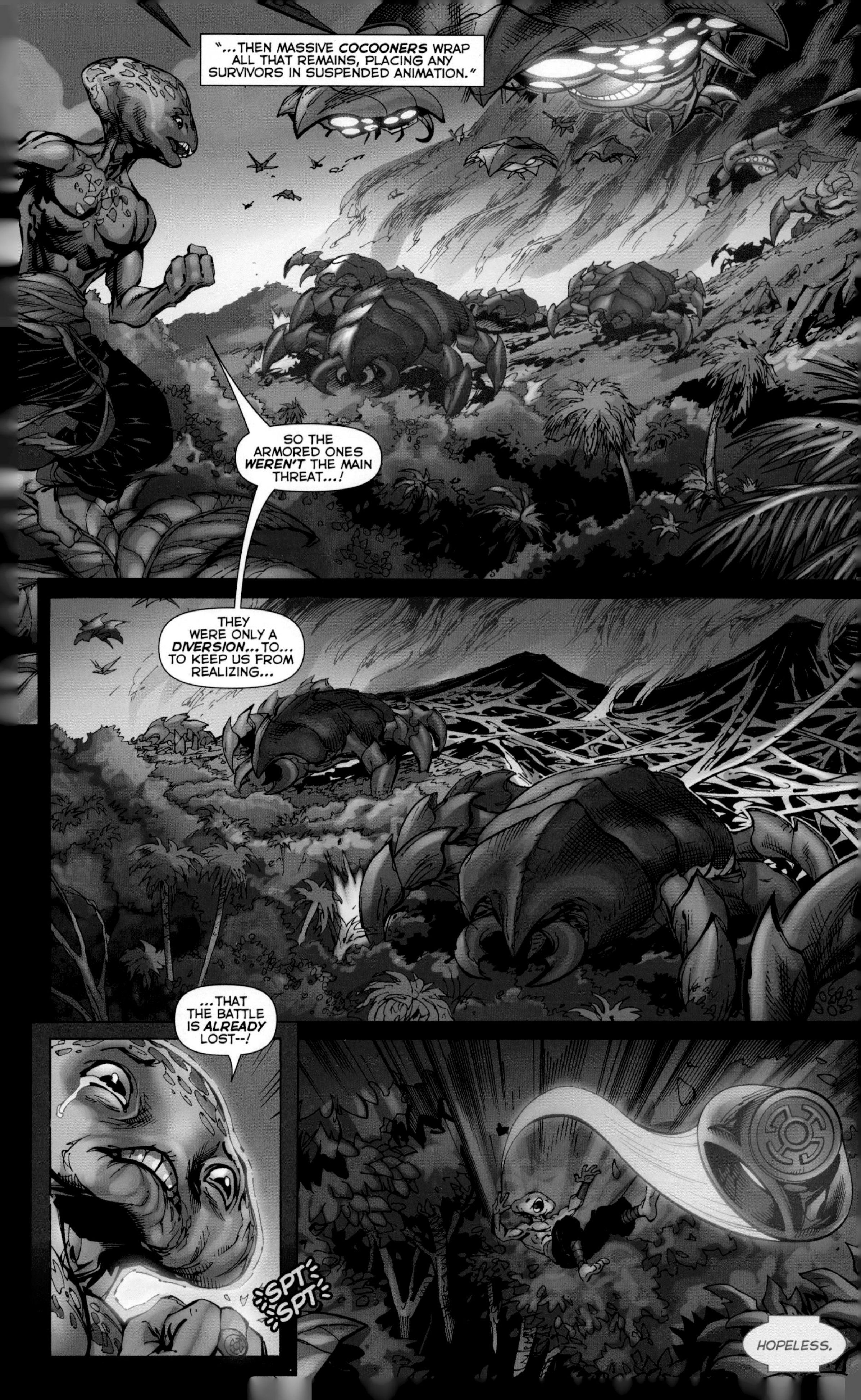
"...THEN MASSIVE COCOONERS WRAP ALL THAT REMAINS, PLACING ANY SURVIVORS IN SUSPENDED ANIMATION."
SO THE ARMORED ONES WEREN'T THE MAIN THREAT...!
THEY WERE ONLY A DIVERSION...TO... TO KEEP US FROM REALIZING...
...THAT THE BATTLE IS ALREADY LOST--!
SPT SPT
HOPELESS.

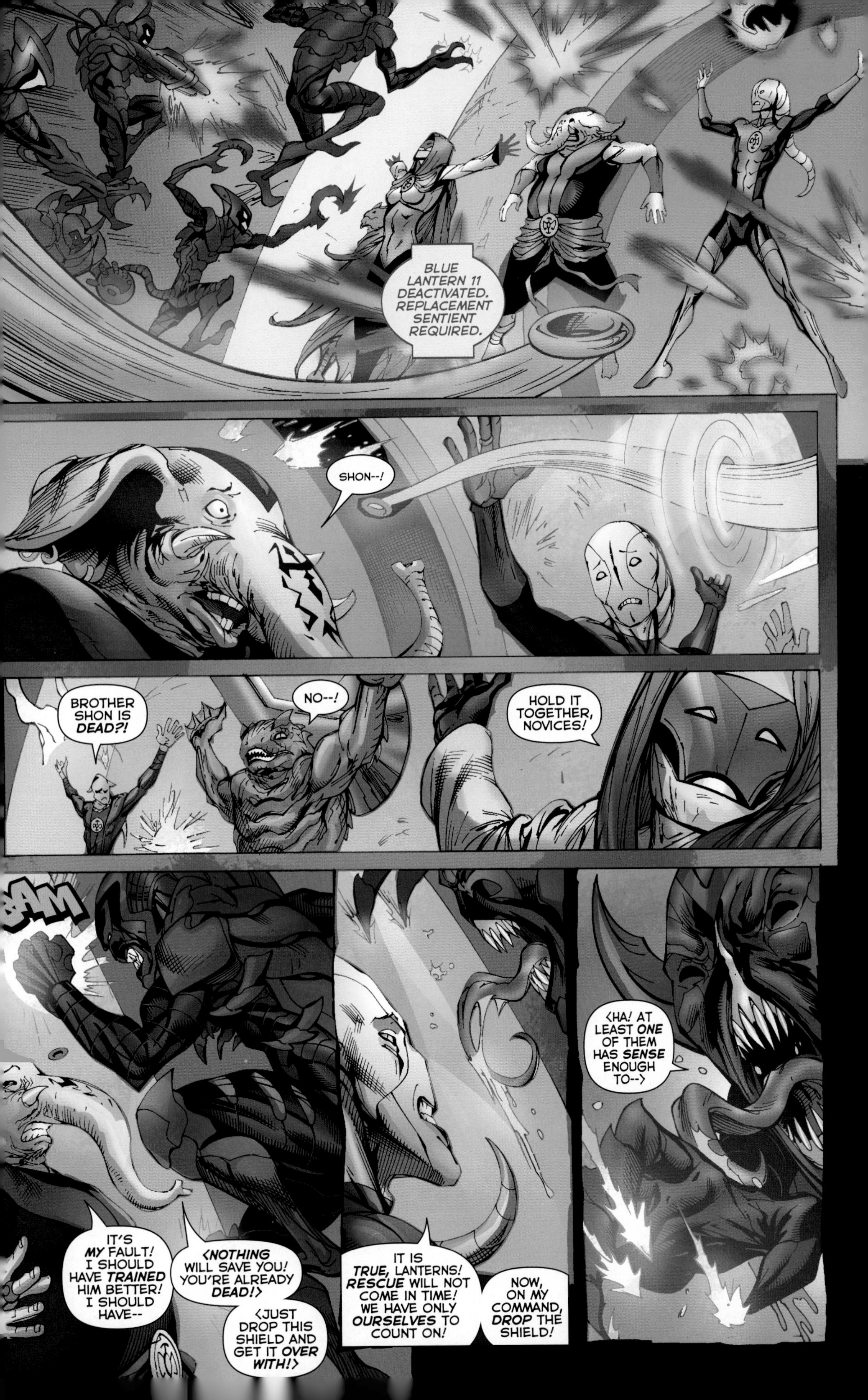

BLUE LANTERN 11 DEACTIVATED. REPLACEMENT SENTIENT REQUIRED.
SHON--!
BROTHER SHON IS DEAD?!
NO--!
HOLD IT TOGETHER, NOVICES!
BAM
IT'S MY FAULT! I SHOULD HAVE TRAINED HIM BETTER! I SHOULD HAVE--
<NOTHING WILL SAVE YOU! YOU'RE ALREADY DEAD!>
<JUST DROP THIS SHIELD AND GET IT OVER WITH!>
IT IS TRUE, LANTERNS! RESCUE WILL NOT COME IN TIME! WE HAVE ONLY OURSELVES TO COUNT ON!
NOW, ON MY COMMAND, DROP THE SHIELD!
<HA! AT LEAST ONE OF THEM HAS SENSE ENOUGH TO-->

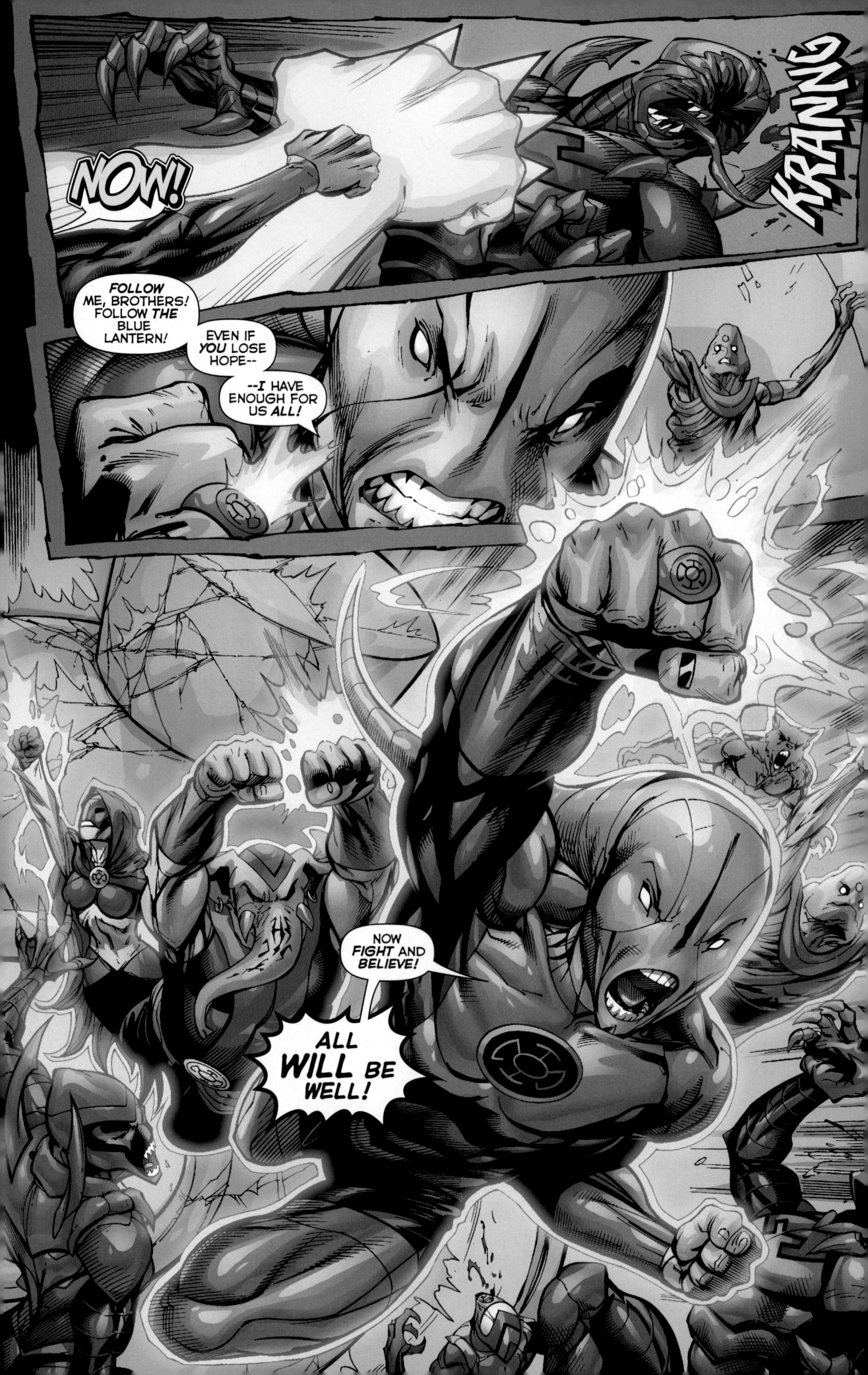
NOW!
KRANNG
FOLLOW ME, BROTHERS! FOLLOW THE BLUE LANTERN!
EVEN IF YOU LOSE HOPE--
--I HAVE ENOUGH FOR US ALL!
NOW FIGHT AND BELIEVE!
ALL WILL BE WELL!
KRANNG

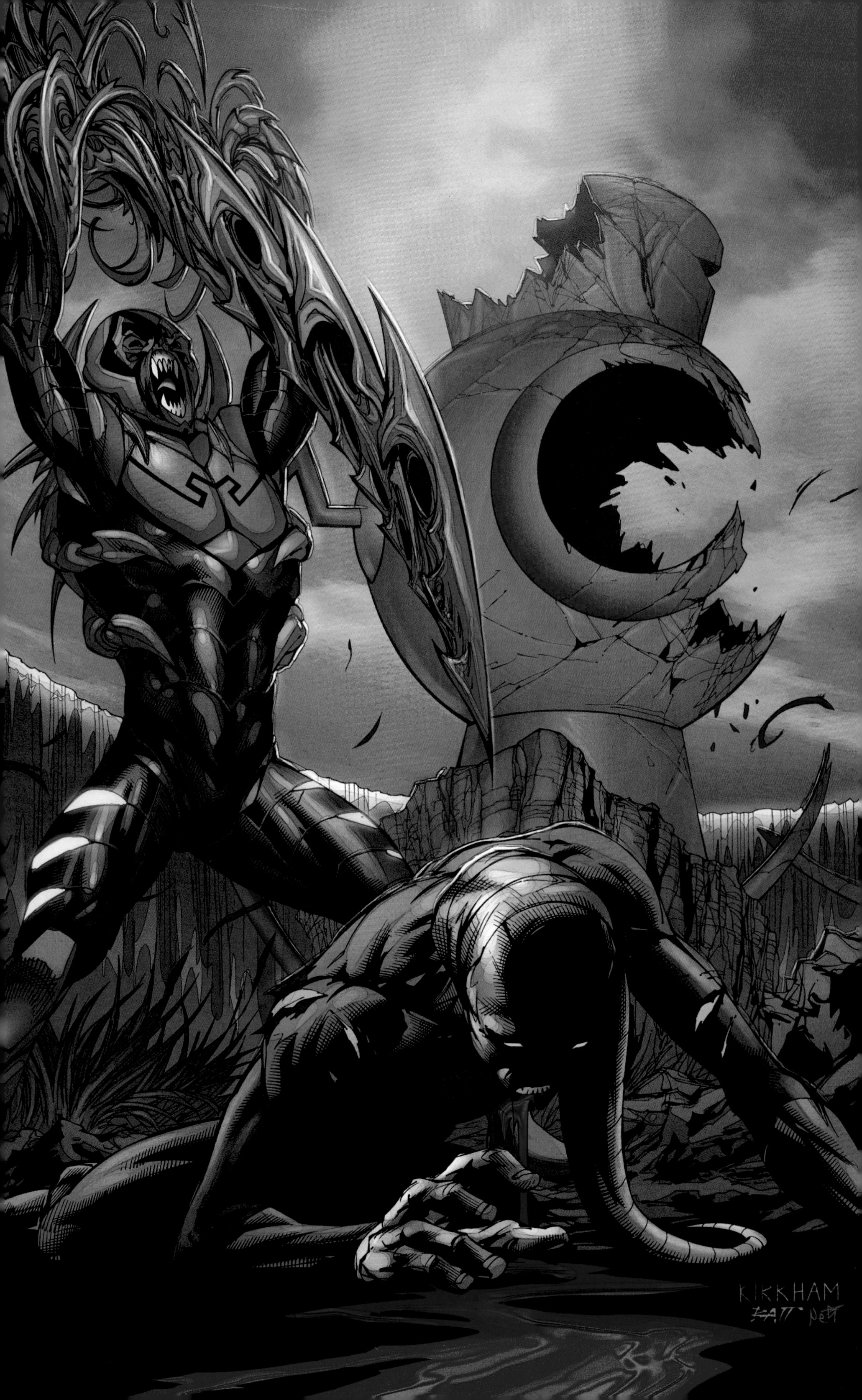
KIRKHAM

BEYOND HOPE: CONCLUSION

TONY BEDARD writer **TOMAS GIORELLO** penciller cover by **TYLER KIRKHAM, BATT & NEI RUFFINO**

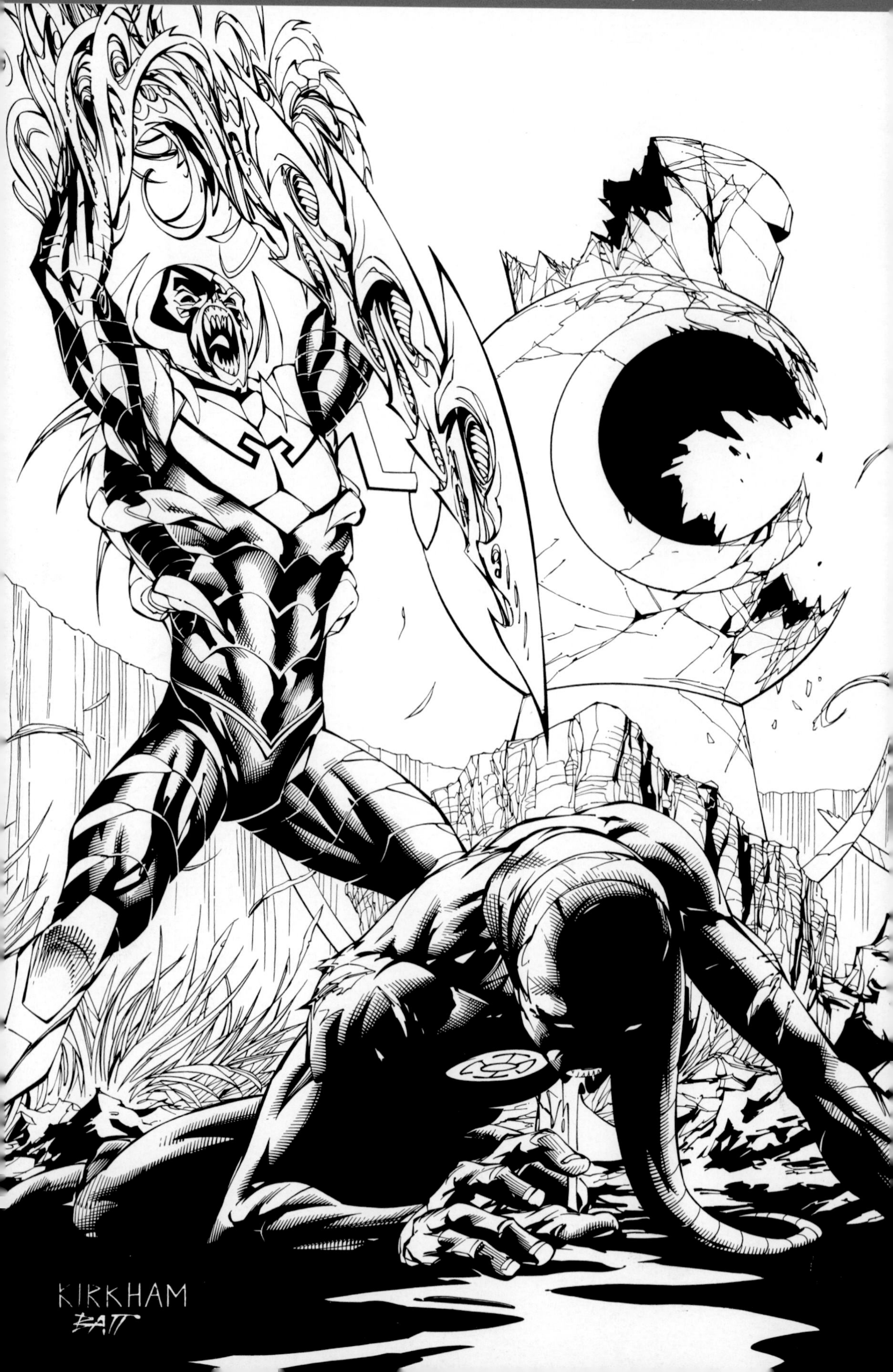
KIRKHAM
BATT

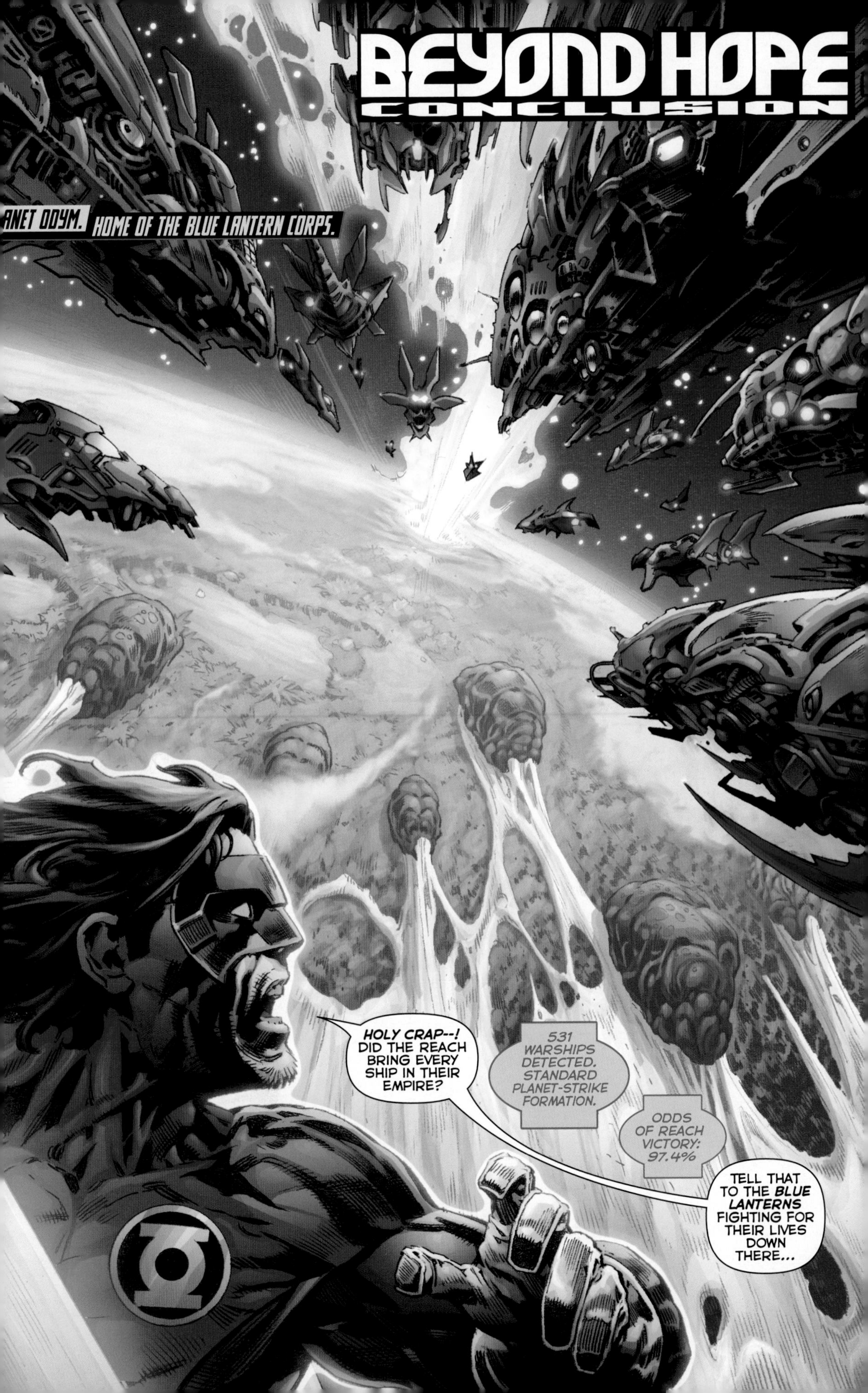
BEYOND HOPE
CONCLUSION
ANET ODYM. HOME OF THE BLUE LANTERN CORPS.
HOLY CRAP--! DID THE REACH BRING EVERY SHIP IN THEIR EMPIRE?
531 WARSHIPS DETECTED. STANDARD PLANET-STRIKE FORMATION.
ODDS OF REACH VICTORY: 97.4%
TELL THAT TO THE BLUE LANTERNS FIGHTING FOR THEIR LIVES DOWN THERE...

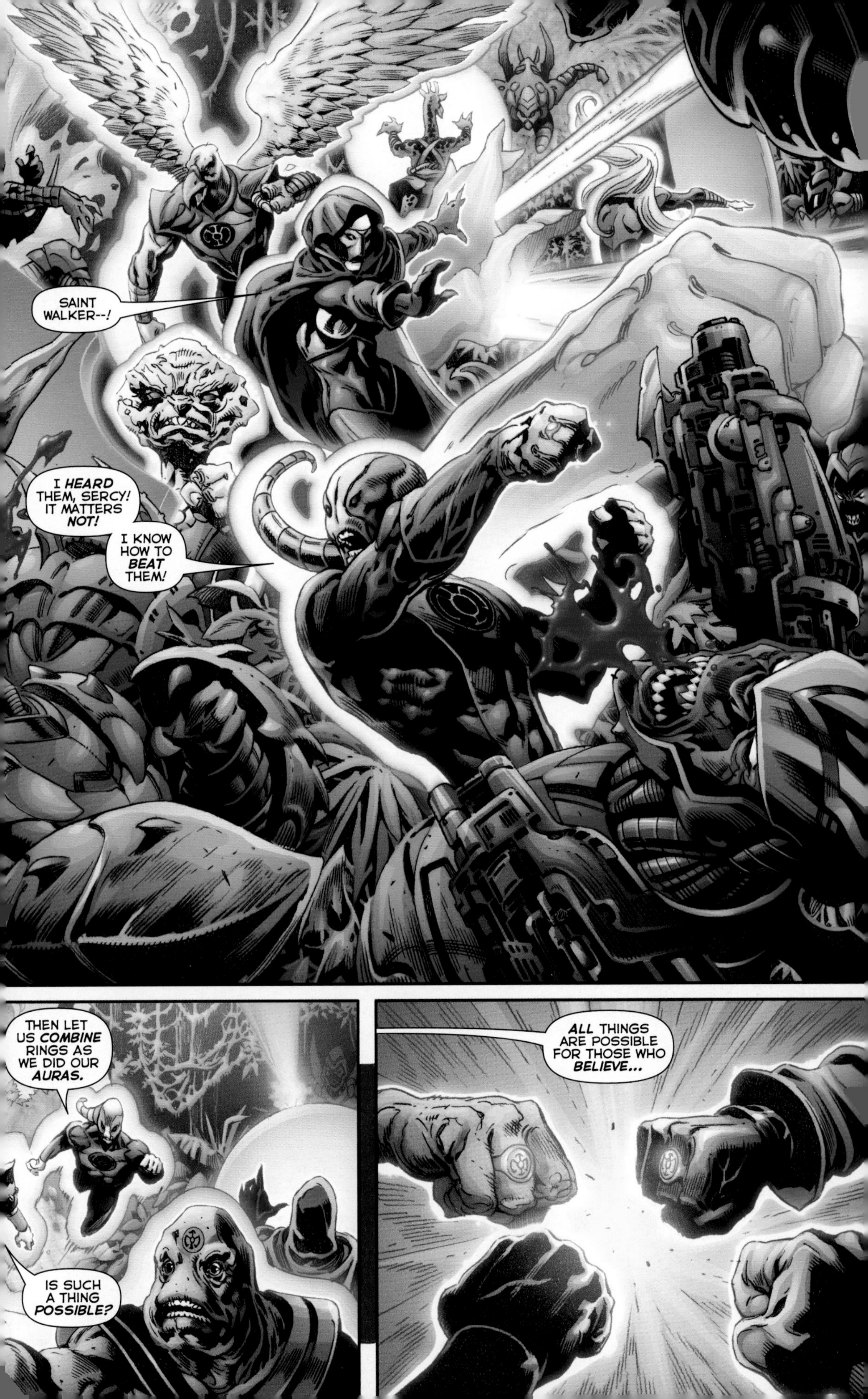
SAINT WALKER--!
I HEARD THEM, SERCY! IT MATTERS NOT!
I KNOW HOW TO BEAT THEM!
THEN LET US COMBINE RINGS AS WE DID OUR AURAS.
IS SUCH A THING POSSIBLE?
ALL THINGS ARE POSSIBLE FOR THOSE WHO BELIEVE...

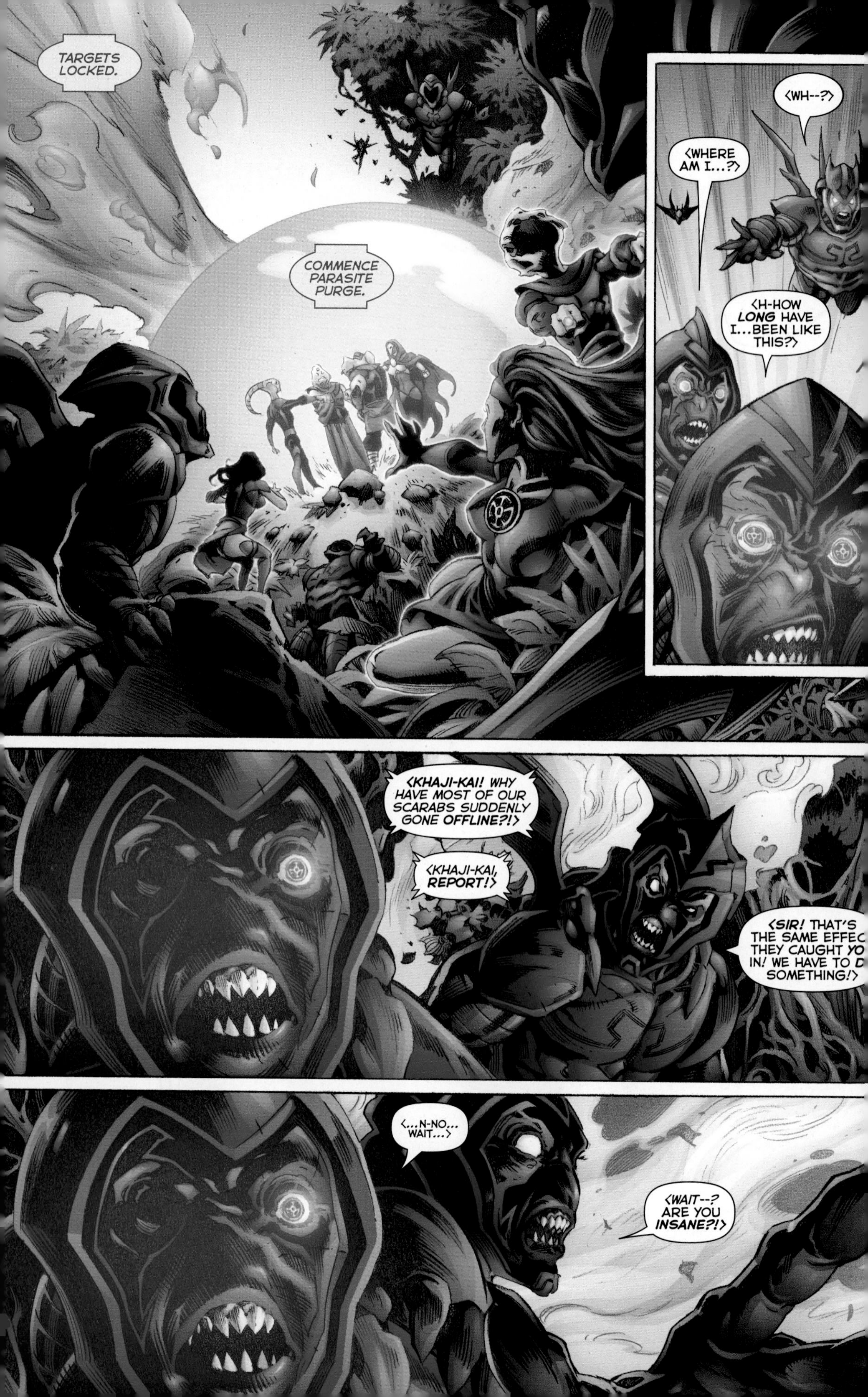

TARGETS LOCKED.
COMMENCE PARASITE PURGE.
<WH--?>
<WHERE AM I...?>
<H-HOW LONG HAVE I...BEEN LIKE THIS?>
<KHAJI-KAI! WHY HAVE MOST OF OUR SCARABS SUDDENLY GONE OFFLINE?!>
<KHAJI-KAI, REPORT!>
<SIR! THAT'S THE SAME EFFEC THEY CAUGHT YO IN! WE HAVE TO D SOMETHING!>
<...N-NO... WAIT...>
<WAIT--? ARE YOU INSANE?!>

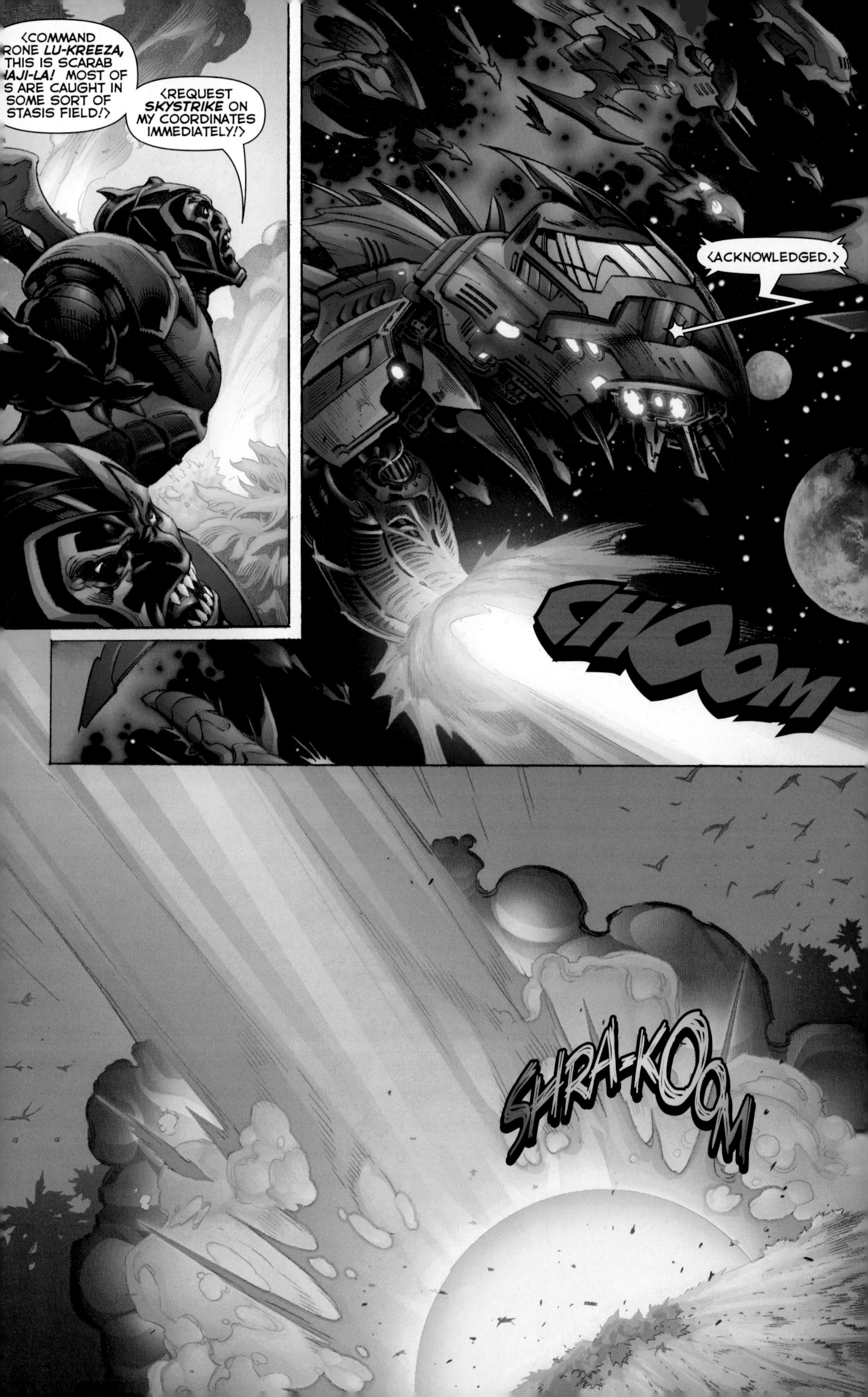
<COMMAND
RONE LU-KREEZA,
THIS IS SCARAB
IAJI-LA! MOST OF
S ARE CAUGHT IN
SOME SORT OF
STASIS FIELD!>
<REQUEST SKYSTRIKE ON MY COORDINATES IMMEDIATELY!>
<ACKNOWLEDGED.>
CHOOM
SHRA-KOOM

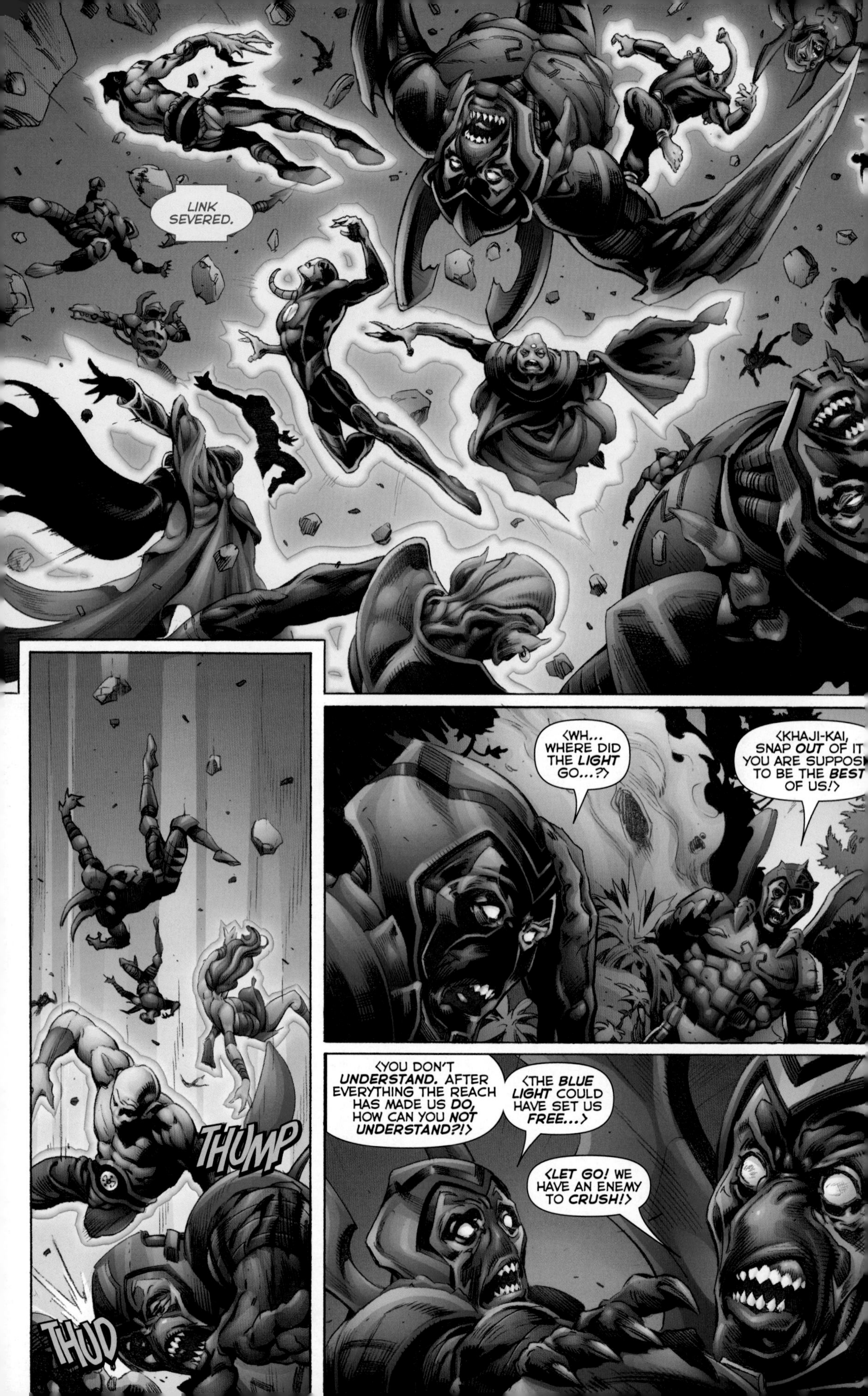
LINK SEVERED.
<WH... WHERE DID THE LIGHT GO...?>
<KHAJI-KAI, SNAP OUT OF IT YOU ARE SUPPOS TO BE THE BEST OF US!>
THUMP
THUD
<YOU DON'T UNDERSTAND. AFTER EVERYTHING THE REACH HAS MADE US DO, HOW CAN YOU NOT UNDERSTAND?!>
<THE BLUE LIGHT COULD HAVE SET US FREE...>
<LET GO! WE HAVE AN ENEMY TO CRUSH!>

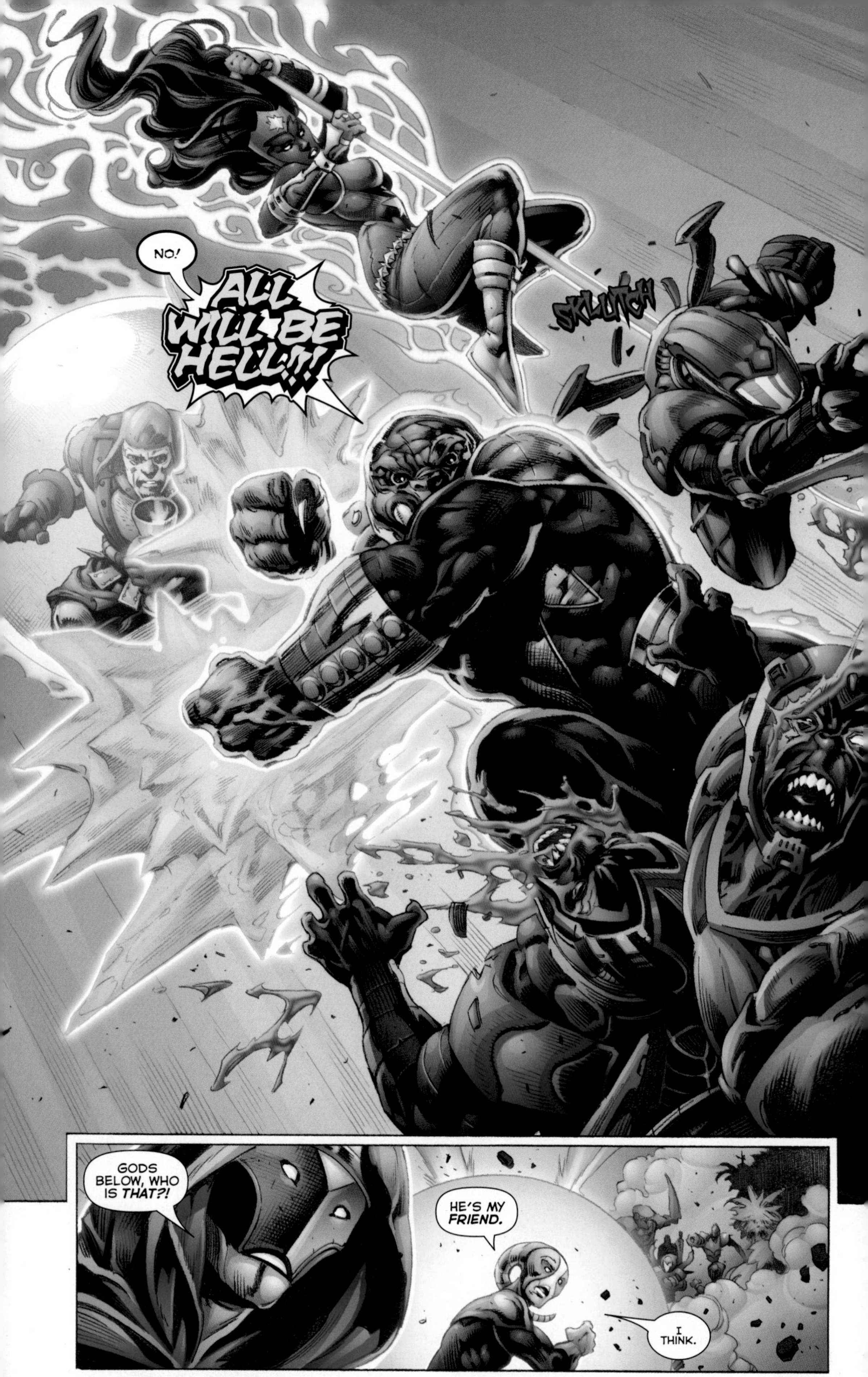
NO!
ALL WILL BE HELL!!!
SKLUTCH
GODS BELOW, WHO IS *THAT?!*
HE'S MY *FRIEND.*
I THINK.

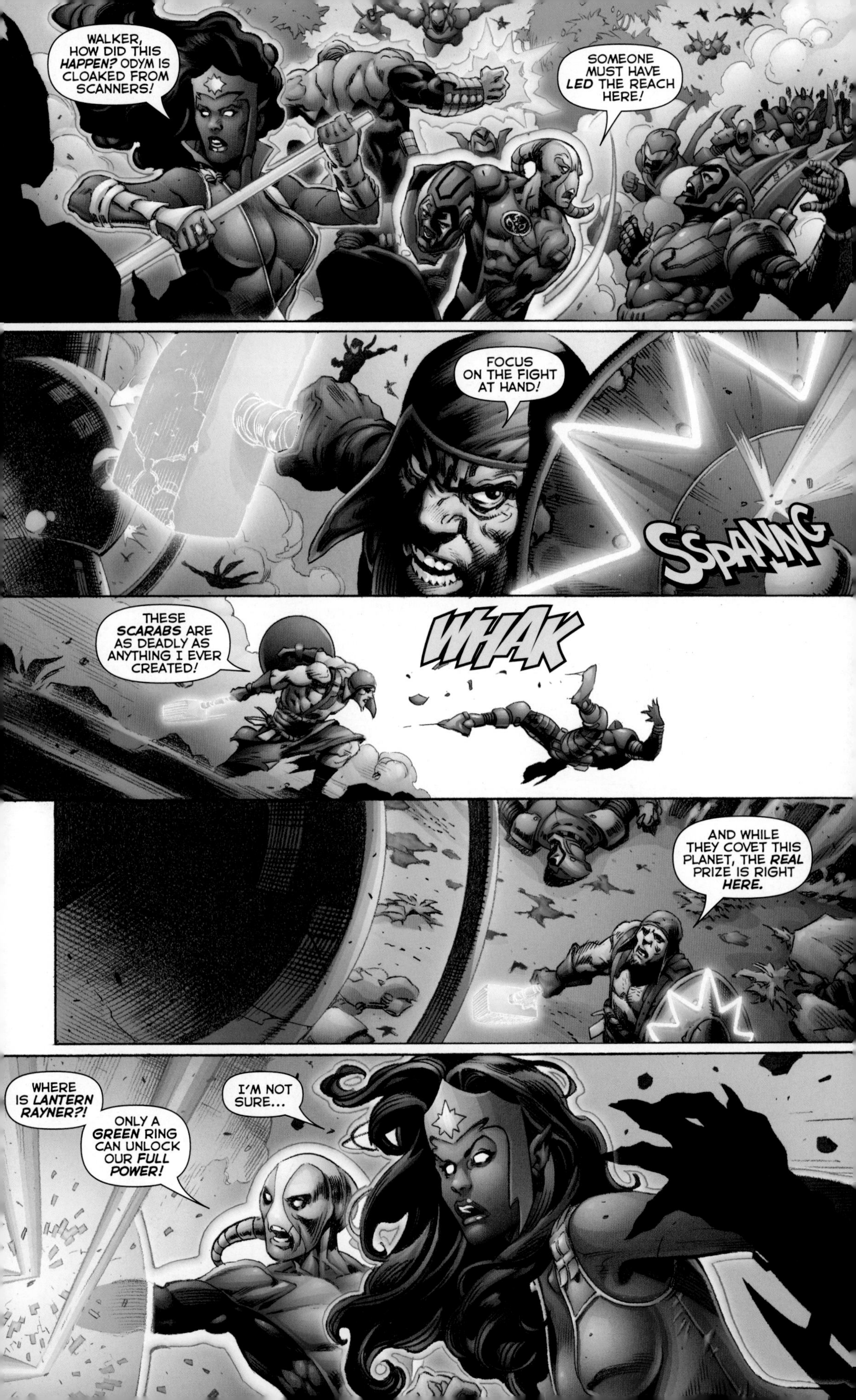
WALKER, HOW DID THIS HAPPEN? ODYM IS CLOAKED FROM SCANNERS!
SOMEONE MUST HAVE LED THE REACH HERE!
FOCUS ON THE FIGHT AT HAND!
SSPANNG
THESE SCARABS ARE AS DEADLY AS ANYTHING I EVER CREATED!
WHAK
AND WHILE THEY COVET THIS PLANET, THE REAL PRIZE IS RIGHT HERE.
WHERE IS LANTERN RAYNER?!
ONLY A GREEN RING CAN UNLOCK OUR FULL POWER!
I'M NOT SURE...

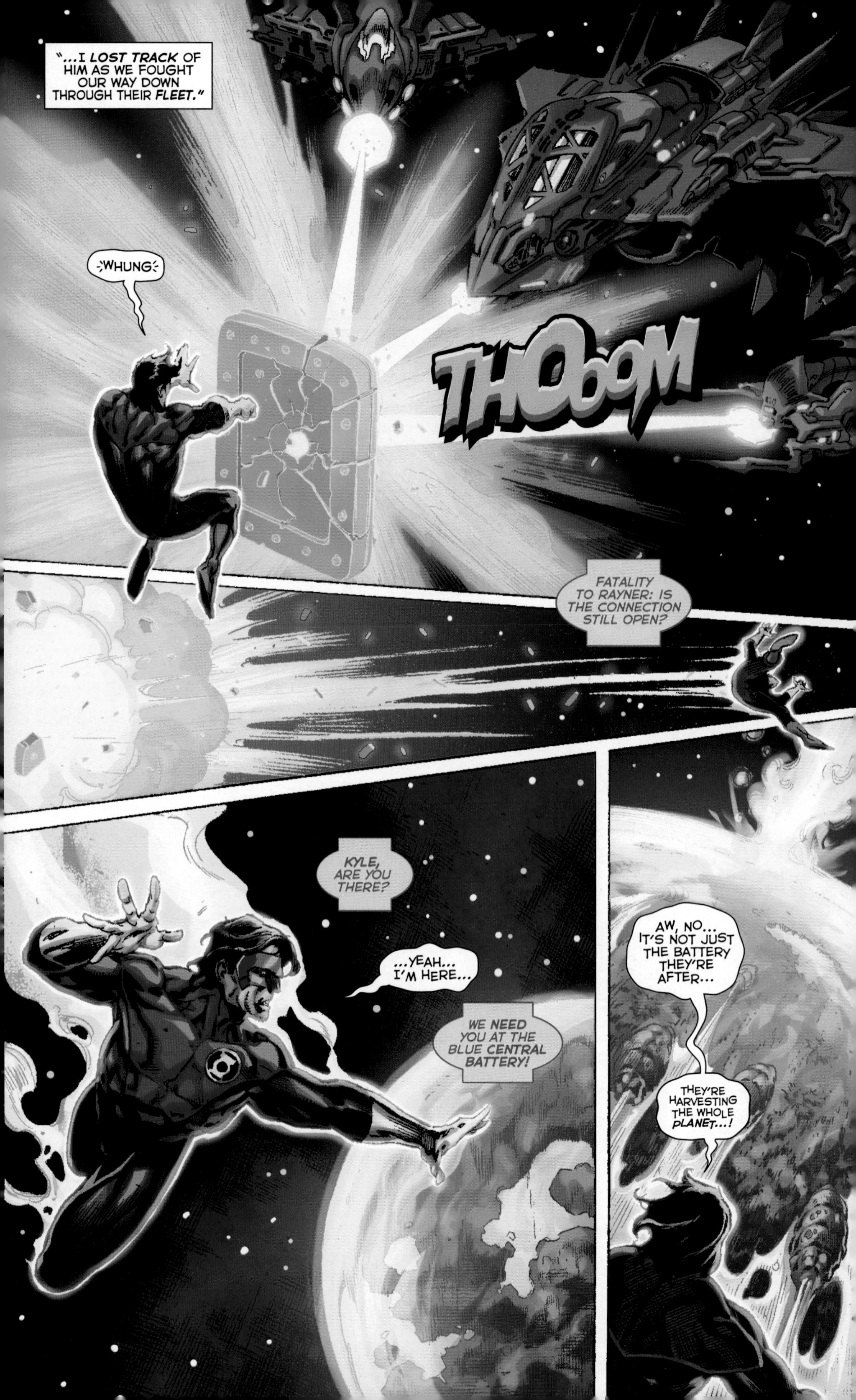
"...I *LOST TRACK* OF HIM AS WE FOUGHT OUR WAY DOWN THROUGH THEIR *FLEET*."
WHUNG
THOOOM
FATALITY TO RAYNER: IS THE CONNECTION STILL OPEN?
KYLE, ARE YOU THERE?
...YEAH... I'M HERE...
WE *NEED* YOU AT THE BLUE *CENTRAL BATTERY!*
AW, NO... IT'S NOT JUST THE BATTERY THEY'RE AFTER...
THEY'RE HARVESTING THE WHOLE *PLANET*...!

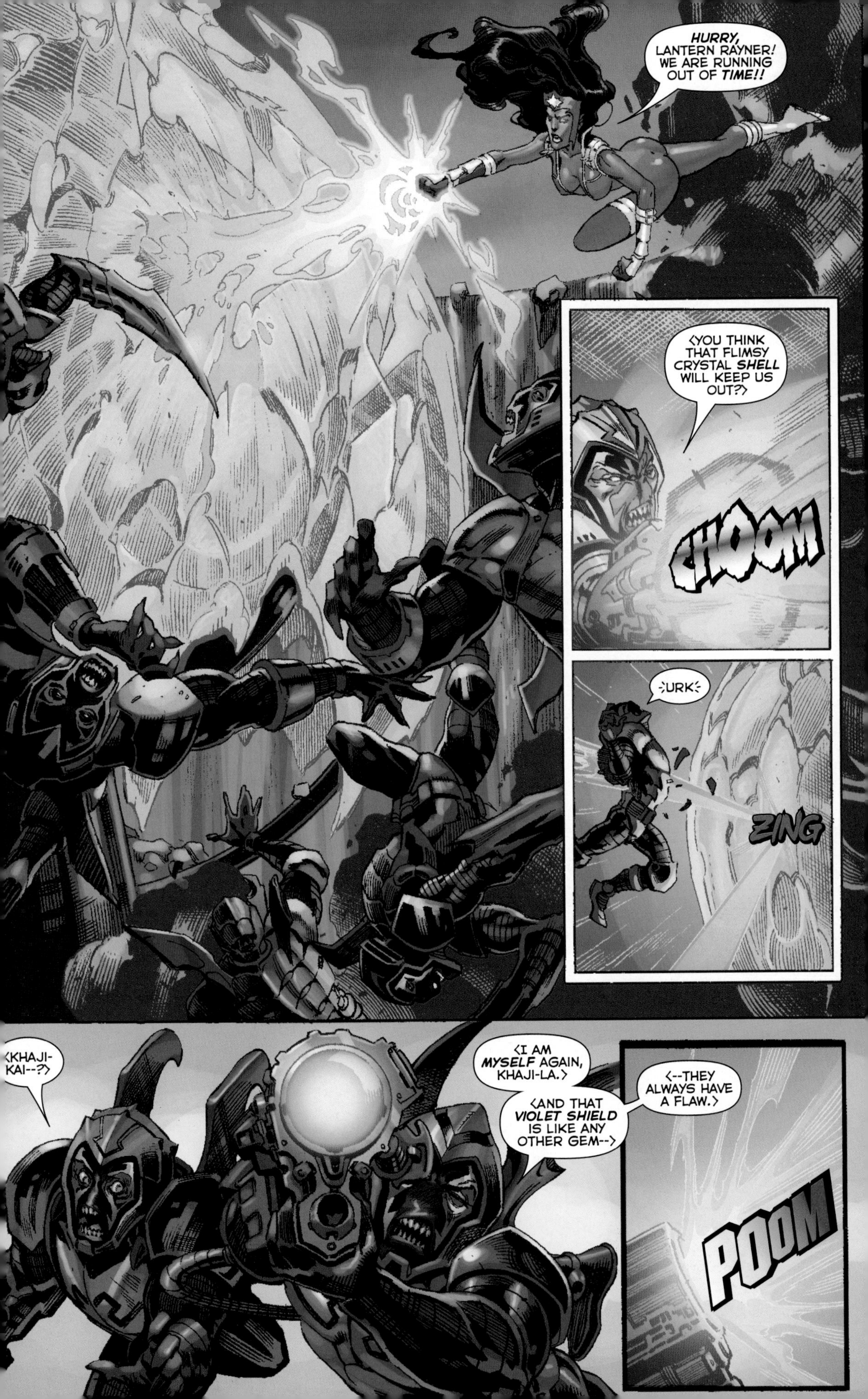
HURRY, LANTERN RAYNER! WE ARE RUNNING OUT OF TIME!!
<YOU THINK THAT FLIMSY CRYSTAL SHELL WILL KEEP US OUT?>
CHOOM
URK
ZING
<KHAJI-KAI--?>
<I AM MYSELF AGAIN, KHAJI-LA.>
<AND THAT VIOLET SHIELD IS LIKE ANY OTHER GEM-->
<--THEY ALWAYS HAVE A FLAW.>
POOM

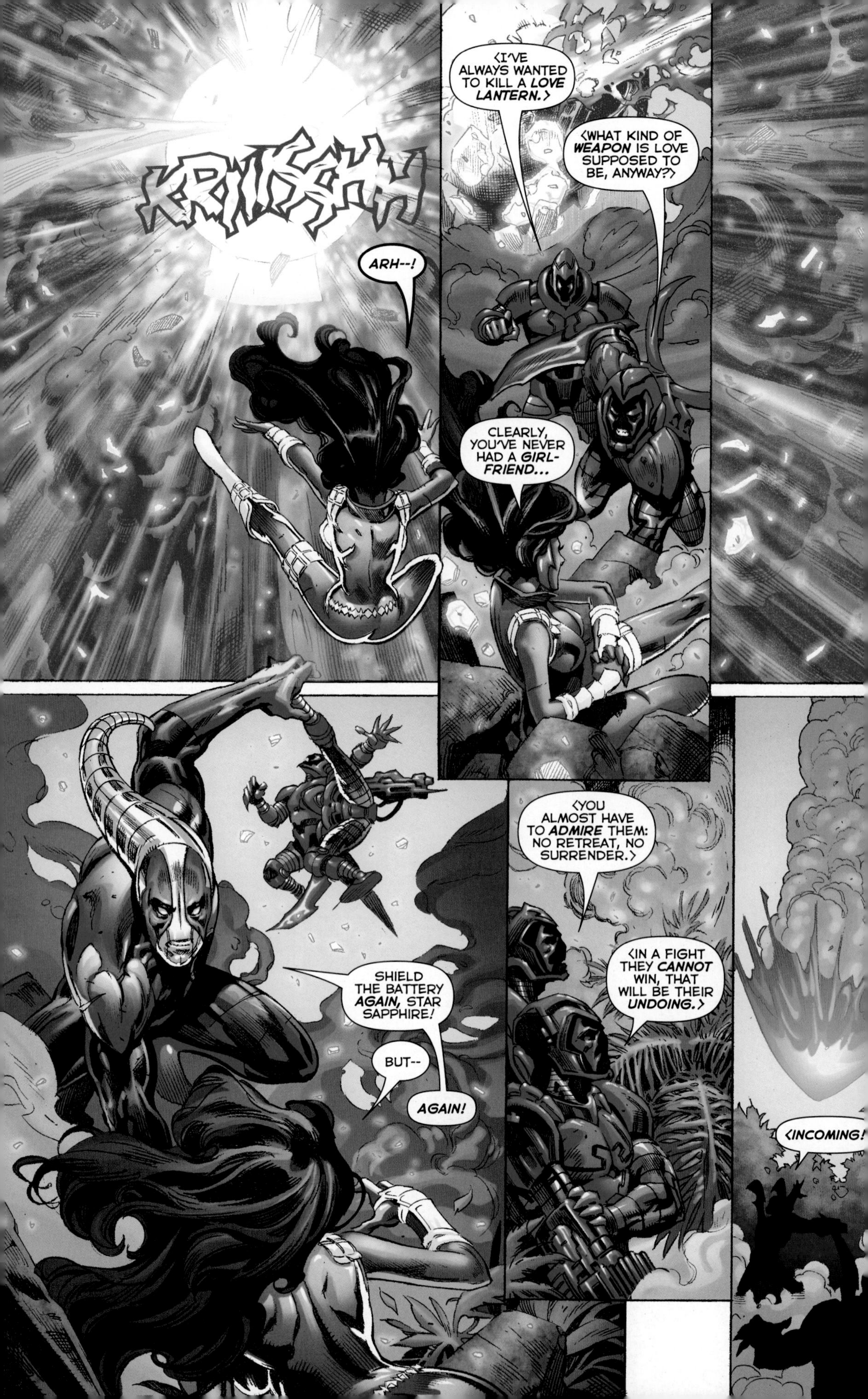
KRUUSSHH
ARH--!
<I'VE ALWAYS WANTED TO KILL A LOVE LANTERN.>
<WHAT KIND OF WEAPON IS LOVE SUPPOSED TO BE, ANYWAY?>
CLEARLY, YOU'VE NEVER HAD A GIRL-FRIEND...
SHIELD THE BATTERY AGAIN, STAR SAPPHIRE!
BUT--
AGAIN!
<YOU ALMOST HAVE TO ADMIRE THEM: NO RETREAT, NO SURRENDER.>
<IN A FIGHT THEY CANNOT WIN, THAT WILL BE THEIR UNDOING.>
<INCOMING!

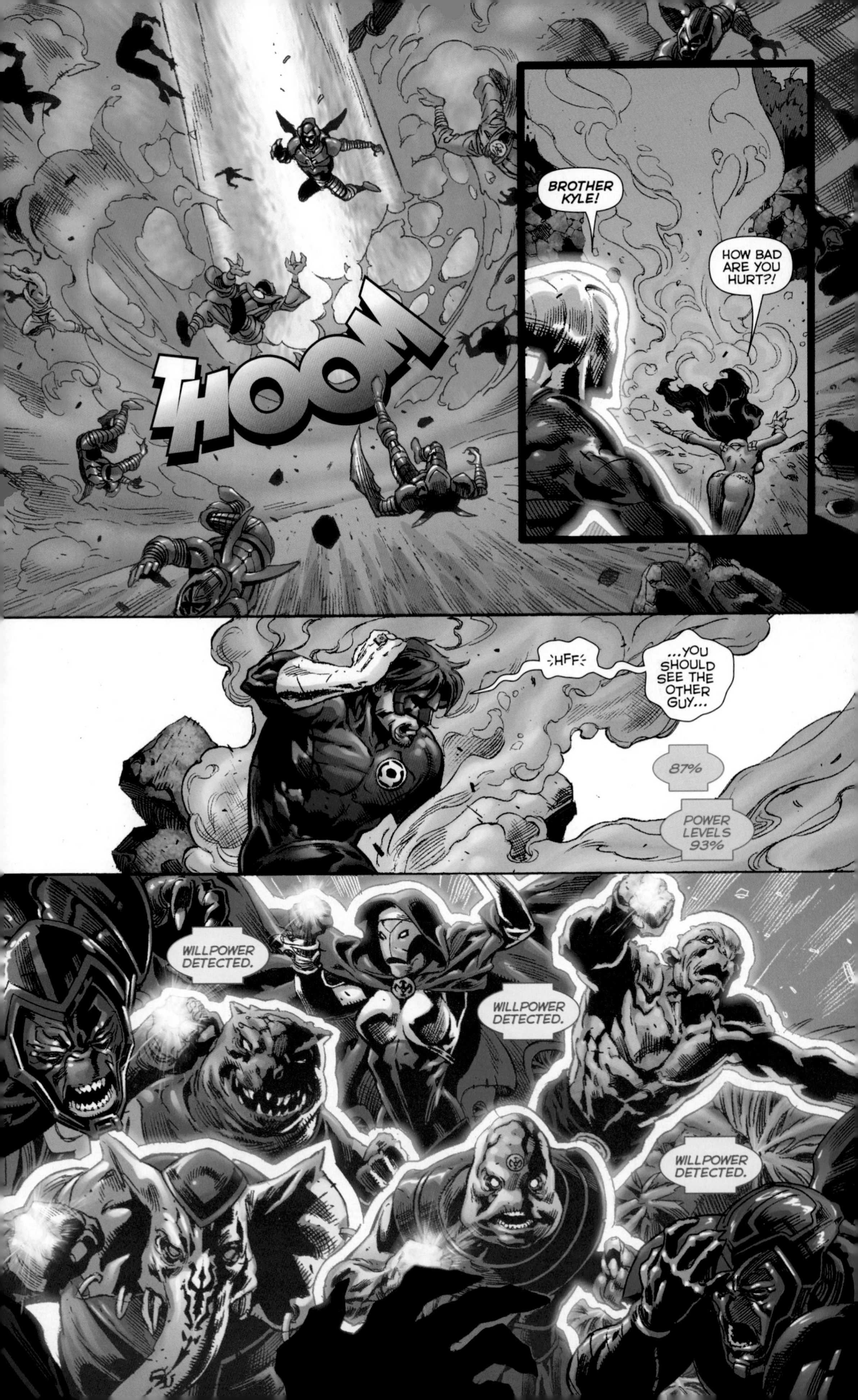
THOOM
BROTHER KYLE!
HOW BAD ARE YOU HURT?!
HFF
...YOU SHOULD SEE THE OTHER GUY...
87%
POWER LEVELS 93%
WILLPOWER DETECTED.
WILLPOWER DETECTED.
WILLPOWER DETECTED.

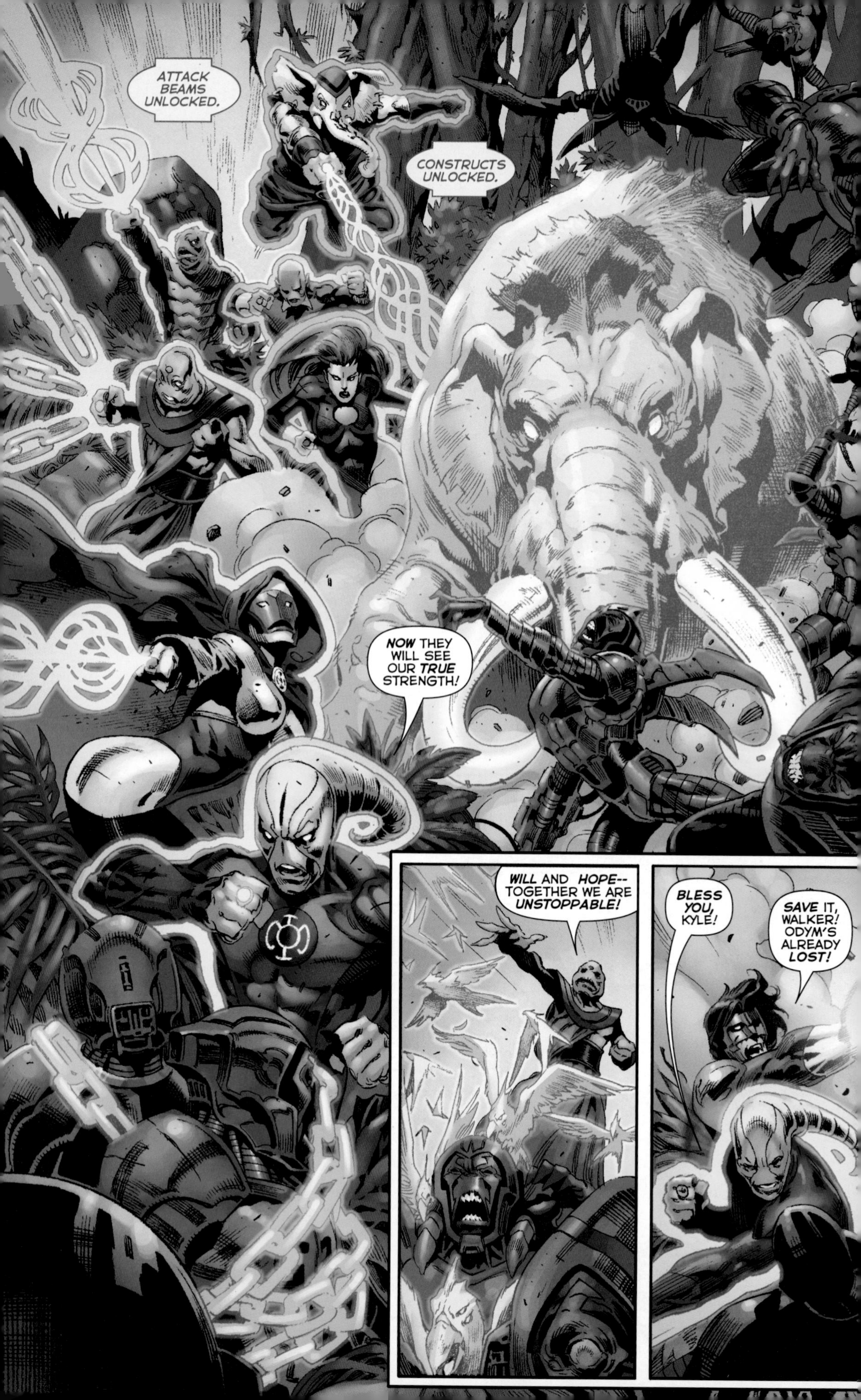
ATTACK BEAMS UNLOCKED.
CONSTRUCTS UNLOCKED.
NOW THEY WILL SEE OUR TRUE STRENGTH!
WILL AND HOPE-- TOGETHER WE ARE UNSTOPPABLE!
BLESS YOU, KYLE!
SAVE IT, WALKER! ODYM'S ALREADY LOST!

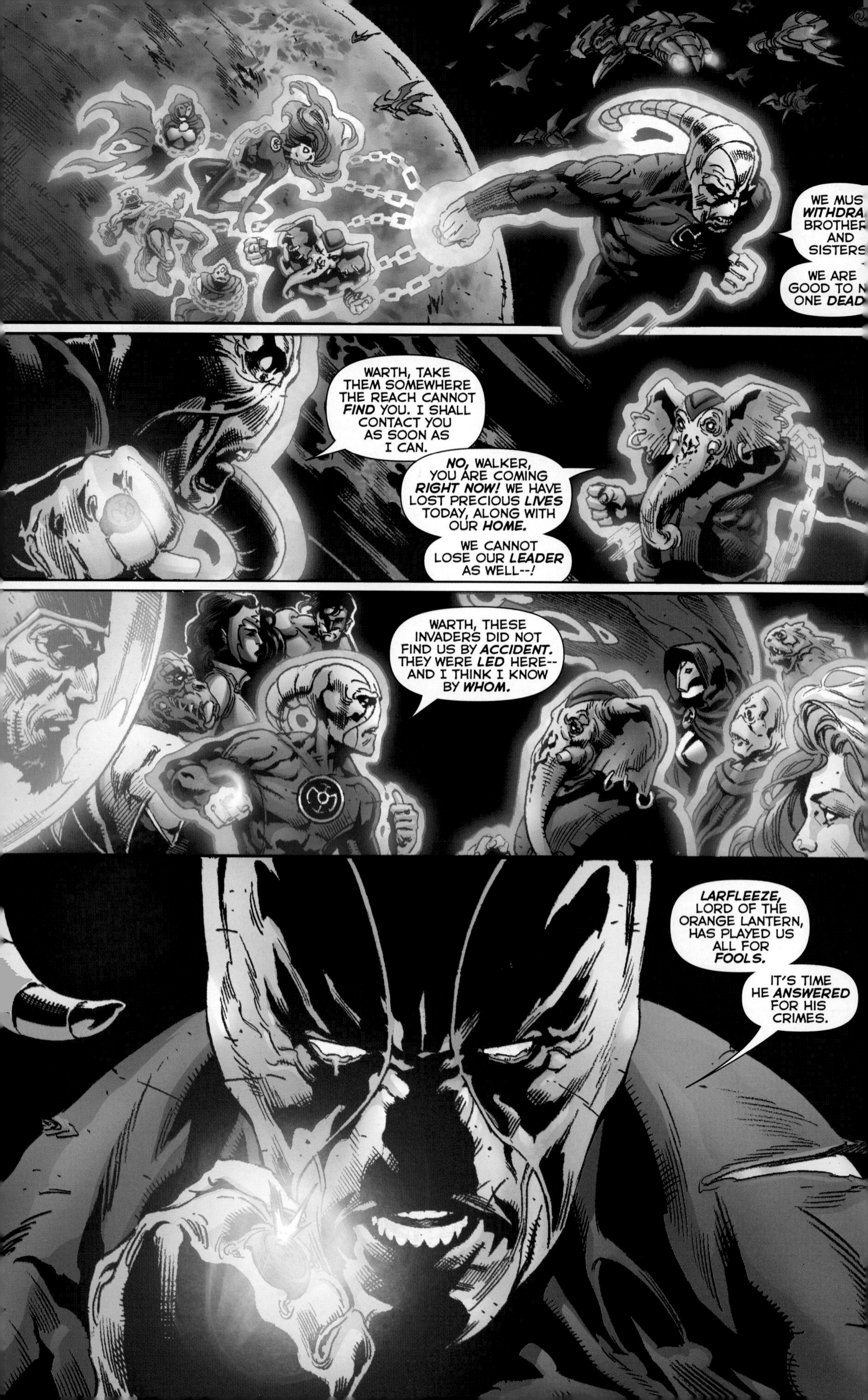

WE MUS WITHDRA BROTHER AND SISTERS
WE ARE GOOD TO N ONE DEAD
WARTH, TAKE THEM SOMEWHERE THE REACH CANNOT FIND YOU. I SHALL CONTACT YOU AS SOON AS I CAN.
NO, WALKER, YOU ARE COMING RIGHT NOW! WE HAVE LOST PRECIOUS LIVES TODAY, ALONG WITH OUR HOME.
WE CANNOT LOSE OUR LEADER AS WELL--!
WARTH, THESE INVADERS DID NOT FIND US BY ACCIDENT. THEY WERE LED HERE-- AND I THINK I KNOW BY WHOM.
LARFLEEZE, LORD OF THE ORANGE LANTERN, HAS PLAYED US ALL FOR FOOLS.
IT'S TIME HE ANSWERED FOR HIS CRIMES.

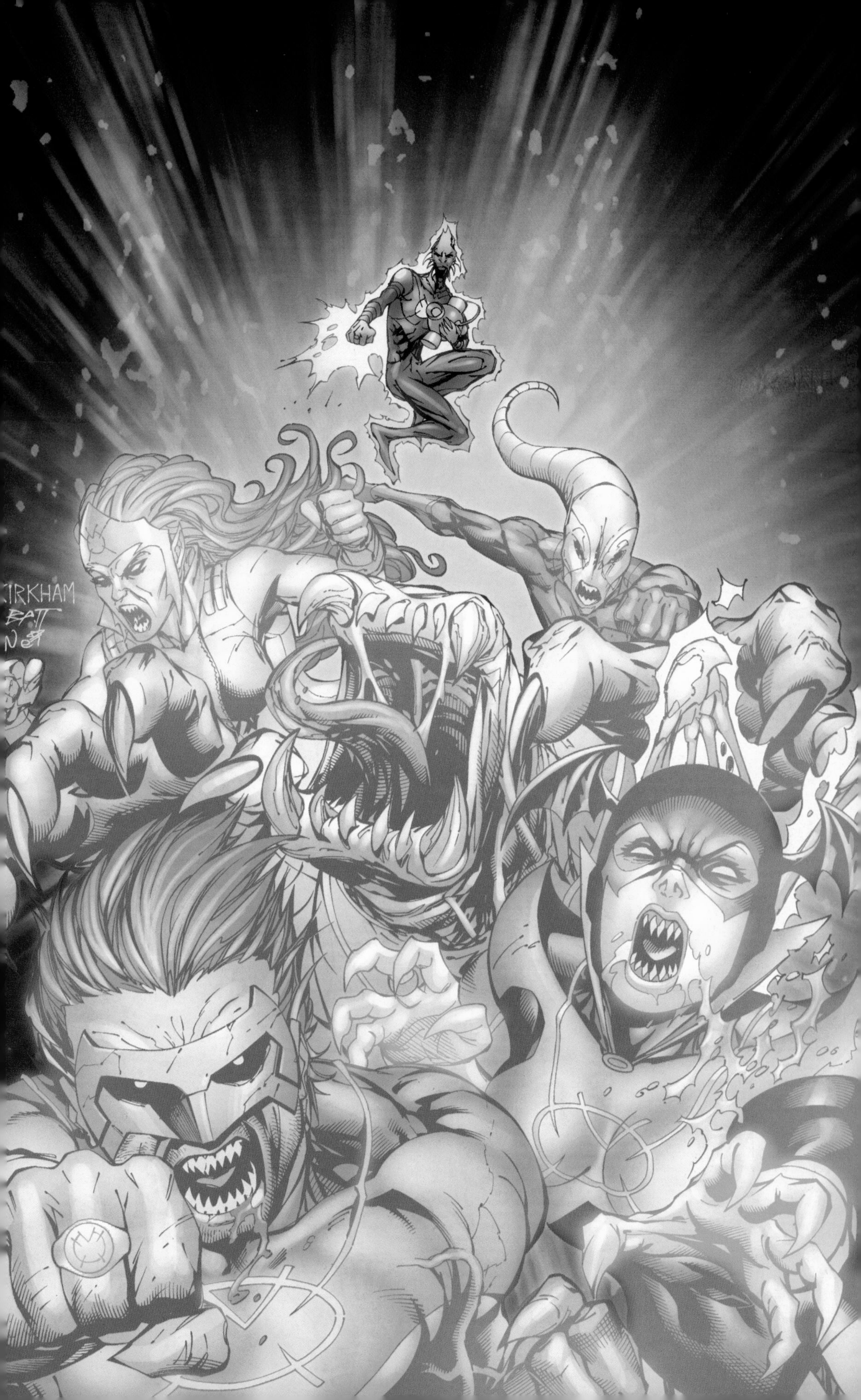
IRKHAM
BATT

OPERATION: AGENT ORANGE

TONY BEDARD writer **TYLER KIRKHAM** penciller **BATT** inker cover by **TYLER KIRKHAM, BATT & NEI RUFFINO**

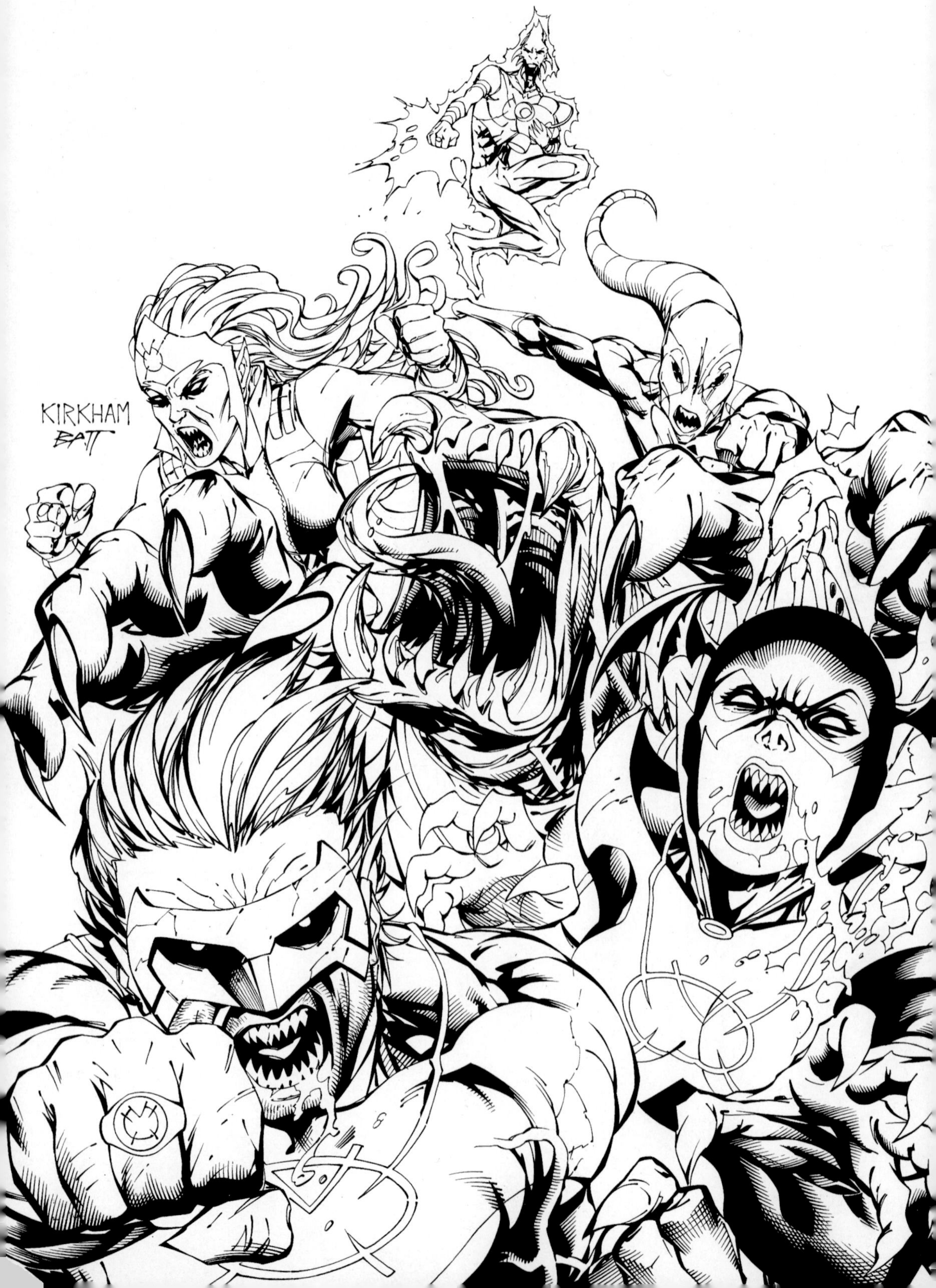
KIRKHAM
BATT

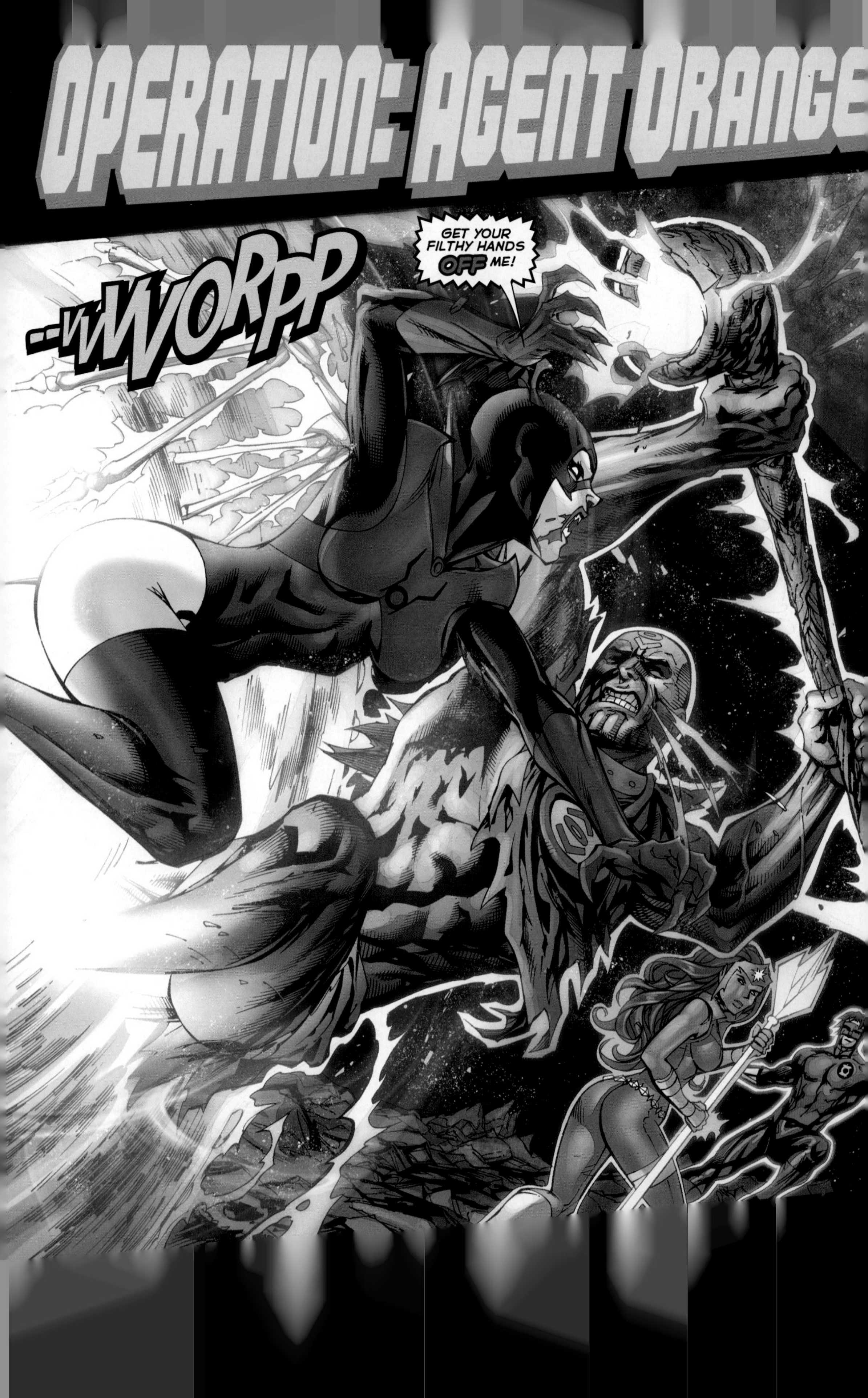
OPERATION: AGENT ORANGE
--VVWORPP
GET YOUR FILTHY HANDS OFF ME!

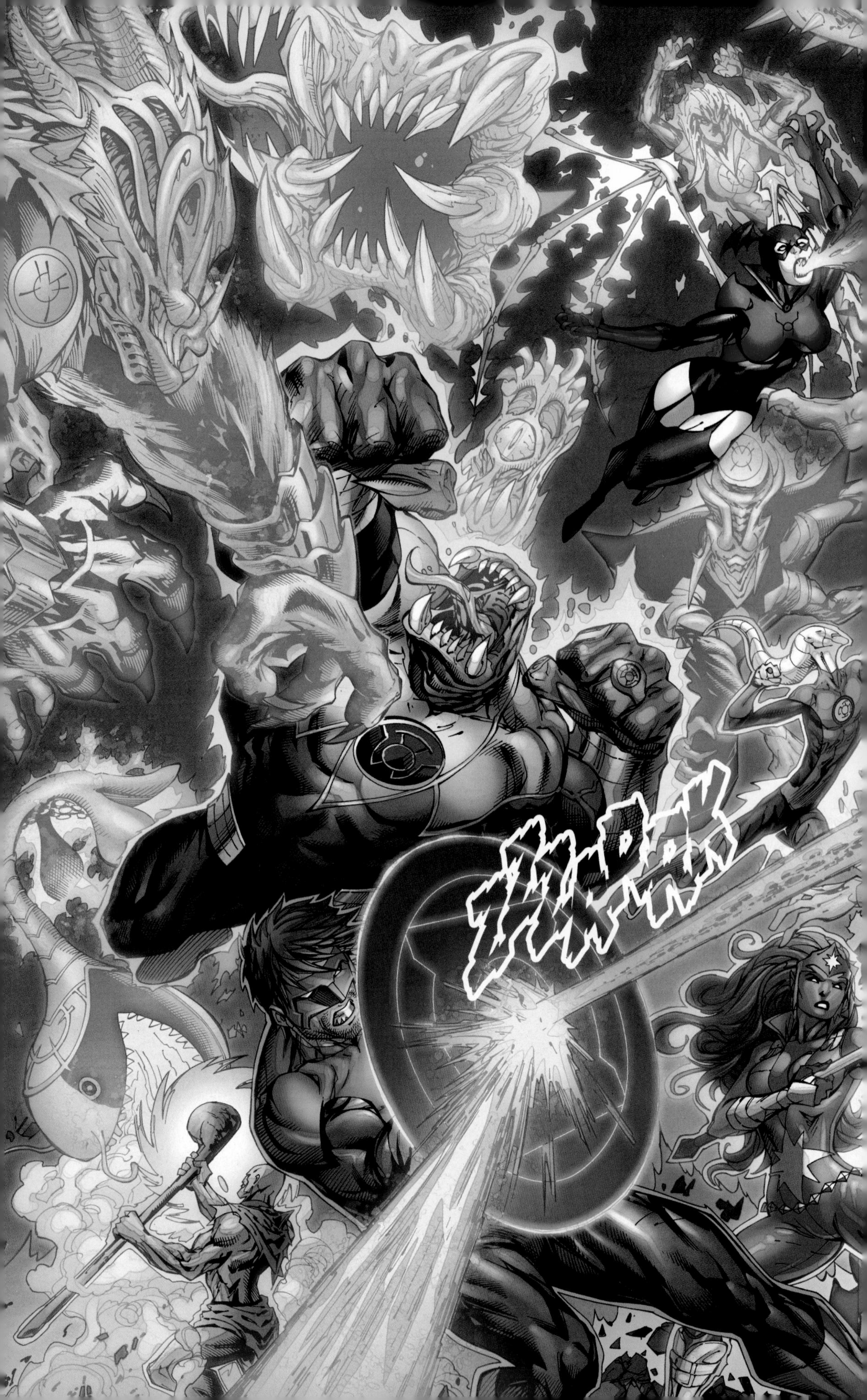

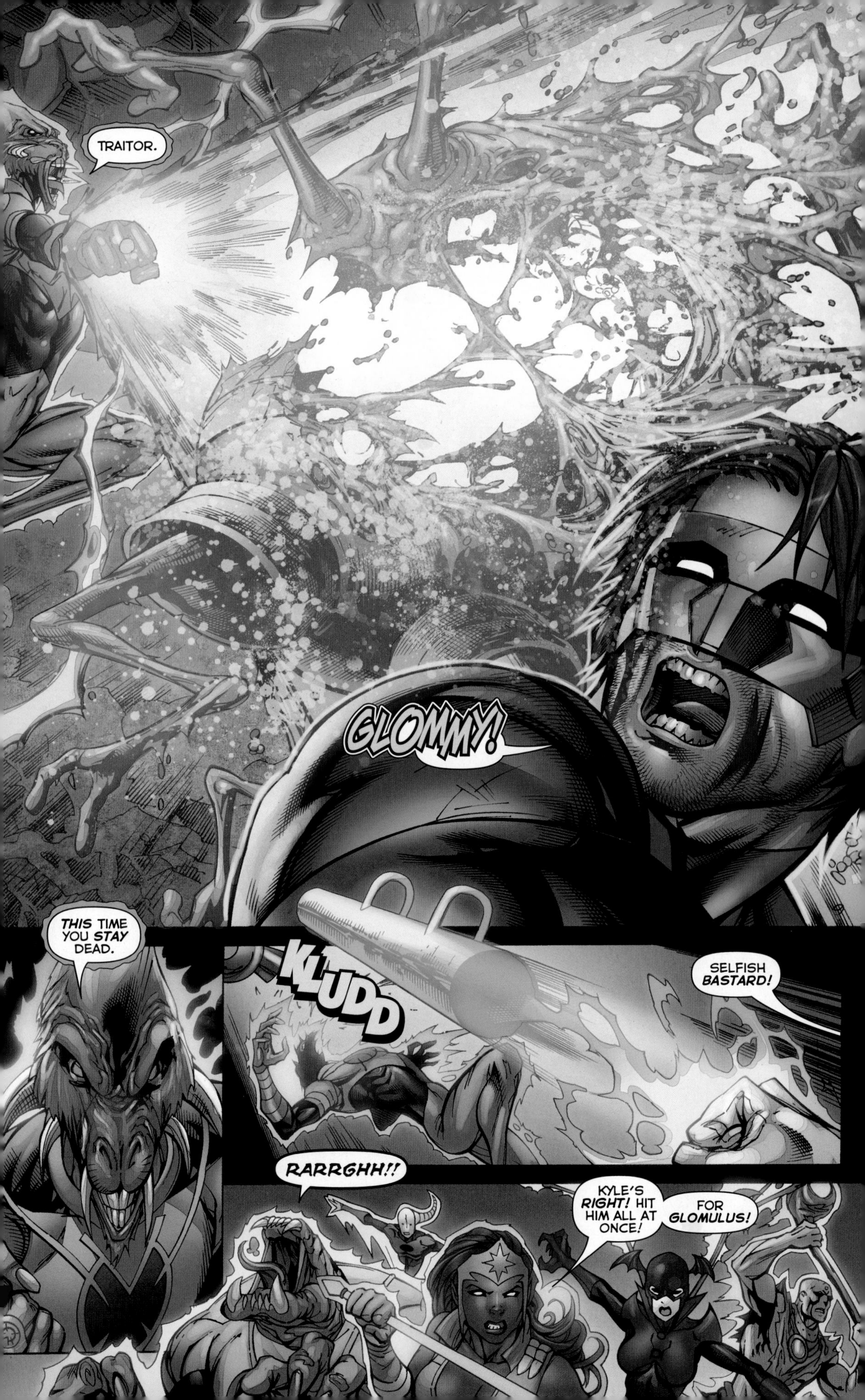
TRAITOR.
GLOMMY!
THIS TIME YOU STAY DEAD.
KLUDD
SELFISH BASTARD!
RARRGHH!!
KYLE'S RIGHT! HIT HIM ALL AT ONCE!
FOR GLOMULUS!

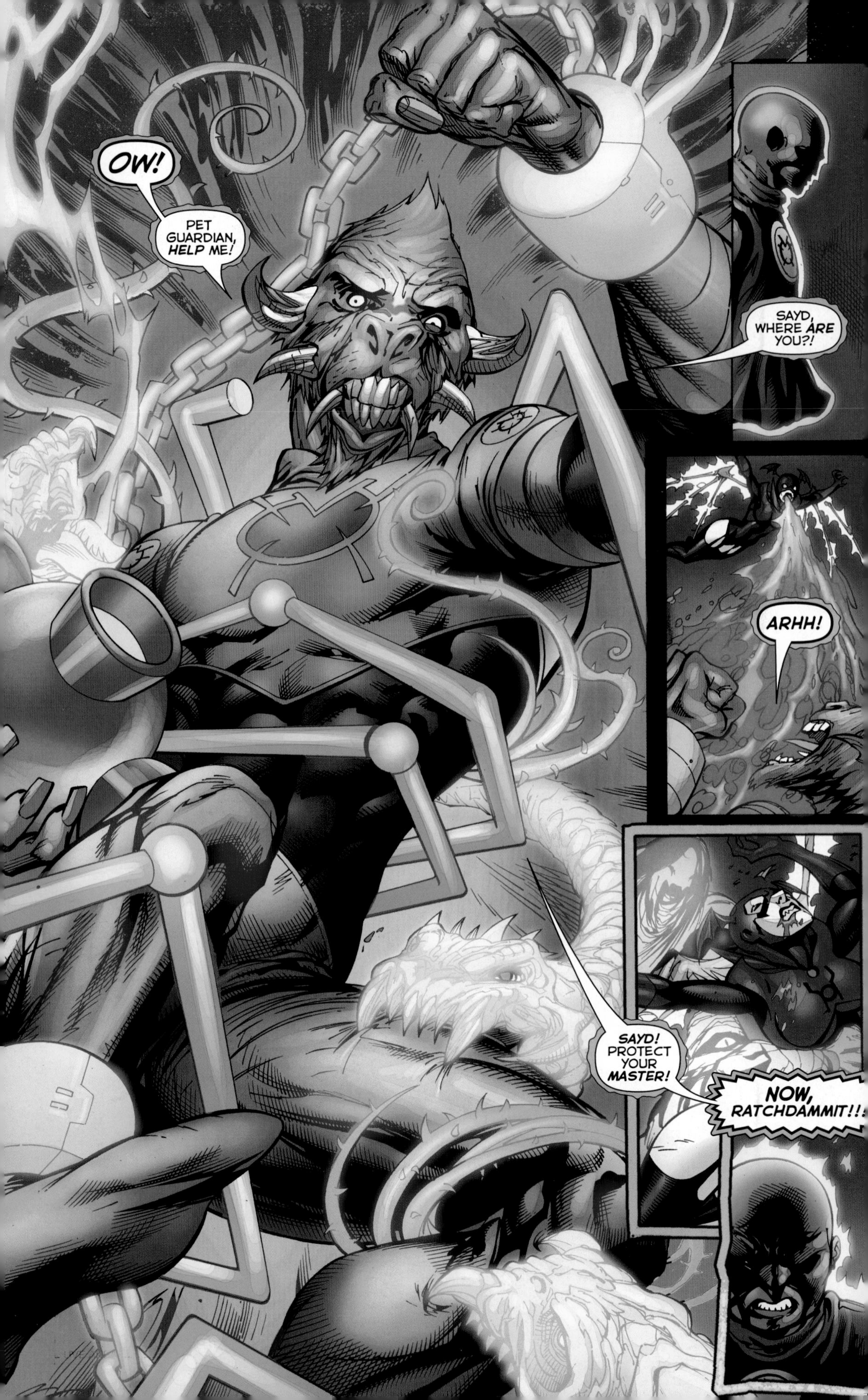
OW!
PET GUARDIAN, HELP ME!
SAYD, WHERE ARE YOU?!
ARHH!
SAYD! PROTECT YOUR MASTER!
NOW, RATCHDAMMIT!!

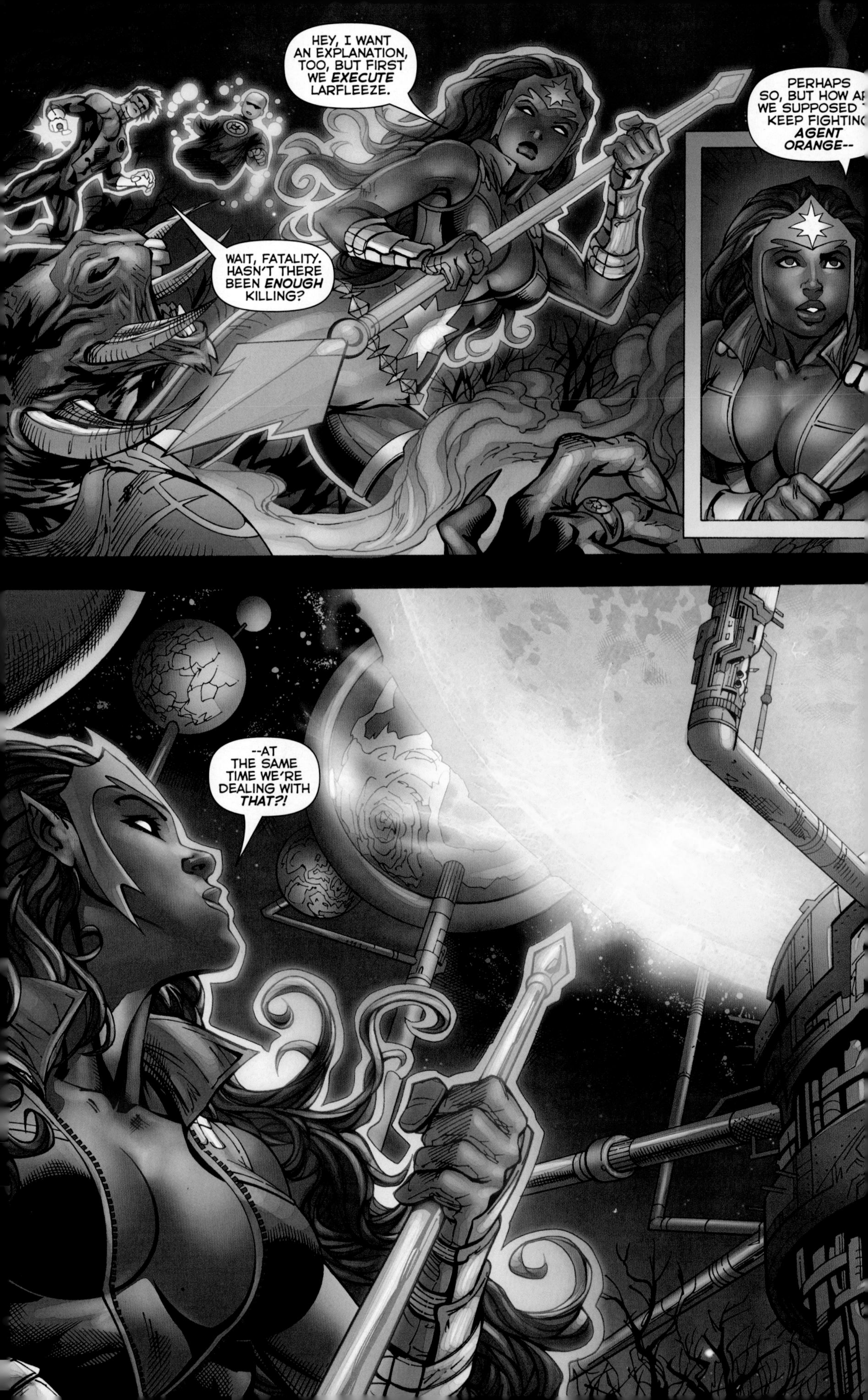
HEY, I WANT AN EXPLANATION, TOO, BUT FIRST WE EXECUTE LARFLEEZE.
WAIT, FATALITY. HASN'T THERE BEEN ENOUGH KILLING?
PERHAPS SO, BUT HOW A WE SUPPOSED KEEP FIGHTING AGENT ORANGE--
--AT THE SAME TIME WE'RE DEALING WITH THAT?!

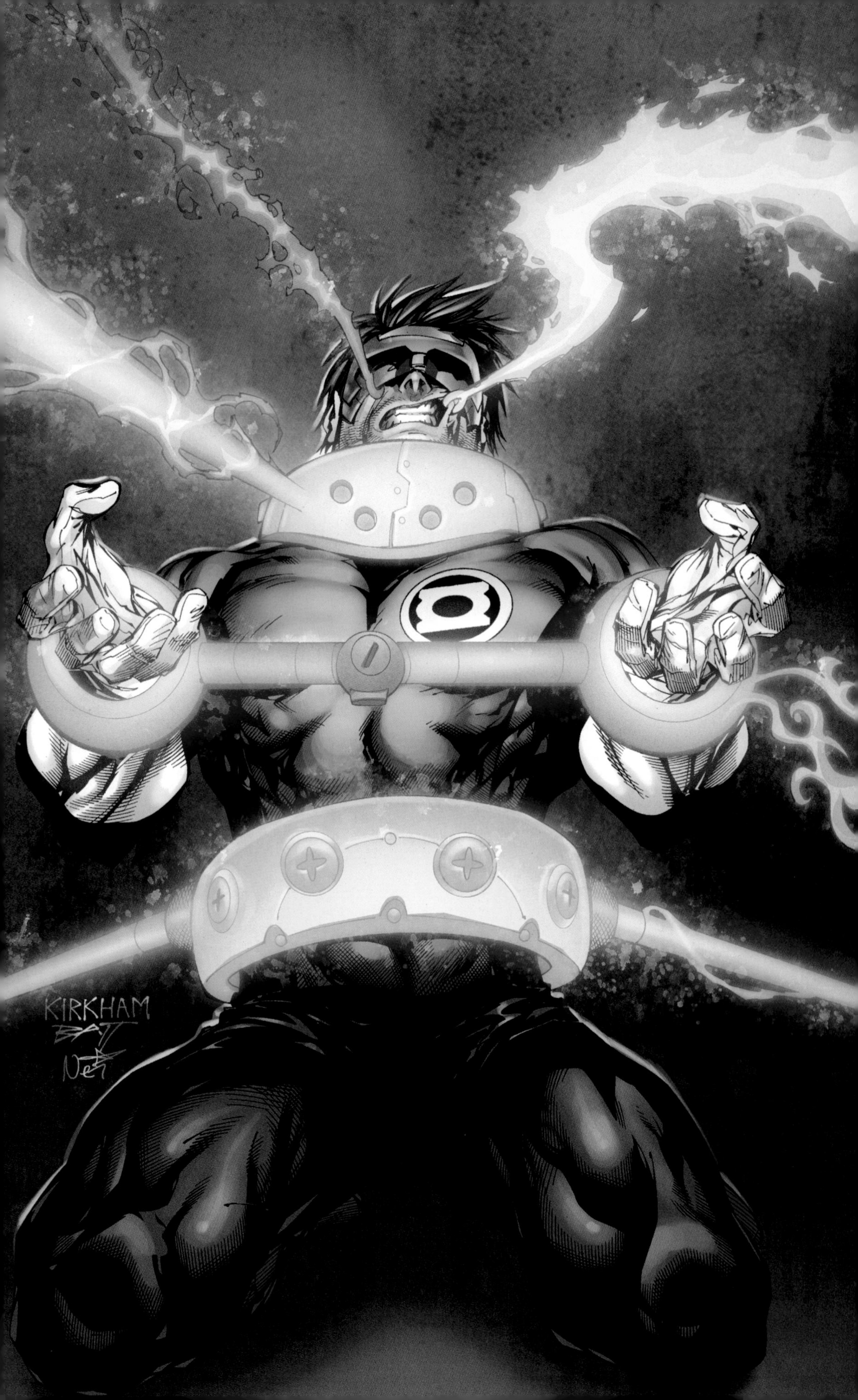
KIRKHAM

IN THE NAME OF LOVE

TONY BEDARD writer **TYLER KIRKHAM** penciller **BATT** inker cover by **TYLER KIRKHAM, BATT & NEI RUFFINO**

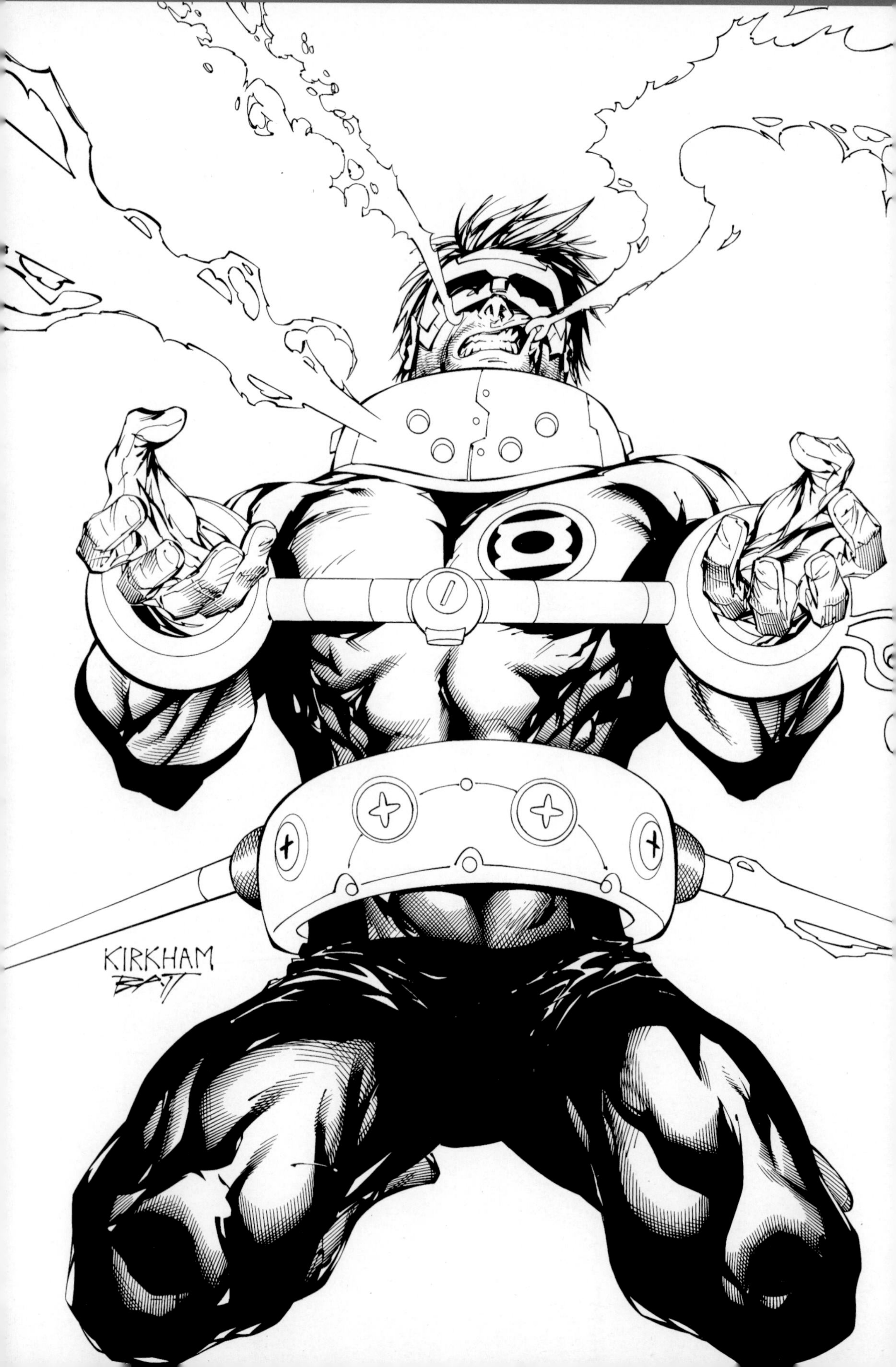
KIRKHAM
BATT

in the name of LOVE

THE FOREST OF WEEDS. OKAARA.

WHY, SAYD? WHY'D YOU DO IT?! WHY LIE TO US?

WHY USE US?!

GANTHET LOVED YOU! AND EVER SINCE HE WENT ALL DARTH VADER, YOU'VE BEEN THE ONLY GOOD GUARDIAN LEFT!

DO NOT PRESUME TO JUDGE ME, KYLE RAYNER. IT IS BECAUSE OF GANTHET THAT I HAD TO DO WHAT I DID!

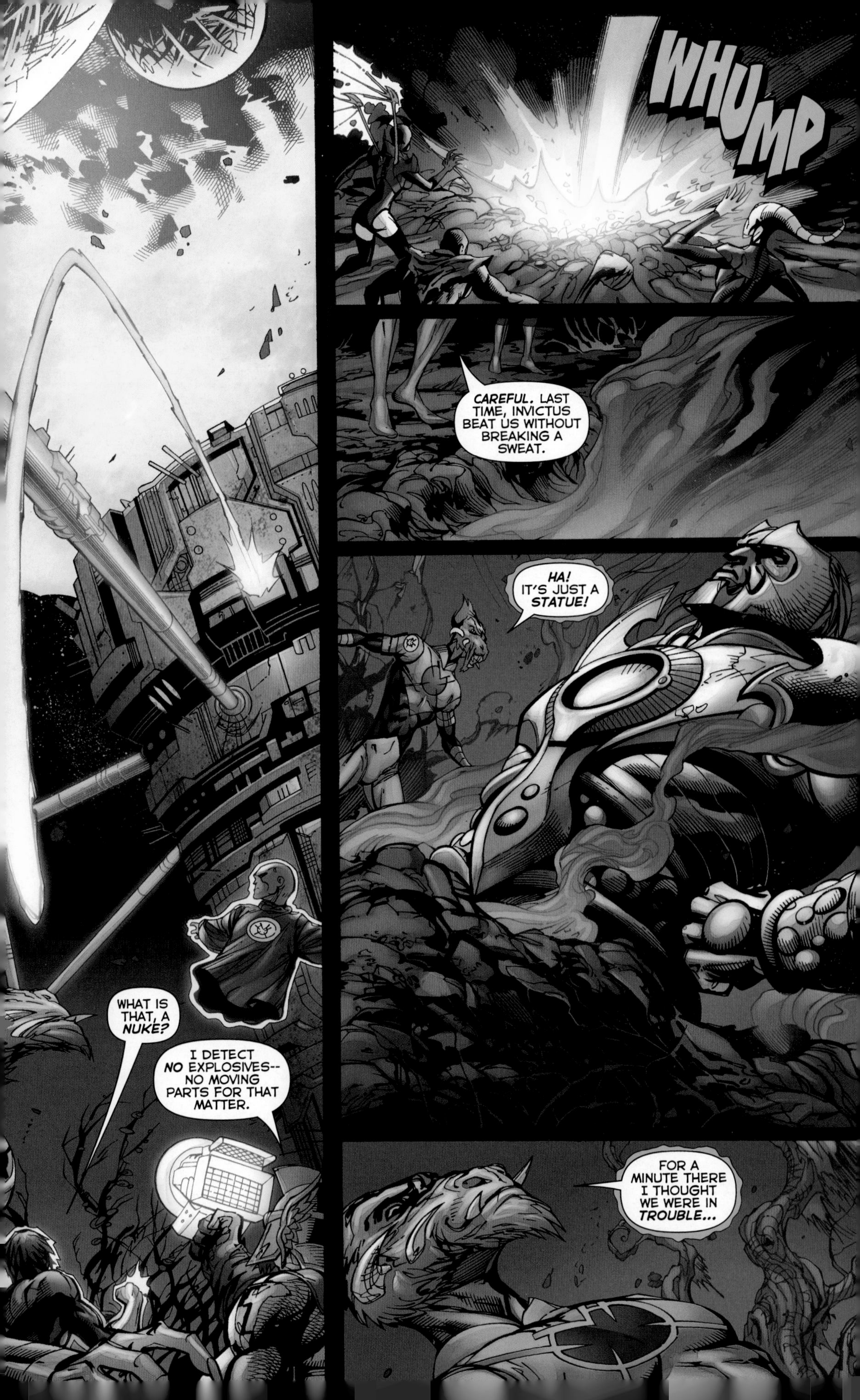
WHUMP
WHAT IS THAT, A NUKE?
I DETECT NO EXPLOSIVES-- NO MOVING PARTS FOR THAT MATTER.
CAREFUL. LAST TIME, INVICTUS BEAT US WITHOUT BREAKING A SWEAT.
HA! IT'S JUST A STATUE!
FOR A MINUTE THERE I THOUGHT WE WERE IN TROUBLE...

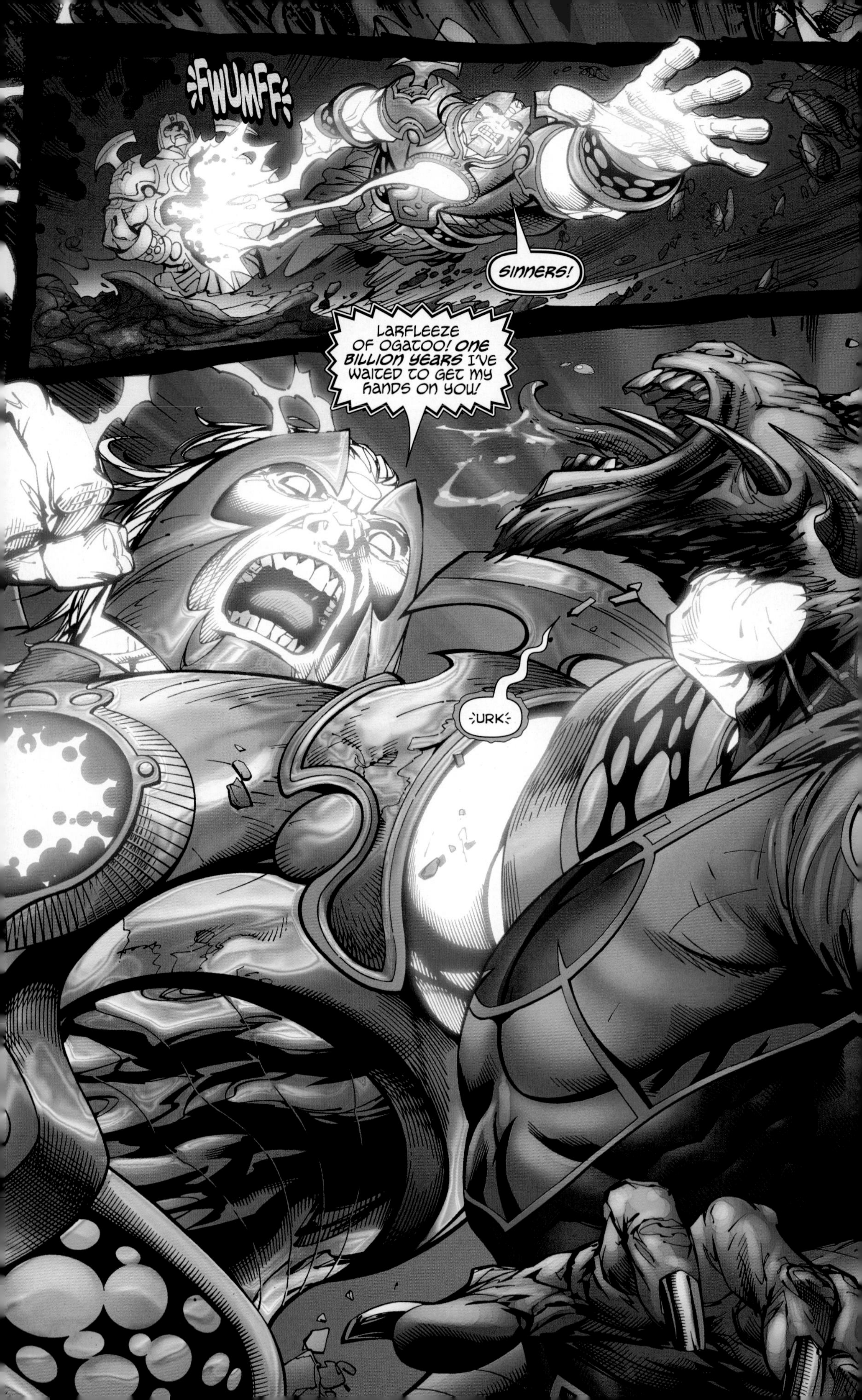
FWUMFF
SINNERS!
LARFLEEZE OF OGATOO! ONE BILLION YEARS I'VE WAITED TO GET MY HANDS ON YOU!
URK

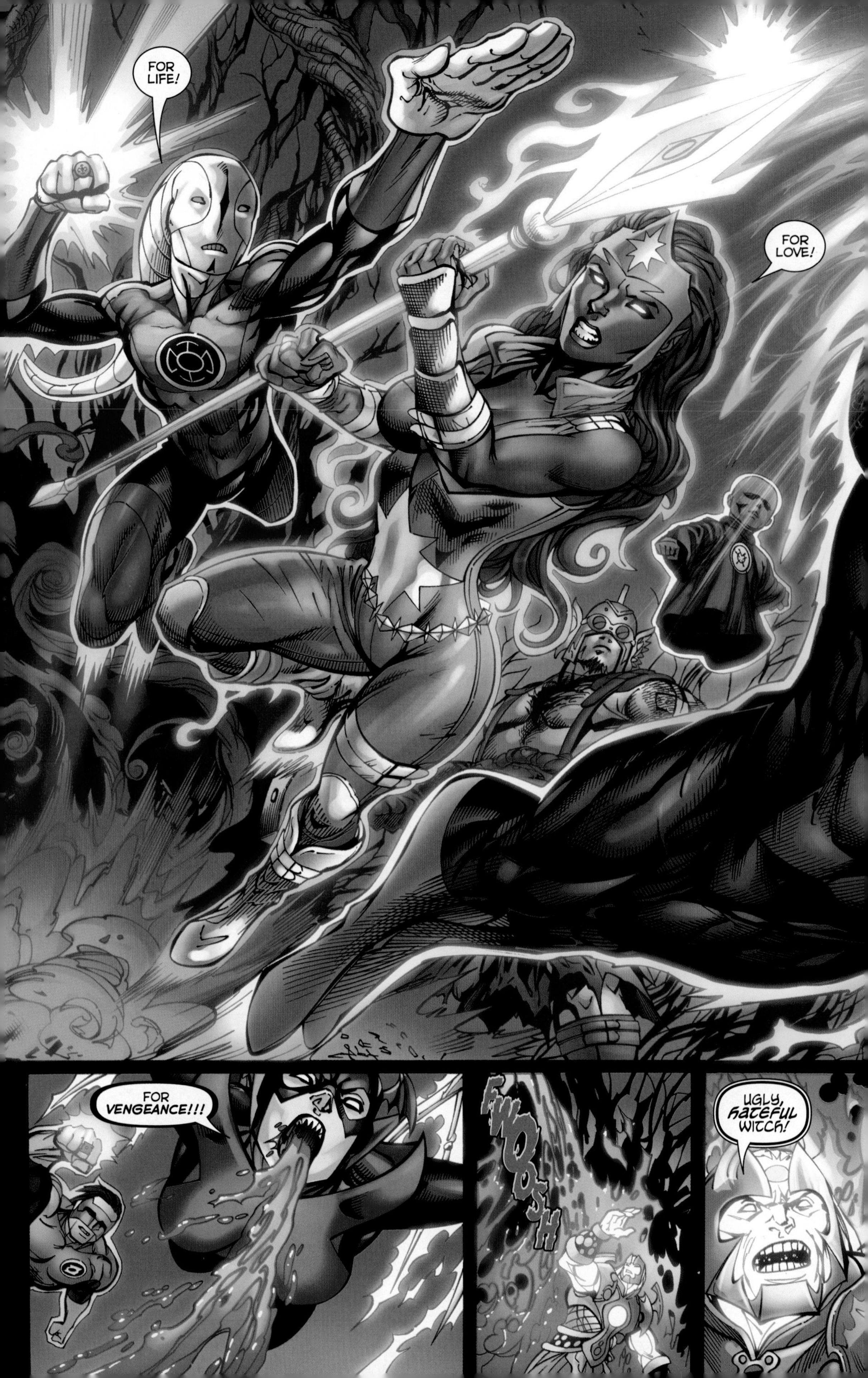
FOR LIFE!
FOR LOVE!
FOR VENGEANCE!!!
FWOOSH
UGLY, HATEFUL WITCH!

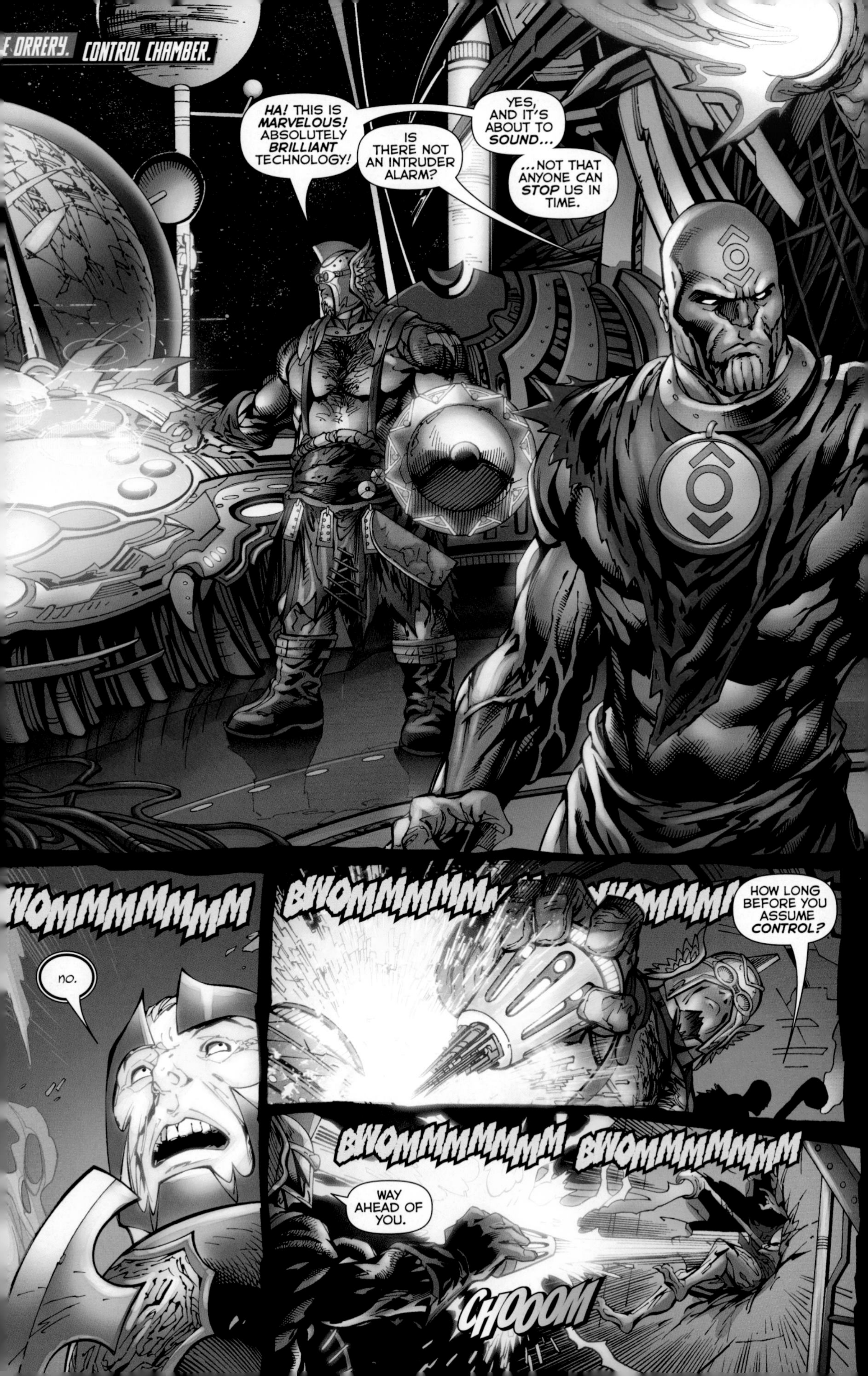
E ORRERY. CONTROL CHAMBER.
HA! THIS IS MARVELOUS! ABSOLUTELY BRILLIANT TECHNOLOGY!
YES, AND IT'S ABOUT TO SOUND...
IS THERE NOT AN INTRUDER ALARM?
...NOT THAT ANYONE CAN STOP US IN TIME.
WOMMMMMMM
no.
BWOMMMMMM
WOMMMM
HOW LONG BEFORE YOU ASSUME CONTROL?
BWOMMMMMMMM BWOMMMMMMMM
WAY AHEAD OF YOU.
CHOOOM

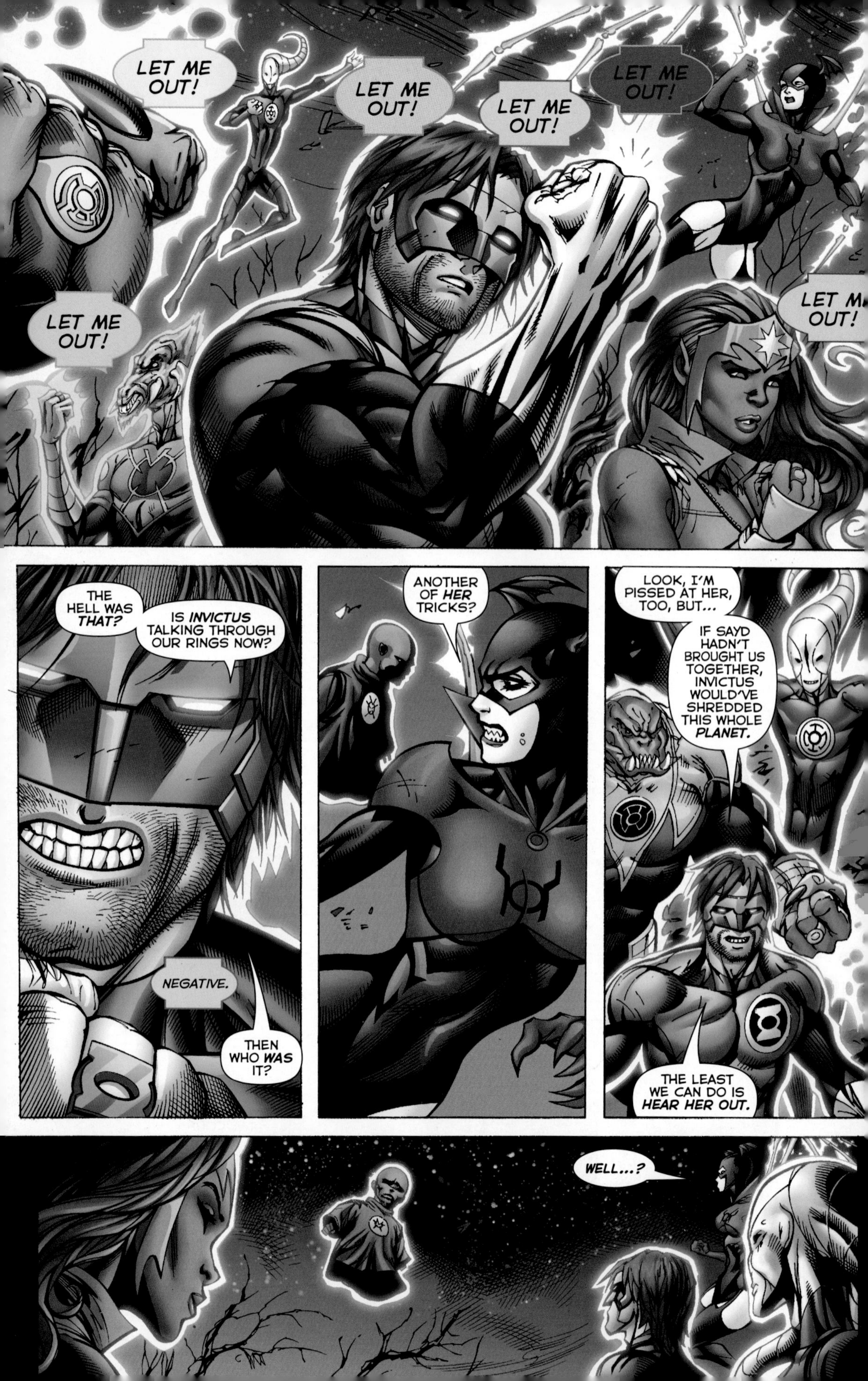
LET ME OUT!
LET ME OUT!
LET ME OUT!
LET ME OUT!
LET ME OUT!
LET ME OUT!
THE HELL WAS THAT?
IS INVICTUS TALKING THROUGH OUR RINGS NOW?
NEGATIVE.
THEN WHO WAS IT?
ANOTHER OF HER TRICKS?
LOOK, I'M PISSED AT HER, TOO, BUT...
IF SAYD HADN'T BROUGHT US TOGETHER, INVICTUS WOULD'VE SHREDDED THIS WHOLE PLANET.
THE LEAST WE CAN DO IS HEAR HER OUT.
WELL...?

GREEN LANTERN: NEW GUARDIANS

PENCILS FOR ISSUE #9 COVER BY TYLER KIRKHAM

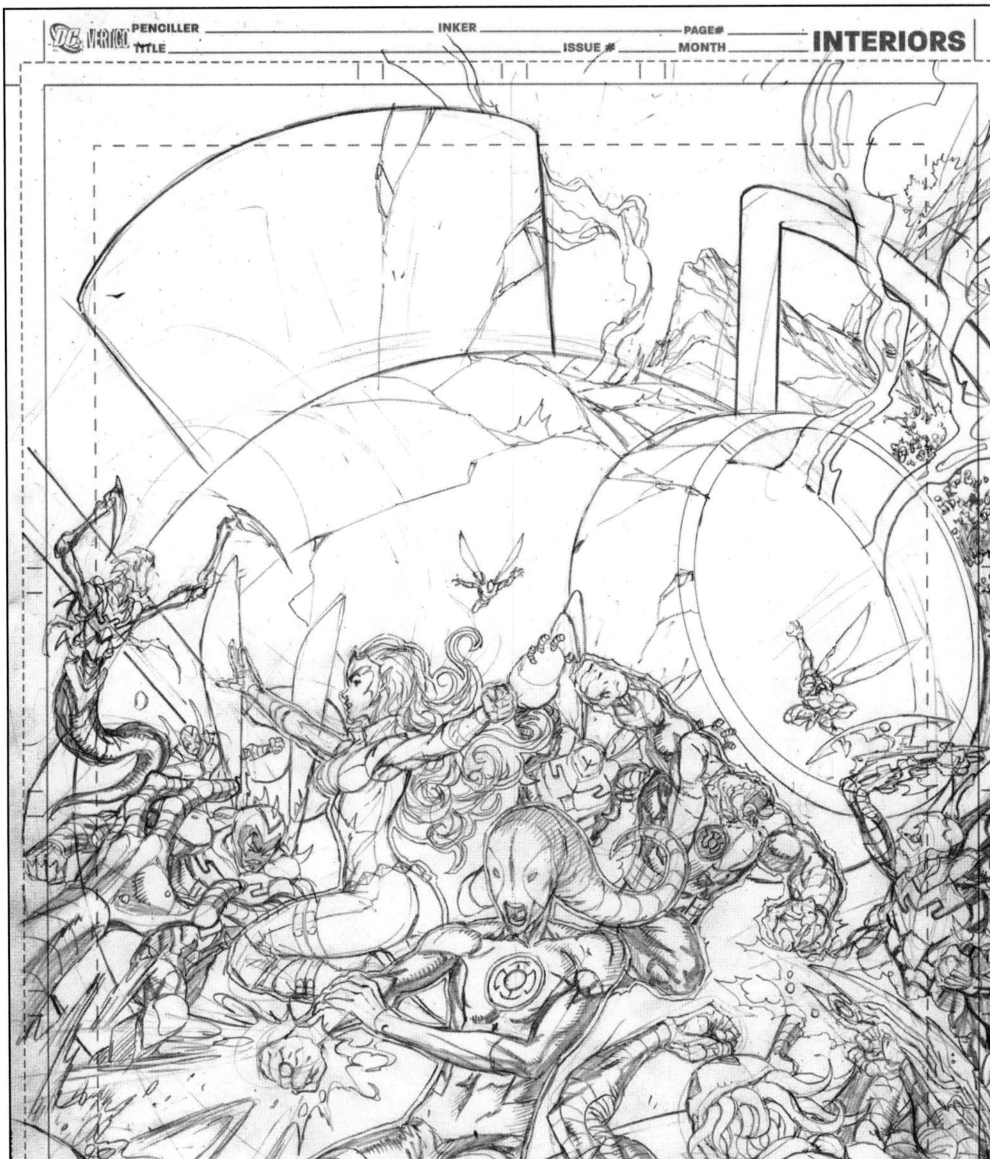
PENCILLER
INKER
PAGE#
TITLE
ISSUE #
MONTH
INTERIORS
LIVE AREA
CROP
BLEED
DOUBLE PAGE SPREAD: CUT AS SHOWN, ABUT PAGE EDGES, TAPE ON BACK, DO NOT OVERLAP
CUT RIGHT-HAND PAGE AT THIS LINE
CUT LEFT HAND PAGE AT THIS LINE

UNUSED COVER FOR ISSUE #10 BY TYLER KIRKHAM, BATT & NEI RUFFINO

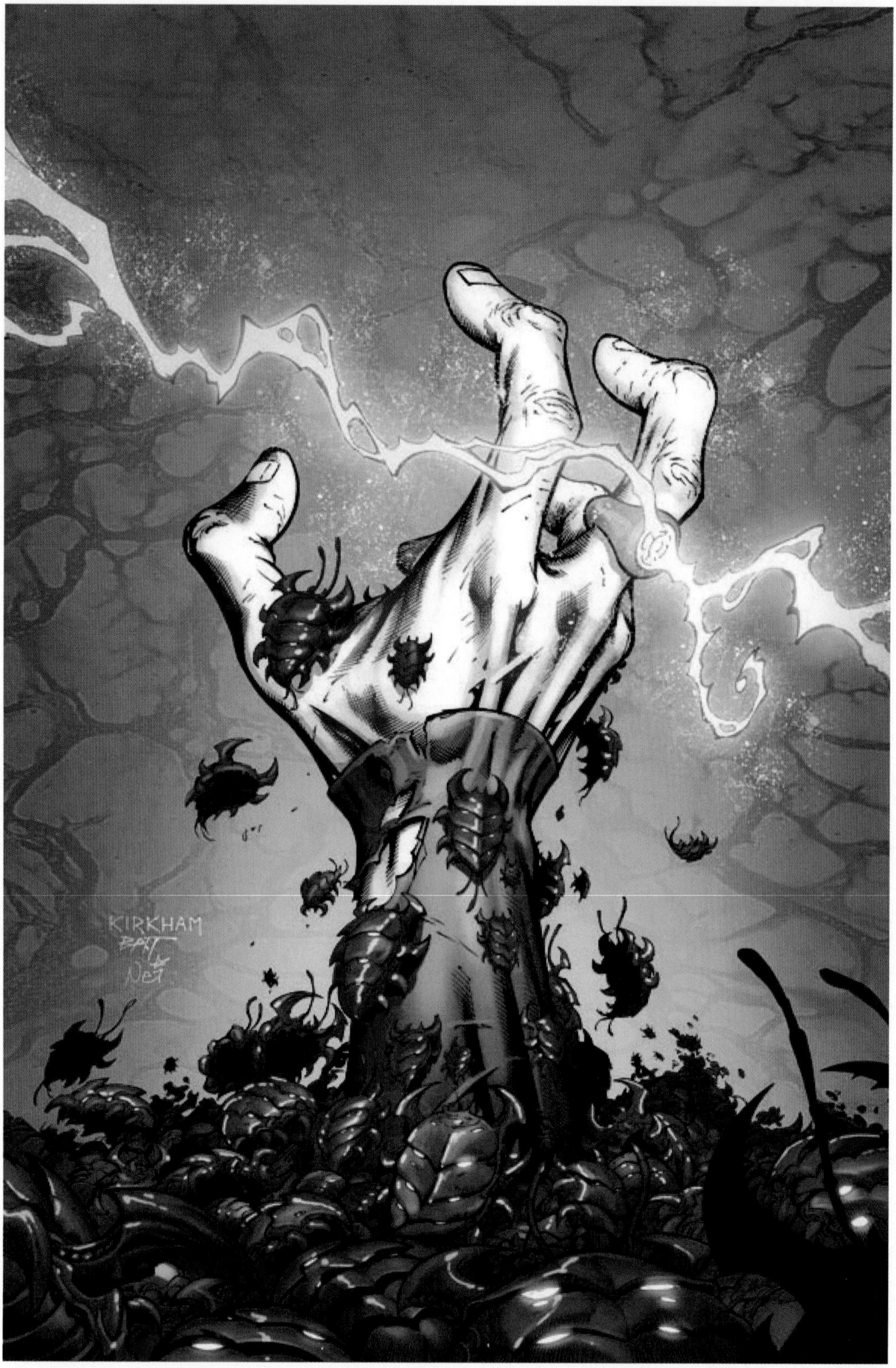
KIRKHAM
BATT
Nei

GREEN LANTERN: NEW GUARDIANS
KYLE RAYNER CHARACTER SKETCH BY TYLER KIRKHAM

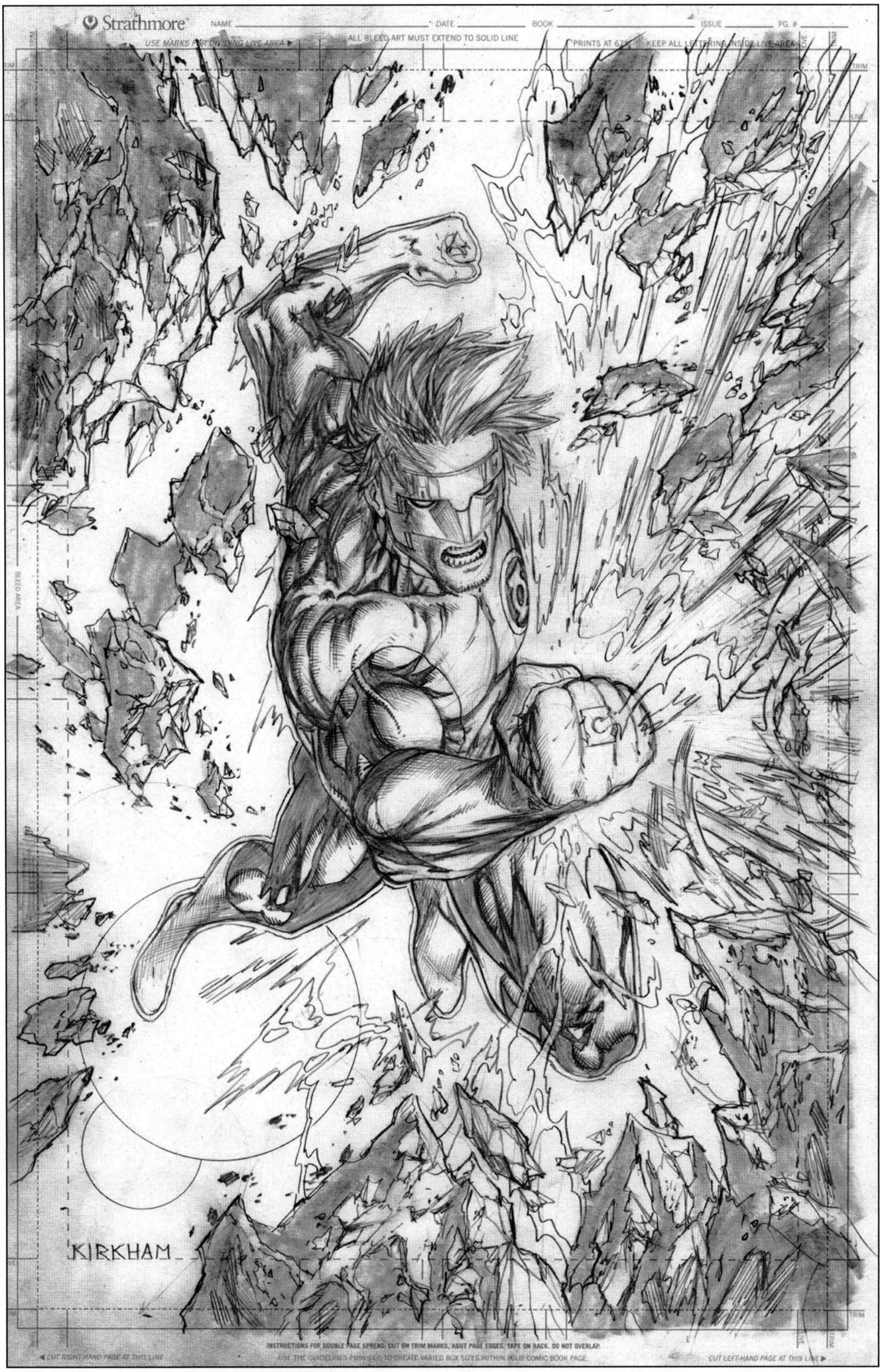
Strathmore
KIRKHAM

FROM THE WRITER OF *JUSTICE LEAGUE* & *THE FLASH*

GEOFF JOHNS
GREEN LANTERN: REBIRTH

GEOFF JOHNS
ETHAN VAN SCIVER

Introduction by
BRAD MELTZER